Women in the Mediterranean

The book addresses the challenges faced by women on the two shores of the Mediterranean from a multidisciplinary and interdisciplinary perspective. While in the European Union's (EU) Mediterranean countries inequality is mostly linked to the social sphere and, in particular refers to labour market dynamics, in the Middle East and Northern Africa (MENA) area, the situation is more complicated as the social and private spheres are blended and cultural and religious factors have a great impact on women autonomy and opportunities beyond the family perimeter. The different challenges women are facing on the two sides of the Mediterranean have sometimes originated incomprehension and misperceptions. Western-supported policies devoted to fill the gap between men and women in the MENA area have overlooked countries' peculiarities simply exporting models tailored for EU's member states. The EU's attempts to strengthen relations with the Mediterranean countries on a multilevel basis have not rescued women from marginalisation. Nevertheless, during the 2011 awakening, women played an important role in activating civil society. They are still considered as a key part of the fight against terrorism and radicalisation, although in some countries their condition has worsened after secular regimes have been downturned. The number of migrant women has increased and, not differently from men, they are looking for opportunities and better conditions of life while Western media tend to present them in a stereotyped way either as traumatized victim and/or as caring mother. There are other misleading common places, which need to be better conceptualised and understood, such as the alleged incompatibility between Islam and women rights. Unfortunately, women's rights are still under attack even in European countries where they are considered consolidated.

The chapters in this book were originally published in a special issue of the *Journal of the Balkans and Near Eastern Studies*.

Leila Simona Talani is Professor of International Political Economy in the department of European and International Studies, King's College London, UK, since 2014. In 2017 she was awarded a visiting Professorship at the Kennedy School of Government of the University of Harvard, USA. She was also appointed as Jean Monnet Chair of European Political Economy by the European Commission in 2012.

Serena Giusti is Assistant Professor of International Relations and Foreign Policy Analysis at Sant'Anna School of Advanced Studies, Pisa, Italy, where she coordinates the Research Group on Eastern Europe, Russia and Eurasia. She is a senior research fellow, Eastern Europe and

Russia Programme, at the Italian Institute for International Political Studies (ISPI) in Milan, Italy. She is member of the OSCE Reflection Group on European Security – Challenges at the Societal Level and of Women in International Security-Italy. She has extensively published (articles and volumes) on the accession of Central and Eastern European countries to the European Union (EU), on European security and defence policy, on the EU's neighbourhood policy.

Women in the Mediterranean

Edited by
Leila Simona Talani and Serena Giusti

LONDON AND NEW YORK

First published 2018
by Routledge
2 Park Square, Milton Park, Abingdon, Oxon, OX14 4RN, UK

and by Routledge
711 Third Avenue, New York, NY 10017, USA

Routledge is an imprint of the Taylor & Francis Group, an informa business

© 2018 Taylor & Francis

All rights reserved. No part of this book may be reprinted or reproduced or utilised in any form or by any electronic, mechanical, or other means, now known or hereafter invented, including photocopying and recording, or in any information storage or retrieval system, without permission in writing from the publishers.

Trademark notice: Product or corporate names may be trademarks or registered trademarks, and are used only for identification and explanation without intent to infringe.

British Library Cataloguing in Publication Data
A catalogue record for this book is available from the British Library

ISBN 13: 978-1-138-48043-8

Typeset in Minion Pro
by diacriTech, Chennai

Publisher's Note
The publisher accepts responsibility for any inconsistencies that may have arisen during the conversion of this book from journal articles to book chapters, namely the possible inclusion of journal terminology.

Disclaimer
Every effort has been made to contact copyright holders for their permission to reprint material in this book. The publishers would be grateful to hear from any copyright holder who is not here acknowledged and will undertake to rectify any errors or omissions in future editions of this book.

Contents

Citation Information		vii
Notes on Contributors		ix
	Introduction: Women in the Mediterranean: Still Discriminated Against? *Leila Simona Talani and Serena Giusti*	1
1	Islamic Feminism(s) in the Mediterranean Area: a Hermeneutical Approach *Barbara Henry*	4
2	Gender, Identity and Belonging: New Citizenships beyond Orientalism *Alessia Belli and Anna Loretoni*	23
3	Women, Globalization and Civil Society in the MENA Area: Between Marginalization and Radicalization *Leila Simona Talani*	39
4	Gender Mainstreaming towards the Mediterranean: the Case of the ENP *Serena Giusti*	64
5	Representations of Gendered Mobility and the Tragic Border Regime in the Mediterranean *Heidrun Friese*	81
6	Back to Basics: Stateless Women and Children in Greece *Mariangela Veikou*	97
7	The Conflict between Education and Female Labour in Turkey: Understanding Turkey's Non-compliance with the U-shape Hypothesis *Miray Erinc*	111
Index		131

Citation Information

The chapters in this book were originally published the *Journal of Balkan and Near Eastern Studies*, volume 19, issue 5 (October 2017). When citing this material, please use the original page numbering for each article, as follows:

Introduction
Women in the Mediterranean: Still Discriminated Against?
Leila Simona Talani and Serena Giusti
Journal of Balkan and Near Eastern Studies, volume 19, issue 5 (October 2017) pp. 461–463

Chapter 1
Islamic Feminism(s) in the Mediterranean Area: a Hermeneutical Approach
Barbara Henry
Journal of Balkan and Near Eastern Studies, volume 19, issue 5 (October 2017) pp. 464–482

Chapter 2
Gender, Identity and Belonging: New Citizenships beyond Orientalism
Alessia Belli and Anna Loretoni
Journal of Balkan and Near Eastern Studies, volume 19, issue 5 (October 2017) pp. 483–498

Chapter 3
Women, Globalization and Civil Society in the MENA Area: Between Marginalization and Radicalization
Leila Simona Talani
Journal of Balkan and Near Eastern Studies, volume 19, issue 5 (October 2017) pp. 499–523

Chapter 4
Gender Mainstreaming towards the Mediterranean: the Case of the ENP
Serena Giusti
Journal of Balkan and Near Eastern Studies, volume 19, issue 5 (October 2017) pp. 524–540

Chapter 5
Representations of Gendered Mobility and the Tragic Border Regime in the Mediterranean
Heidrun Friese
Journal of Balkan and Near Eastern Studies, volume 19, issue 5 (October 2017) pp. 541–556

CITATION INFORMATION

Chapter 6
Back to Basics: Stateless Women and Children in Greece
Mariangela Veikou
Journal of Balkan and Near Eastern Studies, volume 19, issue 5 (October 2017) pp. 557–570

Chapter 7
The Conflict between Education and Female Labour in Turkey: Understanding Turkey's Non-compliance with the U-shape Hypothesis
Miray Erinc
Journal of Balkan and Near Eastern Studies, volume 19, issue 5 (October 2017) pp. 571–589

For any permission-related enquiries please visit:
http://www.tandfonline.com/page/help/permissions

Notes on Contributors

Alessia Belli is research fellow in Political Philosophy at the DIRPOLIS Institute of the Sant'Anna School of Advanced Studies, Pisa, Italy, and legal consultant for asylum seekers, Arci, Comitato Arezzo.

Miray Erinc is a PhD candidate at King's College London, UK. Her main research interests are migration, labour markets and skilled migration, European Union (EU) integration, women and education.

Heidrun Friese is a Full Professor of Intercultural Communication at the Chemnitz University of Technology, Germany. She has published widely on the 'Limits of Hospitality' and (undocumented) mobility in the Mediterranean.

Serena Giusti is Assistant Professor of International Relations at Sant'Anna School of Advanced Studies, Pisa, Italy, and she holds a Jean Monnet Module titled 'The EU's Responses to the Challenges of its Neighbourhood'. She is also a senior research fellow, Eastern Europe and Russia Programme, at the Italian Institute for International Political Studies (ISPI) in Milan, Italy.

Barbara Henry is Full Professor of Political Philosophy at Sant'Anna School of Advanced Studies in Pisa, Italy, where she is the director of the Global Security and Human Rights Laboratory and the coordinator of the PhD in Human Rights and Global Politics.

Anna Loretoni is Full Professor of Political Philosophy and coordinator of the PhD in Politics, Human Rights and Sustainability at DIRPOLIS Institute, Sant'Anna School of Advanced Studies, Pisa, Italy.

Leila Simona Talani is Professor of International Political Economy in the department of European and International Studies, King's College London, UK, since 2014. In 2017 she was awarded a visiting Professorship at the Kennedy School of Government of the University of Harvard. She was also appointed as Jean Monnet Chair of European Political Economy by the European Commission in 2012.

Mariangela Veikou is Researcher at the Public Administration Department, Faculty of Behavioural, Management and Social Sciences, University of Twente, the Netherlands.

Women in the Mediterranean: Still Discriminated Against?

Leila Simona Talani and Serena Giusti

This Special Issue is the outcome of a successful and lively debate, taking place in the course of the Women in the Mediterranean event organized within the context of the Festival d'Europa 2015 in Florence. The panel consisted of women addressing, from a variety of viewpoints, the challenges faced by women on the two shores of the Mediterranean. The thoughts, views and analyses presented in the course of this debate are the inspiration for the present publication. In it, we are aiming at proposing different disciplinary perspectives and methodologies offering a composite, although not exhaustive, picture of such a complex and multifaceted issue. At the roots of this effort is the attempt to give voice to women and to their questions through the contribution of experts in various related fields. What emerges is a kaleidoscope of overlapping images, realities, information, all hinting at the fact that women are still experiencing inequality on both the northern and southern shores of the Mediterranean.

In the EU's Mediterranean countries social patterns have evolved and women now are strongly present on the labour market and have become financially independent. Nevertheless, inequalities persist, as women's employment rate is still lower than men's. For young women it is even harder than for young men to enter the labour market and women are still paid on average less than men for the same job. They are more likely than men to take up part-time jobs or interrupt their careers altogether to care for children or a sick parent. This inequality is also carried on to women's pensions, which are on average lower than men's. The glass ceiling has not disappeared: there are still too few women in leadership positions both in private and public sectors as well as in politics.

While in the EU's Mediterranean countries inequality is mostly linked to the social sphere, and in particular refers to labour market dynamics, in the Middle East and Northern Africa (MENA) area the situation is more complicated as the social and private spheres overlap and cultural and religious factors have a great impact on women's autonomy and opportunities beyond the family perimeter. The different challenges women are facing on the two sides of the Mediterranean have sometimes led to incomprehension and misperceptions. Western-supported policies devoted to closing the gap between men and women in the Southern Mediterranean area have overlooked those countries' peculiarities, simply exporting models tailored for EU's member states. The EU's attempts to strengthen relations with the Mediterranean countries on a multilevel basis have not rescued women from marginalization. Nevertheless, during the 2011 awakening, women played an important role in activating civil society and they are still to play a role in the modernization of their countries. They are considered as a key part of the fight against terrorism and radicalization, although in some countries their condition has worsened after secular regimes have been overturned. The number of migrant women has increased and, no differently from men, they are looking for opportunities and better conditions of life while Western media tend to present them in a stereotyped way either as traumatized victims and/or as caring mothers.

There are other misleading commonplaces, which need to be better conceptualized and understood, such as the alleged incompatibility between Islam and women rights. Unfortunately, women's rights are still under attack even in European countries where they are considered established. These questions are at the core of the articles presented in this Special Issue.

The article by *Barbara Henry* questions some conceptual assumptions which are shaping the contemporary debate on Islamic feminism, such as the incompatibility between the *Qur'an* and women's rights as well as its uniqueness. Feminism, it is argued, consists of an extremely fluid, dynamic and pluralistic set of phenomena. The article offers a deep and analytical account of the variety of feminisms in the Mediterranean in a diachronic perspective. Women have been involved in liberalization movements, engaged in modernization and also recently have been supportive of changes in their societies. Besides the emergence of innovative interpretations of the *Qur'an* there is also the clear will to develop a syncretic and transnational feminism.

The article by *Alessia Belli and Anna Loretoni* points out that Western feminism is not immune from the effects of the use of stereotypes regarding Muslim women. The authors suggest a deconstructive strategy and an intersectional approach that they apply to the case of some Italian and British Muslim women activists. The aim is to show that the agency of Muslim women emerges in different contexts, thus breaking the Western mainstream essentialist perspective. The concept of fluid identity seems suitable for capturing the intertwining of religious, gender and political dimensions. The feminist approach to cultural diversity would then benefit from a perspective of cultural flexibility and transformation, an experience of continuous border crossing, in which principles, rights and values are constantly negotiated, while at the same time they are translated into multifaceted and controversial practices.

The article by *Leila Simona Talani* tackles the question of women's access to technology and their position in the political economy of the countries of the MENA area. If it is true that the area is progressively more marginalized in the globalization process, this particularly affects women as they tend to have fewer of the skills that are necessary to respond to the technological challenges of globalization. Furthermore, despite the different interpretations of the role of women in Islamic societies, the crisis of the Arab states seems to emphasize a more radical approach to Islam and a diminished role played in it by women. The article is centred around a transnationalist interpretation of globalization, which stresses the dynamic nature of this process, its technological and skill content, and its uneven manifestation. After discussing these characteristics of globalization, the author moves to the analysis of the evolution of civil society institutions and social capital in the MENA area to assess how they have been impacted by globalization and where this leaves women.

The article by *Serena Giusti* examines the EU's gender mainstreaming towards the Mediterranean countries. It discusses, in particular, the implications of the European Neighbourhood Policy that promotes gender equality through diffusion of norms. In spite of efforts toward appraising and making it more effective, the EU's gender strategy has generally failed to confront the structural causes of inequality as it has mainly focused on the external aspects of the question while underestimating cultural, domestic and familial impediments. The EU has overlooked national debates on these issues in the partner countries and the contributions of local feminists.

Heidrun Friese in her article underlines that there is also a gendered way to represent migrants, as women are usually described as traumatized victims and/or as caring mothers. Based on the author's direct experience in Lampedusa, the article argues that situations of emergency generate a post-humanitarian discourse and a 'visual humanism' that make pain and suffering a-political and a-historical. And yet social imagination sets female vulnerability against male aggression and the threat of 'invasion'. Within the reiterated gender binarism and its symbolic order, the mother as well as vulnerable children are deprived of threatening agency, of autonomy. They do not menace the political order of the nation and its sovereignty. In other words, the female victim and her suffering do not belong either to historical time or to the political order.

The topic of migrants and refugees is also dealt in *Mariangela Veikou*'s article. She analyses how European societies are coping with the growing refugee crisis in tandem with the on-going economic crisis in recent years. Within this climate, migration risks being seen more than ever as an additional 'burden' that societies have to 'carry' and it is sometimes even questioned why it should be accommodated or respected at all. This paper draws on empirical research from Greece to examine changing European societies, with a particular focus on how the crisis is affecting the most vulnerable members of society, the stateless children and women migrants and refugees.

Finally, in her article, *Miray Enric* notes how the female labour force participation rates are known to be exceptionally low in Turkey by international standards. The general consensus is that the catalyst behind female labour force participation rates is the level of educational attainment. In the academic literature, the relationship between the two factors – education and female labour force participation – is explained under what is known as the U-shape hypothesis. Although female education has increased over recent years, the U-shape is not observable in Turkey. This research scrutinizes the economic and social characteristics of the labour markets in Turkey and finally seeks to demonstrate how women in Turkey are trapped in a vicious cycle. The U-shape theory is insufficient in explaining female labour force participation rates in Turkey. Turkish women face barriers in entering the labour markets, although they are well-educated. They present a form of passive human capital, whose skills are underutilized. Thus, the curve remains an L rather than a U.

Islamic Feminism(s) in the Mediterranean Area: a Hermeneutical Approach

Barbara Henry

ABSTRACT
This article aims at questioning some conceptual assumptions which frame the current debate on Islamic feminism. Firstly, there is the assumption regarding the existing structural incompatibility between the Qur'an and women's rights that needs to be tested by means of methodical hermeneutical tools. Secondly, the thesis affirming the uniqueness and univocity of the movement should also be questioned. The article argues that the syntagma 'Islamic feminism' should be approached as the 'indicator' of an extremely fluid, dynamic and pluralistic set of phenomena which has not yet assumed, and may never assume, its final conformation.

1. Introductory remarks and outline of the article

What we need nowadays is a different way of configuring the interwoven relations between juridical, cultural and political contexts, which have been in a permanent state of flux in the Middle East and North Africa (MENA) region since the end of 2010. In particular, we need to work at local and global levels, and even at the glocal level,[1] given that we are dealing with gender asymmetries, gender discriminations, feminist resistance and feminist agency in the various civil societies and constitutional frameworks throughout the world, with a special focus on Islamic countries. In the specific case of MENA countries, the attitude suggested in 1996 and reiterated later by the well-known constitutional law scholar Abdelfattah Amor is useful. According to Amor, any grounded analysis of the Islamic State arrangement nowadays cannot rely on a hypothetical constitutional frame of a sole presumed Islamic State of the origins, but it concerns the peculiar Islamic variations of models simply borrowed from Western constitutionalism, which are very remote from ancient paradigms of any kind.[2]

New vocabulary and categories should be generated in a renewed relation with the traditional glossary in order to grasp the interwoven and blended, multifaceted set of relations between particularity and universality, and between colonial burden and unexpected free paths of behaviour and agency, which are to be strongly recommended and implemented. This comes out against the old kind of imperial universalism, but in favour of an embedded/located universalism. More than ever it is a matter of nomenclature, considering the relation between power and knowledge ('the power of giving names'); this impacts on the phenomena evoked by the syntagma Islamic feminism through positive and negative self-ascriptive processes on the part of the protagonists. This is because of the strict relation existing among the ubiquitous/ambiguous powers at work via the classification/labelling procedures and the power of agency/resistance/erosion assumed by the targeted groups. Both ascriptive power and counter/competing power (not simply reactive) are at work in different symbolic and material arenas, with different outcomes. For example, this phenomenon is widespread in non-Arab Islamic countries *and* also communities, such as in Iran, Malaysia, South Africa and the United States.

The contextuality of the frames together with the biographical/cosmopolitan trajectories of the protagonists are to be carefully taken into account in their transformations as a significant variable. The syntagma itself is an overall, handy label[3] which has had mixed fortunes since the 1990s. The syntagma has sometimes been accepted with reluctance or even rejected[4] by feminists advocating, via Islamic discourse, the endorsement of women's rights in Islamic countries, such as the much lamented Fatima Mernissi.[5] It has even been used strategically or operationally on behalf of a more effective and multifaceted 'women's movement' in a post-colonial and transnational framework, in order to improve winning allegiances among women (the Iranian intellectual Valentine Moghadan). Nevertheless, we can say that Margot Badran, Riffat Hassan, Amina Wadud, Asma Barlas, Laleh Bakhtiar, Asma Lamrabet, Ziba Mir-Hosseini and Fatima Naseef, each in a different way due to national, linguistic and academic socializations, have claimed or agreed indirectly to be part both of the movement and the ideal/methodical constellation labelled as Islamic feminism. Others have proclaimed an Islamic feminist self-identification from the start, such as the activists of the Iranian journal *Zanan* since 1992, first of all the founder Shala Sherkat, the Sisters of Islam in Malaysia, with the indefatigable Zainah Anwar, and some exegetes from South Africa like Shamima Shaihk.

Figures like that of the American Mirian Cooke, the Egyptian-American Leila Ahmed, the Iranian-American Nayereh Tohidi, the first two being sympathetic academics, the second a scholar and supporter, are an example of how plural and variegated the voices, the tones, the nuances, the attitudes and the evaluations can be.

This is all very relevant for the case, which is inscribed as a multivariate, pluralistic, fluid indicator of changes in the post-colonial era, in which the glocal effectiveness and resonance of ideas and movements is certainly wider than in the past.

Moreover, the Islamic feminist constellations of knowledges, taxonomies, codes and practices must always be considered not in general but in contextual and genealogical terms. Why is this so?

Because it is here that we find deposited the most important and decisive moments, also contrasting with one another, and the most important components of the historical-conceptual framework of the last two centuries and of contemporary history, together with the disciplines born to understand them. We cannot be exhaustive here, but we can in a cursory manner trace some routes. We can construct the matrix of Islamic feminism beyond colonialism and post-colonialism, and the liberation movements (including post-colonial and gender studies), Islamic and post-Islamic constitutionalism, the autochthonous feminism, which germinated in the first years of the last century in Egypt and Iran (*al-Nahda*).[6] We shall also consider the return of religion as a collective and emancipating political phenomenon, such as the women's Islamist movements (explicitly non-feminist in their strong aversion to the colonial legacy and the image of the woman established in Western society) are one of the consequences.

The following three sections (2-4) will thus be dedicated to the interweaving of native and national feminisms, using the device of colonial knowledges still in use and the auto-ethnographic dismantling of colonialism. Starting from the space for intersection that has been created by the crossroads of these focalizations, the fifth section will face new phenomena of a hermeneutic nature, associated with the re-employment of the notion of *ijtihad* in the interpretation of the Qur'anic *surahs* and of the tradition and sayings of Muhammad (Hadith) after centuries of marginalization of these writings, together with the self-defining opacity of the phenomenon (why not Muslim feminism?) and the links with religious democracy renewed in the post-secular period by certain currents of Islamic constitutionalism. The sixth and last section invokes a critical internal-external voice, which since 2002 has invited caution without however ignoring the 'positive' core, because it destabilizes from within the symbolic structures of male power of this feminist constellation[7] which remains an open musical score with continual counterpoints, that continually reformulate the issue (see 3, 5, 6).

2. Changing frames, stable constraints. Islamic feminism as a successful case of auto-ethnography

Some years ago it was suggested that 'We in the world are in an age of Occidentalism', in which the direction of the classifying and defining perspective has changed consciously and been implemented systematically.[8] There is no doubt that in the upper spheres of the scientific establishment, the model of intellectual elite prevailing until the middle of the last century was made up of white male Western scholars and scientists. The (only so far presumed) transformation is that this elite has been successfully replaced by something that is constituted by more gender-sensitive, if not feminist, decolonized and decentralized currents and energies. Even if the unlimited validity of the hypothesis is controversial, the phenomena under investigation exemplify a case of a gender-sensitive, decolonized, culturally embedded set of methods, world representations, theoretical skills, practices and symbolic energies, all embodied in a community of female scholars. It is a toolkit encompassing the new model of glocal intellectuality.

Having said that, despite the expectations of some pivotal and visionary scholars there is still a long way to go before such a model takes root in curricular and academic policies, and especially in the disciplinary mainstream of the social sciences. Such an epistemic revolution is slow to permeate into the common consciousness and become mainstream knowledge, with levels of awareness existing throughout almost all Western societies (European and not).

On the one hand, it should not be forgotten that it is only in the last few decades that the depositories of the cultural heritage of the European West have been observed and studied methodically and in the institutions in which knowledge is produced by those who were once subject to processes of domination. It is not by chance that most of the intellectuals giving support and a scientific element to the movement are or have been academics and theologians (Amina Wadud, Miriam Cooke, Afsaneh Najmabadi, Margot Badran, Asma Lamrabet, Leila Ahmed, Nareye Tohidi and Fatima Mernissi among others) who are active at national and international/transnational research institutions.

On the other hand, this delayed emergence of occidental centres of research and dissemination does not at all mean, as will be confirmed further on, that until the 1980s the epistemic colonial machinery had produced its own world representation with no counterpart or any proactive contribution from the side of the colonized cultural and pragmatic energy and resources. Moreover, the processes of colonization never really occurred on a *tabula rasa*, in a *terra nullius*. On the contrary, they occurred against the background of pre-existing socio-institutional histories, gender patterns and social structures. Even when these were destroyed or radically assimilated, they influenced the colonial symbolic and material patterns of domination. First of all, we had the gender pattern of subjugation coming to terms with different types of stratified discrimination and creating ways to counterattack. Resistance, and micro-resistance, is often used by women, who act by resorting to the simulacrum of the patriarchal discourse. They empty it from the inside, by means of micro-systems of autonomous creation, of development of marginal subjective identities, indeed, but which are still female, and of specific types.[9] They are therefore forms of 'sabotage from within'. It is an act of epistemic presumption (typical of the colonial cognitive machinery) to exclude the possibility of women being able to use strategically a screen and an icon that is prejudicial to them. On the contrary, in many cases they accept such features outwardly, while at the same time eroding them from within. The notion of auto-ethnography defines such situations of cultural interchange, which is not free of domination and of reversal influence between the poles of the relation.

This is even truer for women's narratives and discourses. If the canonical descriptive language, according to Foucault,[10] is a cognitive power structuring the master narratives and the world representations in a given time and space, the rival languages (codes, patterns, styles) are inevitably plural and can work either reactively or proactively in different phases and in different proportions, depending on the degree of subalternity, submersion, marginality and invisibility to which the languages' speakers were relegated.

An example of what is meant by the quoted processes of 'giving names to things and living phenomena' is what initiated practices of symbolic creation through the construction of the nomenclature of all realities, natural and social, during colonial times. The specific antithesis between female and male roles was rewritten *in loco*; the transformation of the pre-existing urban structures, including the resetting of the hiatus between private and public, was pursued in such a way as to redefine the identity of populations and transform with this the internal structure of autochthonous, in most cases resilient, patriarchalism.

If such a resilient and interwoven apparatus of practices and knowledges is not carefully unpacked and deconstructed, all the legitimate claims to be defending the lasting, unassailable nucleus of women's rights and women's emancipatory strategies against its conservative detractors, Islamic or simply traditional, could be nullified by means of a twofold rhetorical trap. Firstly, it labels any 'feminism' as a degrading Western colonial imposition, and secondly, it creates a dichotomy between women's equality and religious belief/'religiously inspired' life conduct. Such entangled narratives have to be considered in terms of an auto-ethnographic re-appropriation of equality and freedom; so far, they are valuable emancipatory means for the women combating patriarchalism. In order to do this, a profound revisiting of the lexicon of rights should be undertaken and the harm inflicted on the subjugated in their self-representations and self-ascription should be taken into consideration. Such moral 'disablements' affecting women's self-image are the most long-lasting, also because they have not yet been recognized as such, not even since the beginning of the

Arab uprisings. This means going far beyond Norberto Bobbio's well-known book *The Age of Rights*, or a 'situated/frantic (glocal) ideal' of emancipation.[11] The author is able to say that women's rights have been acquired only because specific groups of women, in embedded contexts, have struggled hard for them, often damaging their lives; this has happened with enormous differences in terms of initial conditions, of trade-offs between costs and benefits, of durability and efficacy of results. This is more than evident, as historical and living cases show, in examples coming from the global, and in the present case glocal, different shapes of the so-called Islamic feminisms. Nevertheless, all the women's rights embodied by the feminists have been endorsed by remaining culturally burdened and shaped characteristics, which possess a historical and contextual connotation. To give an initial definition of what is at stake, let us resort to the following statement by Margot Badran:

A core definition of Islamic feminism is to be detected in the writings and work of Muslim (believers in Allah and his Prophet, having a public projection or not) protagonists; those scholars interpret their outcomes as a feminist discourse/practice and derive it from the Qur'an, seeking rights and justice within the framework of gender equality for women and men in the *totality* of their existence.[12]

This justifies why the reference to the previous roots and shape of women's activism in the MENA region is of crucial relevance to unpacking the new syntagma. The *Nahda* movements (nineteenth century) must be briefly observed through the auto-ethnographic lens in order to allow the profile of Islamic feminism(s) to emerge more vividly in the (perhaps only presumptive) contrast with the previous type of emancipatory movements. The combination of a historical approach (II) with both an analytical (III) and hermeneutic approach (IV) is adopted in order to shed light on the different variables and elements of the phenomenon under investigation. Moreover, the three approaches interwoven disclose some resilient characters of the contemporary Islamic versions of secularism (II, III), of pluralistic theology and of feminism (IV, V).

3. Islamic awakening and autochthonous feminisms in MENA countries: anticipations of the contemporary feminist approaches

Towards the end of the nineteenth century, in the MENA region there was affirmation of what Renata Pepicelli defines as 'the autochthonous tradition of feminism within an Islamic context',[13] emerging in correspondence with the movements of Islamic modernism (*Nahda*). This, in turn, proliferated between the nineteenth and twentieth centuries with characteristics that were not greatly different from contemporary Islamic feminisms in terms of their inspiration, theological and political outcomes and national peculiarities.

Against the backdrop of the social, political and cultural changes that had stimulated[14] the dominant Islamic communities and local realities of the Mediterranean basin between the end of the twelfth and the nineteenth centuries (and which concluded with subjection by the European powers), there was the need for radical renewal in an anti-colonial direction. It should not be forgotten that there had been at least two golden ages of Islamic culture and politics (not to mention the great philosophers such as al-Ġazālī and Averroè, who acted as a support between Aristotle and Thomas Aquinas). The second is the true seat of interpretative rationalism, the period of the *Mu'tazilites*, between the eighth and tenth centuries; this is very important and today intentionally ignored by the de facto and *de jure* alliance among supporting schools of exegetic literalism and authoritarian regimes of the region, the first among these countries being Saudi Arabia. The so-called 'Islamic rebirth' (*al-Nahda*) in reality has behind it a renaissance, which is an authoritative source of all the new developments in terms of philosophical theology, including feminist developments. The *Mu'tazilites* supported nature as created by the Qur'an, a work revealed by God but to be historically contextualized, like a text arranged not only to be commented on, but also to be interpreted, understood and analysed, it having been written in human language.[15] At that time (eighth-tenth centuries) the Qur'an was translated into other languages, precisely to make possible with new interpretations the transposition of the minimum unchanging nucleus into manifold ethnic and social variations. What prevailed within a fierce debate among different schools of thought, which were also concrete social and political factions, was the notion of an 'uncreated Qur'an', which also became the dogma for Sunni Islam, through the victory of the As'arites. The history of this debate is unknown and obscured by the majority of contemporary Sunni scholars; they continue to pass off the concept of the 'eternity of the Qur'an' as divine truth, a concept which accidently emerged victorious from a conflict between interpretations and factions. Similarly, as regards the nineteenth century reawakening, there was little recognition of an anteriority of this socio-political struggle in theological guise between interpretative freedom and exegetical closure. The nineteenth century awakening after all did not set objectives primarily of an interpretative kind but of a political, social and institutional sort, in a nationalistic form. However, it was inserted thanks to the feminine components of the movement within the context of the discussion on religious reform.

The *Nahda* was born in Egypt between the nineteenth and twentieth centuries, and spread throughout the region, propagating instances of a 'return to the origins' in its full sense—religious, cultural and political—instances aimed at facing the great challenges posed by modernity and by the Occident which embodied overwhelming and hegemonic features. These tendencies that were generically included in the *Nahda* phenomenon have been the object of detailed studies and analyses, and are today classified respectively as 'movements of awakening', 'reformist movements', 'modernist movements' and radical or fundamentalist 'movements'—it depends on the representation of the golden age of Islam and on the methods used for the return to this authentic origin of the theological, juridical, political, cultural and philosophical constellation initiated by Muhammad and consolidated for 13 centuries until today.[16]

That having been said, the first 'autochthonous feminist' was indebted to the specific modernist ideology characterizing the movements of national liberation, in turn influenced by the instances of renewal of the institutions in a secular sense. Therefore, from the very beginning, a vision, also renewed, of the *saeculum* is central in that it is the exclusive setting in which faith in Allah and in his Prophet may be exercised by members of the *ummah*, the community of the faithful, which already during this period laid claim (again, as at the time of Muhammad) to its own specific and unique function of exercising earthly power. The Arabic term for the noun 'secularism' was *almaniyya*, which comes from *alam* ('world'), a concept by which reference is made to the (non-conflictual) separation of religious institutions from state institutions, ideally contemplating reference to all religious confessions. It is to this secularism, closely associated with the specificities of the national pathways to liberation from colonialism, that we refer; it is within this context that Islamic 'secular' feminism is founded. With this context there is associated indissolubly the core of religious modernism, according to which there emerges, on the one hand, a distinction between the fundamental Islamic doctrines and its social teachings and laws and, on the other hand, the precept by which Muhammad Abduh, to whom we shall refer later, and his direct followers are the specific and unequivocal references. These doctrinal cores are essential: faith in God, in revelation occurring by the intercession of prophets of the Old and New Testaments and concluding with Muhammad, with the duty of justice, moral responsibility and the Last Judgement starting from spiritual and moral equality among believers. The law and social ethics therefore came to assume the characteristics of historical applications of universal principles prescribed by the Qur'an. Since with the transformation of situations, of behaviours, of human aspirations the law and ethics are also destined to change, the duty of the Muslim innovators became that of bringing the laws and changeable customs into alignment with sacred and unchanging principles. This concept of Islam enabled the supporters of these ideas to accept the ideas of modernity, even if it was within a nationalistic and anti-colonial context, and corroborated their awareness in terms of respecting their faith.

Among the initial supporters of women's emancipation as a pillar of national liberation *and* religious reawakening, we find intellectuals and jurists, whose voice necessarily had a wider appeal with respect to the purely female counterpart of the movement; this was a minority part but nonetheless important and, given the enormous asymmetries, still more revolutionary. Among these are the Lebanese-Egyptian Zaynab Fawwaz (1860–1914), the Egyptian Aisha al-Taymuriyya (1840–1902), the Syrian-Lebanese Mayy Ziyada (1886–1941) and finally the Egyptian Malak Hifni Nasif (1886–1918). By means of their prolific literary production, they all gave voice to demands regarding the right of access to education, participation of women in the public sphere and the right to employment, in addition to the right to participate in prayers in places of worship.

On one side, these pioneers prompted the appearance, only 30 years later, of what has been defined as the embryo of a first 'feminine consciousness' in these societies. On the other, the most influential voices (as was inevitable in a largely patriarchal structure with greater segregation the higher the socio-economic status of the women)[17] were those of exponents of the modernist current such as the Egyptians Muhammad Abduh (1849–1935) and Qasim Amin (1863–1908), and the Tunisian al Tahir al Haddad (1899–1935). These put at the centre of their claims the progress of the nation, of which female emancipation was an indispensable means (not an end). The Egyptian jurist Qasim Amin, in particular, in his most famous work *Tahrir al-ma'ra* ('The Liberation of Women') of 1899, considered to be the first text to promote 'state feminism' in the Arab world,[18] affirms that the causes of Egypt's backwardness of are due to the subordinate role of women within the family and the society.[19] Amin maintained that females should receive the same education as males, so as to cope better with family duties and also to gain access to positions in the public sphere, to those positions that, if well-filled, would ensure the progress of the country. For this purpose, the religious customs associated with use of the veil, polygamous marriage and the general state of segregation of women should be abolished to make way for a process of national modernization, which would fail without being able to make use also of the female contribution. These ideas (due to their instrumental and subsidiary aspects) prompted widespread criticism and objections from the currents of feminine thought and activism existing in the same period and also from the exponents of the contemporary feminism originating in the Mediterranean area.[20] However, a great merit of Amin was that of opening a productive debate which induced reflection on the prospects of gender as a new challenge for the Arab societies of the time.[21] In this sense, and according to this chronology, one must speak of feminism(s) in the Arab world.[22] They were movements of a nationalistic, modernist and secular stamp, but, again to be underlined, *not* also laicist. Margot Badran, shedding light on the autochthonous roots of the contemporary Islamic feminism, reflects on how the instances that generally prompted debate in those years were strongly indebted to the ideologies of the end of the 1800s, when

> women anchored their feminist discourse firmly within the discourse of religious reform, most notably Islamic modernist discourse, and at the same time within the nationalist discourse, pairing their own liberation and advance with that of the nation, a trend in late nineteenth and early twentieth century women's struggle in parts of the Middle East that included other Asian societies.[23]

These first demands, ascribable to what has been defined by Badran, one of the foremost contemporary Islamic feminists, as the category of 'feminism of the century of nationalism', were characterized by the tendency to adopt the modernization of institutions and emancipation of the fatherland as the main aims through which the efforts of the activists could be channelled.[24] We must recall the semantic breadth and politico-cultural implications, in the sense of a form of national and non-secular 'government of the people', of the Arabic term indicating the noun 'secularism'. In describing the period of social and cultural unrest that characterized Egypt in the aftermath of the British occupation, Badran adds that far from elaborating a true feminist awareness—which would emerge officially only in 1923, on foundation of the Egyptian Feminist Union—the term *nationalism* was used both by women, who declined to accept the concept according to an interpretation focused on feminine emancipation, and by men, whose nationalism betrayed an immediate patriarchal stamp, taken for granted and never thematized as such.[25] The ideological border between the feminist cause and nationalist cause was therefore something of a fine line, but certainly the former was subordinate both lexically and practically to the latter. The contribution of feminist activism to the Egyptian nationalist party *Wafd* was fundamental during the struggle for independence. And yet the first official demand of Egyptian women dating back to 1910, voiced during the nationalist congress in Brussels, and expressly demanding an end to the British occupation of Egypt, was read by a man because it was legally impossible for the proposer to appear in public.[26] Therefore, one should not be surprised if, following Egyptian independence, the hopes for social affirmation on the part of women were frustrated and feminism as 'public independent discourse was silenced'.[27] The Egyptian women, initially active participants in the struggle for liberation, were soon marginalized in the name of national unity. To witness the birth of an autonomous feminist reflection in the Arab world it was necessary to wait until the first half of the twentieth century, following spread of the education system and the emergence of a new consciousness that was originally more feminine than feminist. The appearance of the pivotal movements, circles and associations whose exponents explicitly avoided the monopoly of masculine language dates to the period between the end of the 1800s and beginning of the 1900s. This was when diffusion of print media and access to the school system enabled an increasing number of women to build the embryo of a 'feminine conscience'[28] and to face the issues associated with the new role of the woman in Islamic societies.[29]

A brief summarizing reflection enables us to say that the secular feminism of the end of the nineteenth century always kept its demands within an Islamic framework, because the concept of secularism was not conceived as synonymous with exclusion of religion from the social sphere, but only as a consensual separation (neither indifferent nor hostile) between religion and the state, according to the modernist model. This is a distinction which was not at all taken advantage of in favour of the civil and political progress of women by the nationalist front of the victorious and patriarchal *Nahda*. It was the nationalism and patriarchalism, latitudinarian in mentality and practices and in institutions of every kind, and not religious faith as such which inhibited the legitimate instances of emancipation typical of the autochthonous, Mediterranean feminisms. This is true if an auto-ethnographical and self-reflexive reading based both on historical documents and witness accounts and on a combined theoretical-practical interest is of any value. In contrast, at the current moment some contemporary secular feminists in the Islamic area (Iran) do not consider this connection relevant. They set in a contrastive secular framework with respect to religions[30] their reflection on human rights as an instrument of affirmation of the female gender within a democratic civil society, which is aware of the risks of its evolution in a repressive direction. As asserted by Valentine Moghadam, an Iranian feminist takes a position of neither rejection nor acceptance towards Islamic feminism, 'although religious reform is salutary and necessary, it is important to recognize its limitations. Women's rights and human rights are best promoted and protected in an environment of secular thought and secular institutions'.[31]

Of what kind of secularism are we speaking, then? Does it have any sense to counterpoise once again (laicist) secularism to the demands for rights of women believers on religious and liberal-democratic bases? Or should we try to encourage some of the affected subjects to rephrase the thesis on secularism in Islamic discourse?

4. Secular state, Islam, women's rights: against a dual citizenship

The emergence and rapid spread of extremely violent forms of radicalism (e.g. Isis in Syria, Iraq, Libya, Europe, Nigeria and Mali) represents not only an urgent threat, but also a deep exegetic shake-up which challenges traditional Islamic thought taken as a whole.[32] In particular, the question is whether these tensions indicate the incomparability of cultural and/or religious traditions of the Muslim world with Western perceptions of women's rights and democratization, or whether that framing of the issue itself is problematic. Could it be that truly and universally feasible, instead of merely Western, conceptions of human/women's rights and democratization are in fact compatible with Islamic traditions? These are the same questions posed (see below, 5), and answered negatively by Moghadam, who supports a solution which seems to be incompatible with the over-quoted Islamic definition of secularism enforced during the 'old' *Nahda* experience. This could mean even the rejection of any type of democracy which aims at being 'religiously inspired', and not simply religiously dependent/derived. This is a crucial question. If it is easy to reject a theocracy (the second case), it is more difficult to tackle and to reject *ipso facto* the first typology, which includes numerous and various democratic systems throughout the world, Western democracies included.

In order to favour a better outcome with respect to the common objective, it is necessary once and for all to invert the historically consolidated priorities (see section 3) among the instances, putting the case of feminine and anti-patriarchal emancipation first whenever the others are considered variable, even if relevant. In this case, the variables are the notions of an Islamic secular state and religiously characterized secular democracy, a concept and political arrangement that appears to be the inevitable background of Islamic feminisms, not only in the Mediterranean countries but worldwide.

For this reason, we shall make a brief reference to the thinking of Abdullahi An-Na'im, even if this important figure has not yet been in direct discussion with feminist scholars. In *Islam and the Secular State*, especially in the opening chapter of the study, the world-famous legal scholar An-Na'im points out the relation between Islamic faith and the modern 'secular state', especially in a democratic context.[33] As An-Na'im declares: 'In order to be a Muslim by conviction and free choice, which is the only way one can be a Muslim, I need a secular state'.[34] By 'secular state' he means a political regime which both prohibits the public 'establishment' of religion and encourages the 'free exercise' of faith. A secular state, he notes, is

> one that is neutral [though not indifferent or hostile] regarding religion, one that does not claim or pretend to enforce *Shari'a*—the religious law of Islam—simply because compliance with *Shari'a* cannot be coerced by fear of state institutions or faked to appease their officials.

At the same time, secularism for An-Na'im characterizes a regime which 'facilitates the possibility of religious piety out of honest conviction' and 'promotes genuine religious observance, an observance operative in civil society rather than on the level of formal state structures'. With these formulations, *Islam and the Secular State* opposes both an overt 'politicization' and restrictive 'privatization' of faith. The stress on secularism in an Islamic sense, we read, does not mean 'the exclusion of Islam from the formulation of public policy and legislation or from public life in general'. On the contrary, 'the state (in order to be a genuine secular Islamic regime) should not attempt to enforce *Shari'a* precisely so that Muslims are able to live by their own belief in Islam as a matter of authentic (not coerced) religious obligation'.[35] First, in contrast to a laicistic ideology he acknowledges that 'the religious beliefs of Muslims' (whether as public officials or private citizens) are liable to 'influence their actions and political behavior' —an influence which necessarily blends the idea of a strict 'neutrality' as employed by many Western liberal thinkers. Second, in conformity with liberalism, 'people cannot truly live by their convictions' if rulers use the 'extensive coercive powers of the state' to impose religious doctrines. Third, reframing partly liberal assumptions, the state cannot be 'completely neutral (indifferent)' because as a public institution it is 'supposed to be influenced by the interests and concerns of its citizens'. Consequently, the modern principle of 'the religious neutrality of the state' acquires a dense connotation: state institutions should 'neither favor nor disfavor any religious doctrine or belief'. Nevertheless, the real objective of such neutrality is precisely 'the freedom of individuals in their communities to accept, object to, or modify any view of religious doctrine or principle'.[36] According to An-Na'im, apostasy should then be inconceivable as a crime according to the criminal law of any state in the world. We should add that even atheism or agnosticism must be envisaged and guaranteed—and this is also in opposition to the Western tradition *if* the *Epistula de Tolerantia* of John Locke is taken literally, that is to say without a hermeneutical–historical reframing. A similar critical acknowledgement is called for in the case of 'Western' modern democracy, if considered from a genealogical/interpretative point of view.

Given the fact that democratic life is nurtured by the motivations, beliefs and desires of ordinary citizens, and that these aspirations in turn reflect the religious beliefs and cultural customs of people, it follows that democracies cannot be the same everywhere but are bound to vary in accordance with beliefs and customs prevalent in different societies or regions.[37]

But what happens if the prevalent beliefs are or become again patriarchal, as is the case in many MENA countries nowadays? What about the restoring of dual citizenship for Muslims and for non-Muslims? What about the recurrent claims for a differential approach (equity and complementarity instead of equality, or equal dignity in separate roles) to women's status? Again, the 'women's rights issue' reveals itself to be a typical *experimentum crucis* for democracy and for secularism, in both cases, in a latitudinarian meaning and on a glocal scale, according to the auto-ethnographic approach.

5. What do they all have in common? The reopening of the door of interpretation of the Holy Book

The discourse on gender equality (irrespective of roles) in the Islamic world is centuries old. Contemporary protagonists of the debate regarding the emancipation of women believe that the first 'revolt of women' can be traced back to the times of the Prophet. It is told that a certain number of women protested about harassment by their spouses, and we can recall the wives of Muhammad, Sukayana bint al-Husayn, Um Salama e Aïcha, as symbols of female activism and freedom.[38]

Nevertheless, some aspects are new. Primarily, two main connotations are visible in the kaleidoscopic facets of the phenomenon labelled as Islamic feminism(s). There are two 'souls'. One is mainly theological, aiming at innovative interpretations of the Qur'an for the sake of genuine faith, no less than of the egalitarian, emancipatory message inherent in it. The other is associative, pragmatic, syncretic and transnational, aiming at the overwhelming of dichotomies, such as *local* versus *global*, *west* versus *east*, even the dichotomy 'secular feminism versus religious feminism, and Western feminism versus non-Western feminism'. According to this, an author like Valentine Moghadam can be situated on the left side of the constellation, even if she would accept this attribution only for the sake of a transnational post-colonial allegiance among 'decent' partners of the struggle against patriarchalism all over the world.

Despite this distinction between theologians and transnational intellectuals, this is only true from an ideal-typical point of view. Both are present in the works and declarations of the protagonists, all engaged in the promotion and safeguarding of the equality and dignity of all women worldwide, but ensured and respected in their contextual specificity, according to the codes immanent in their life-worlds. A step towards a more rigorous framing of what a religious *lifeworld* could be is merely asserting the relevance of a diverse terminology. Why Islamic and not Muslim feminism, given that the genuine individual faith in Allah and his Prophet is the turning point? Islam is a system of thought, of discourse, of traditional practices, of power and institutional devices. Muslim faith and life experience is irreducibly individual and variable. This is not simply a matter of words. It is not by chance that the doctrine of an Islamic secular state is grounded on the free choice to be a believer, declared in the Qur'an as a sine qua non condition to being a member of the *ummah*. How has it evolved since its beginnings, in the last decades of the past century, and who are the players? I could quote, for instance, the self-definition as Islamic feminists of Wadud, Cooke, Najmabadi, Lamrabet and Badran. More often than not Badran has been referred to with respect to the reconstruction of the roots of secular and feminine conscience. She is a graduate of al-Azhar University and Oxford University, and at the present moment one of the representatives of this constellation, under the motto of a 'holistic Muslim feminism', which could agree with the outline we referred to at the beginning (see section 2), and which could serve as a stipulative, but not uncontroversial definition.

A core definition of Islamic feminism is to be detected in the writings and work of Muslim (active believers in Allah and his Prophet) protagonists. Those scholars interpret their outcomes as a feminist discourse/practice and derive it from the Qur'an, seeking rights and justice within the framework of gender equality for women and men in the *totality* of their existence. Islamic feminism explicates the idea of gender equality as part and parcel of the Qur'anic notion of equality of all human beings and calls for the implementation of gender equality in the state, civil institutions and everyday life. It rejects the notion of a public/private dichotomy (incidentally absent in early Islamic jurisprudence) conceptualizing a holistic *ummah* in which Qur'anic ideals are operative throughout.

Badran is thus expressing clearly what she has called the theological (more distinctive and problematic) 'soul' of the constellation. Of course, the borders of the two fields are not clear-cut, but porous and blurred.[39]

With respect to the problems of compatibility of religion with women's rights and democracy, a proposal of mediation has been reached from a non-Western point of view, which is secular and religious, but not laicist. So far it has been necessary to provisionally resort to linguistic categories and dimensions associated with exegesis of the sacred texts, and with the terminology of theology, not only Islamic, but monotheistic, involving the three religions of the Book.

It is no longer possible to ignore or fail to appreciate the fact that thousands of women, both Muslim women believers and feminists, are reflectively active worldwide in order to improve their condition and that of others in the direction of greater equality and justice. This scenario has come about, also with a theoretical contribution through the work of great women reformist theologians, and male theologians, such as the much-lamented N. Abū Zaid, Muslim and reformist theologian. However, he does not enter into discussion with the feminists because he charges them to remain on the path of Islamic tradition and continue to interpret the Qur'an as a text. In his view the Qur'an is a plurality of discourses where many interlocutors are involved.

Nevertheless, the feminists (Wadud, Naseef and Hassan among others) are engaged especially in hermeneutics (*ta'wīl*) rather than exegesis in the form of the literal commentary (*tafsir*). Hermeneutics is the main method of open interpretation (free access of believers to the text of the Qur'an—and also to the sayings of the Prophet and the Sunnah), as we can see, for instance, in Amina Mernissi and Hidayet Tuksal, it is more than ever the basis for the transformation in favour of the instances of gender equality of Islam. The three effective hermeneutic methods of intervention can be listed as (a) rigorous re-examination of the phrases in order to reveal the permanent core and eliminate the ephemeral and spurious skin, as in the case of the Creation of Adam and Eve; (b) exact citation of the unmistakable formulations regarding gender equality; (c) critical deconstruction of the *surahs* in which the contextual and contingent difference of gender has been passed off as affirmation of male superiority.

For all the protagonists of this renewed hermeneutic line (of derivation, syncretically understood, *mu'tazilite* or *ṣufi*), we must recognize that, although the Qur'an is the word of God, we are dealing with a historical text, oral, proclaimed and put down in writing at a specific moment of history, in the social context and language of the time. Only starting from the presupposition of this historical and general philological awareness can we interpret the text of the Qur'an correctly and grasp the essence of the message, which transcends its historical context, and retrace its meaning for the believers of today.

This must be clear, in order that the sense, the original (and therefore dated) context and particularistic character of the times of Muhammad do not prevail over the universal, cosmopolitan and multilingual (not only Arabic) significance of the text. On the contrary, the historicized analysis of the life and sayings of the Prophet is a fundamental hermeneutic means of repositioning things in the right and appropriate place. The fundamental nucleus is in the following reading of the notion of equality, combining the three religions of the Book, which comes under the fourth chapter of the Qur'an, dedicated to women from a literary point of view, whilst from a hermeneutic viewpoint it is dedicated to equality and justice, the two cornerstones, the essential doctrine of Islam, referred to by Islamic modernism. Man and woman were created by a single soul. God divided them into two and this couple originated the entire human species.

The verse of the Qur'an (4: 1) speaks of *min nafsin wāḥidatin* (from a single soul, according to Abū Zayd[40]), and in the Hebrew verse of Genesis we find the Hebrew term *nefes* = spirit, living breath, a degree more original than the *ruach* but assimilable in that both refer to the bringing to life by the breath of God. This formula of *nafsin* is valid indistinctly for both Adam and Eve (we recall that the doctrine of original sin is particularly unfavourable for Eve), but has not had for Islam the same weight that it has assumed for Hebrew-Christian culture. We can say that '*male and female* was created the human being'. The version (the second of the two in Genesis) whereby Eve is created from Adam's rib was integrated *ex post* in the exegetical tradition.

On the other hand, considering the laical and revolutionary seventeenth century transcription, the French term *homme* also originally meant 'being human' and to this day does not indicate univocally a 'male human'. However, it is in this last meaning that the term has absorbed also the second gender, assimilating it, and imposing itself as the only meaning for two different meanings, the masculine and the feminine. The place of this misappropriated validation was the particular herald of momentous consequences: the *Declaration of the Rights of Man and of the Citizen* of 1789 was the model of language of rights beyond what could have been imagined at the time. Also for this reason the verses of the Qur'an that formulate the relation between human species and the distinction of gender roles are read and deconstructed in parallel by some Islamic and/or Mediterranean feminists. However, this is carried out in total autonomy and without reverence, with respect to the language of universal Western rights, without being advocates of literalism as are the Salafists. The opposite is true. Reading the parts with respect to the whole, the whole with respect to the parts, using socio-historical analysis together with linguistic methodology, anthropology, cultural studies, sociology, literary criticism and historiography is the way to give again the right place and appropriate meaning to the unchanging doctrine. This will distinguish the everlasting nucleus from the obsolete, dated and misleading stratifications, which, if not historicized, are impediments to the attainment of justice, freedom and equality.

A decisive example regards the cornerstone *surah* of the patriarchalism of Islam, *surah* 4 (al-Nisa'i), *aya* 34. The patriarchal exegesis translates it as the unchanging and unconditioned superiority of husbands with respect to their wives. This erroneous and distorted interpretation conditions logically and semantically the most specific references to patrimony, inheritance, the single and married conditions and violence within the household.

The theme of male superiority (*quawwamuna'ala*) is in reality an issue of responsibility, similar to 'providing for someone', to economic maintenance and to protection of female subjects during the vulnerable stages of breast-feeding and looking after the children.

This is a vulnerability and dependence which varies across the centuries and in socio-political contexts, as affirmed for example by Amina Wadud, Riffat Hassan and Fatima Naseef. In particular, they vary in relation to the capacity of women to work and maintain themselves independently and become head of the family. Furthermore, Badran suggests a synoptic reading of the *surah* 9, *aya* 71 (Al-Tawbah), in which it is said that believers, men and women, must protect each other: 'The believers, men and women, are protectors (*'awlliya*) of one another.'[41]

If these are the criteria and the salient examples of the Islamic feminist theological reworking of the reading of the Qur'an, through a reopening of the *ijtihad*, the personal reading of the texts, our initial warnings become understandable: (a) do not close the issue, because the search for counterpoints within feminist theological hermeneutics with an interreligious tone has just begun with the studies of the Lebanese Hosni Abboud on the 'revolutionary' role of Mary in the Qur'an; (b) do not lose sight of the complications—the twists, the asymmetries, the varied facets—of the picture, due to the discarding, or caesura, of previous versions by both women's movements on a world scale and also by the new autochthonous feminisms emerging in Islamic countries before and up to the 1990s.

In particular, there is still a need to face the radical criticism of those who, having experienced from the inside patriarchal Islamic life-worlds, do not envision the conceivability of the syntagma.

For some, not only misinformed citizens, overburdened by stereotypes, but also not only Western but originally Muslim feminists, it is considered an oxymoron, a contradiction in terms. An example is that of Ayan Hirsi Ali, screenwriter of *Submission*, the film for which Theo van Gogh was murdered. She declared that the Shari'a, the Islamic law, is an enemy of democracy, just like Nazism, and consequently an enemy of women's rights in that they are citizens *pleno iure*.

On the one hand, the theologians of the movement could counter-argue by using the above-cited An-Na'im, among others, saying that the Qur'an explicitly states that compliance with the Shari'a cannot be coerced by fear of state institutions or faked to appease their officials. Even the Qur'anic formulation (II, 256) is considered by supporters of the contemporary Tunisian movement *al-Nahda* and by the well-known theorist and politician R. al-Gannushi as no less than incontrovertible grounds for freedom of religious belief, founded in the above-cited *surah*. 'There is no constraint in Faith.'

On the other hand, it is just as true that only by accepting the vision of *coherent* religious secularism in the separation between constitution and the socio-political dimension like that of An-Na'im can one avoid *de jure* and de facto dual citizenship, for believers and non-believers, of which the 'moderate' Islamist R. al-Gannushi theorized the constitutional model in the 1990s, well before Tunisia had the real possibility of putting it into effect. This is total freedom of professing faith, from which however there descend different accesses to public positions among believers and non-believers, together with different obligations of behaviour. The distinction is between a general citizenship and a special citizenship, between a Muslim citizen, for whom certain behaviours (and not only food) are forbidden, and a *dhimmi* (a protected person, in the sense of a non-Muslim citizen in an Islamic state, as was the case for Christian and Jews in the medieval millet system), for whom the main public positions are forbidden.[42] The content of the programme of the secular feminists, although sensitive to new ideas of the Islamic feminisms, focus exactly on this point, in order to avoid the ownership rights of freedom and equality for women *passing through* adhesion to the Qur'anic faith and the consequent membership of Islam as a traditional patriarchal apparatus.

6. Internal criticism of Islamic feminism: a dense conversation, not a third way

Valentine Moghadam, a legitimate component of the movement so far as it is a transnational and inclusive phenomenon, envisaged the evolution of Islamic feminism in Iran after the Islamic Revolution and formation of the Islamic Republic of Iran. In comparison with Leila Ahmed and other scholars, Moghadam expressed her critical attitude to the formation of Islamic feminism more than 14 years ago. It is not a paradox because she is indebted to the most secular variant of feminism in the Islamic world, Iranian feminism, which nowadays, not without the restless activity of a global figure such as the Nobel prize winner Shirin Ebadi and her worldwide network, is more culturally and politically active, and more demanding than ever. It is no surprise at all that she is vindicating the specificity of the Iranian autochthonous way to feminism. This is a path enriched by the encounter *in loco* of both colonial and Western feminism and by diverse ideological contaminations. This can become clear only if we take seriously the contextual specificity and embedded richness of the particular version of Western or Arabic feminism which is the Iranian version of 'women's emancipation'.

Moghadam already in 2002 framed the debate with attention to the objections and assertions of both sides, conceding neither that Islamic feminism is the best option nor that culturally specific feminism or feminism *inspired by Islam* is invalid per se. Nevertheless, she is a secularist. On the one hand, Moghadam said that 'Islam, like other monotheistic religions ... may inspire civil codes, political processes, social policies, and economic institutions'; on the other hand, like many other scholars, she does not explain where the difference lies between Islam-inspired and Islam-derived nations and laws. She does make it clear, however, that 'it is not possible to defend as feminist the view that women can attain equal status only in the context of Islam' because this 'is a fundamentalist view'. Moghadam, therefore, continues to assert that feminism needs to act in a secular (laical) way in order to balance the dominant tendency towards regression to repressive (public and private) practices against women carried out by social and political institutions. She further points out that it is particularly Islam which puts feminist movements in danger because Islam and the 'Islamic state ... defines citizenship rights on the basis of sex and religion'.[43]

The main point, again, is whether this result remains a specific Islamic constitutional view among others, restricted to some of the emerging Islamic movements, such as the contemporary *al-Nahda* in Tunisia, and therefore subject to interpretation or even rejection from competing constitutional views. Only if we consider the winning trends in political national struggles can we then be more sympathetic towards Moghadam's concerns. But can we envisage a better strategy than the one of fighting the enemy with its own weapons?

Ideologists and representatives of Islamic feminism, as we have seen above (IV), focus on *ijtihad*, or the ability to freely use individual reason to interpret the holy texts of Islam, which allows for a reinterpretation of the Qur'an that depicts this fundamental source of religious faith as a doctrine granting women's rights. This is a practice of decentring the still dominant elite (the male clergy) from their hegemony of interpretation and replacing this by a gender-sensitive, female and feminist, decolonized and decentralized intellectuality (see above, 1). This use of *ijtihad* may even contribute to creating a new kind of feminism, which is culturally specific and nevertheless transnational and glocal.

Nayereh Tohidi, another significant and critical Iranian proponent of Islamic feminism, quoted by Moghadam, argues that this reframing of both Islam and feminism allows women to reinterpret, for example, the veil as a means of facilitating social presence rather than seclusion, by transforming the compulsory dress code into fashionable styles.[44] We should not forget how this attitude of syncretic and pragmatic struggle can improve and facilitate the interreligious allegiances among feministic theologians (see above, 5). Let us remember (see above, 1) that latent oppositions, resistances and micro-resistances in particular are often used by women, who act by resorting to the simulacrum of the patriarchal discourse. They empty it from the inside, by means of micro-systems of autonomous creations, of development of marginal subjective identities, which remain female, but are of specific types. If, in other words, Islamic feminism allows for both religious interpretation and slow but erosive subversion of the oppressive Islamist law and politics of Iran, with Moghadam we could claim that the open, even conflicting discourse between new cultural feminisms and older feminism is more crucial and effective than one side dominating the debate. Is there then the possibility of creating a pragmatic allegiance for the sake of the women between a feminism only inspired by Islam and the women's movements strictly derived from an Islamic identity (however, very differentiated)? In this case, as a humble proposal, we could refer to the first as 'Islamic feminism' and the second as 'Islamistic women's groups'. In this case, feminism does not derive from an Islamic fixed identity but it is able to bargain among negotiable and non-negotiable issues and frame day by day the allegiances established. This is for the sake of a transnational post-colonial allegiance among 'decent' partners in the struggle against patriarchy all over the world.

7. Some final considerations

Women's rights are and can be under attack again even in countries where they are considered already established and have been consolidated for decades, like in some countries of the EU. Women's rights are not granted per se, and no country is immune to different scales of exposure to this deceitful socio-political and cultural infection, to use a medical metaphor, from the latent and insidious danger of the revival of gender discrimination, direct or indirect, or of detrimental types of gender asymmetries, and neither of the West(s), in the plural, are safe. Nowhere can female and new cultural feminist movements, together with older ones, allow themselves to disengage. Moreover, they are compelled not only to struggle in the political arena at the different dimensional scales, national, transnational and glocal, but even their 'must' is that of elaborating from the scientific point of view some new, effective analytical tools to anticipate with more acute sensitivity the unforeseen menaces against women's freedom and women's self-determination in insurgent political frames never seen before.

Disclosure statement

No potential conflict of interest was reported by the author.

Notes

1. *Glocalization*: this is the concept that puts the binary logic in a critical position. The binary logic interprets reality by means of the mutually excluding terms of homogeneity-heterogeneity, integration-disintegration. On the contrary, Robertson understands differently the relationship between universalism and particularism and states that their thick, multi-dimensional, dynamic and open interaction opposes a globalization understood merely as global homologation from above. R. Robertson, *Globalization: Social Theory and Global Culture*, Sage, London, 1992.
2. A. F. Amor, 'Constitution et religion dans l'État musulmans [Constitution and religion in the Muslim States]', in AA. VV. (Préface Henry Roussillon, Conférence inaugurale Jean Imbert), *Constitutions et Religion*, 4, Académie international de Droit Constitutionelle, Epuisé Presses de l'Université des sciences sociales de Toulouse, Tunis, 1996, p. 53; Nouveau tirage Académie Internationale de Droit Constitutionnel, 2007, 1060, Tunis B.P. 72, 1013, Menzah IX (Tunisie).
3. A. Vanzan, *Le donne di Allah. Viaggio nei femminismi islamici* [The women of Allah. Journey through the Islamic Feminisms], Mondadori, Milan, 2010, pp. 1–4.
4. M. Badran, 'Islamic feminism. What is in a name?', in *Feminism in Islam*, OneWorld, Oxford, 2009, p. 244.
5. F. Mernissi, *Women in Islam. An Historical and Theological Inquiry*, trans. Mary Jo Lakeland, Oxford, Blackwell, 1991.
6. R. Pepicelli, *Femminismo Islamico. Corano, diritti, riforme [Islamic feminism. Qur'an, rights, reforms]*, Carocci Editore, Rome, 2010, p. 14.
7. V. M. Moghadam, 'Feminism and Islamic fundamentalism: a secularist interpretation', *Journal of Women's History*, 13(10), 2001, pp. 43–45.
8. S. Shimada, 'Aspetti della traduzione culturale: il caso dell'Asia' ['Some aspects of cultural translation: the Asia case'], in B. Henry, E. Batini and I. Possenti (eds), *Mondi globali* [Global Worlds], ETS, Pisa, 2000, pp. 137–159; N. Labanca, 'Una visione postcoloniale' ['A postcolonial vision'], in G. M. Cavallarin et al. (eds), *Gli ebrei in Cina e il caso di 'Tien Tsin'*, prefazione di N. Labanca [The Jews in China and the 'Tien Tsin' case, preface of N. Labanca], Belforte, Livorno, 2012, p. 18; E. Said, *Globalizing Literary Study*, Publications of the Modern Language Association of America, 116, 2001, p. 65.
9. C. Bartoli, 'Subalternità, rappresentazioni sociali e rappresentanza politica'['Subalternity, social representations and political representation'], *Ragion pratica*, 2, 2004, p. 23.
10. M. Foucault, *Society must be Defended. Lectures at the Collège de France, 1975/1976*, Picador, New York, 2003; J. Murdoc, *Post-structuralist Geography*, Sage, London, 2006; Said, op. cit.
11. N. Bobbio, *L'età dei diritti* [The age of rights], Einaudi, Torino, 1992.
12. Badran, 'Islamic feminism', op. cit., p. 242; M. Badran, 'Toward Islamic feminisms: a look at the Middle East', in Asma Afsaruddin (ed.), *'Hermeneutics of Honor': Negotiating Female 'Public' Space in Islamicate Societies*, Harvard University, Center for Middle Eastern Studies, Cambridge, MA, 1999, pp. 159–188.
13. Pepicelli, op. cit., pp. 31–32.
14. Such as the closure towards the individual interpretative effort (*ijtihad*) that occurred in the tenth century.
15. N. āmid Abū Zayd, *Testo sacro e libertà. Per una lettura critica del Corano*, Introduzione di N. zu Fürstenberg [Holy Text and Liberty. On behalf of a Critical Reading of the Quran, Introduction of N. zu Fuerstenberg], a cura di F. Fedeli, Marsilio, Vicenza, 2012.

16. E. Pace, *Sociologia dell'Islam* [Sociology of Islam], Carocci, Roma, 1999, pp. 165–172.
17. 'The segregation of women still practised in the first decades of the twentieth century, was considered a symbol of prestige and social status. Only in the higher classes, where the women could afford not to work, delegates the servants to carry out the domestic chores, was it in fact possible to observe the almost total exclusion of women from the public sphere.' Pepicelli, op. cit., p. 33.
18. The first text in favour of female emancipation should really be attributed to the jurist Murqus Fahmi who in 1894 privately published *Al-mar'a fi al-sharq* [The Women in the East]. However, the general picture and objective, both of an instrumental character, do not change. Cf. I. Segati, 'Feminisms in the Arab world between secularism and Islamism. Origins and characteristics to orientate in the contemporary academic debate', unpublished final paper, 2012.
19. M. Badran, 'Dual liberation: feminism and nationalism in Egypt: 1870s-1925', *Feminist Issues*, 3, 1988, pp. 15–34.
20. Opinions contrary to those of Amin have been expressed by some feminist authors such as the Egyptian Malak Hifni Nasif and, more recently, Leila Ahmed, who have questioned the specific recommendations of the jurist to abandon the use of the veil (*Nasif*), and the instrumental use of the condition of Muslim women with the aim of discrediting the whole Islamic cultural universe, with respect to the occidental world 'more advanced on the road to progress' (Ahmed). Cf. L. Ahmed, *Women and Gender in Islam*, Yale University Press, New Haven, CT, 1992, particularly Chapters 9 and 10; C. L. Ahmed, *Oltre il velo: la donna nell'Islam da Maometto agli ayatollah* [Beyond the veil: the 'woman' inside the Islam from Muhammad to the ayatollah], La Nuova Italia, Firenze, 1995; see Segati, op. cit., p. 8.
21. M. Badran, 'Between secular and Islamic feminism/s, reflections on the Middle East and beyond', *Journal of Middle East Women's Studies*, 1(1), 2005, p. 7.
22. Ibid., pp. 6–7.
23. Badran, 'Between secular', op. cit., p. 8.
24. Badran, 'Dual liberation', op. cit., p. 16.
25. Ibid., p. 17.
26. Badran, 'Dual liberation', op. cit., p. 24.
27. Pepicelli, op. cit., p. 41.
28. The author Shahrzad Mojab counterposes the use of this term to the more organic and conscious feminist movement that emerged later. See S. Mojab, 'Theorizing the politics of Islamic feminism', Special issue: 'The realm of the possible: Middle Eastern women in political and social spaces', *Feminist Review*, 69, 2001, pp. 124–146.
29. The centre of diffusion of these movements was Egypt, where between 1892 and 1925 we could count at least 24 women's journals, and where in 1923, due to the work of the feminist Hoda Sha'rawi, the Egyptian Feminist Union (UFE) was founded, the first organization aimed at the female right to education and work, the reform of the Code of the personal statute and at universal suffrage, which would be recognized in 1956. Other organizations followed in Palestine and Morocco, in the wake of the Egyptian example, and these attempted to systematically reconcile feminist demands with national contexts which included the ideology of the modernist movements of the *Nahhda* of the end of the nineteenth century.
30. H. Ahmed-Gosh, 'Dilemmas of Islamic and secular feminists and feminisms', *Journal of International Women's Studies*, 9(3), 2008, pp. 99–116.
31. V. M. Moghadam, 'Islamic feminism and its discontents: toward a resolution of the debate', *Signs*, 27(4), 2002, p. 1162.
32. The urgent issues of the compatibility of human/women's rights with Islamic thought and especially Islamic regimes have again become of crucial relevance worldwide. More precisely, the turmoil provoked by the Arab uprisings have revived an ongoing debate on the relationship between secularism and religion, on the role of constitutionalism and women's rights within Islamic contexts. In the MENA region and the Arab (Islamic) world in general, the relationship between states and religion are undergoing a profound process of internal redefinition, with revolutionary developments that, for example in Tunisia, have brought a new promising

Constitution, while in Libya has led so far to the dismantling of any form of the rule of law, in the hope of a real endorsement of the proclaimed institutional change in the very near future. See F. Dallmayr, 'Whither democracy? Religion, politics and Islam', *Philosophy and Religion,* 'Reset', Web Magazine, Istanbul Seminar, Wednesday, 29 August 2012.

33. A. A. An-Na'im, *Islam and the Secular State: Negotiating the Future of Shari'a*, Harvard University Press, Cambridge, MA, 2008, pp. 1–2.
34. Ibid., p. 2.
35. Ibid., pp. 4–6.
36. Ibid., pp. 3–4.
37. Dallmayr, op. cit., n. 15.
38. Badran, 'Between secular', op. cit., p. 6.
39. Badran, 'Islamic feminism', op. cit., pp. 246–247.
40. One can accept here, due to the clear assonance with the Hebrew term *nefes* (soul), the solution proposed by Ḥāmid Abū Zayd, op. cit., p. 42. Cf. the note by the editor, F. Fedeli, who motivates the choice and directs it to a traditional and patriarchal setting which recognized in that 'person' the first human, Adam. Ibid., p. 67.
41. Badran, 'Islamic feminism', op. cit.,, pp. 248–249.
42. R. al-Gannushi, *The Right to Nationality Status of Non-Muslim Citizens in a Muslim Nation*, Islamic Foundation of America, Springfield, USA, 1990. See A. Santilli and P. Longo, 'Tunisia: models of Islamic state compared. *Al-Nahda* and *Hizb al-tahir* between Islamic democracy and universal caliphate', *The History of Political Thought*, Special issue: 'The ambiguous concept of Islamic state', 3, 2014, pp. 399–422.
43. Moghadam, 'Islamic feminism and its discontents, op. cit., p. 1162.
44. VIbid., p. 1147.

Gender, Identity and Belonging: New Citizenships beyond Orientalism

Alessia Belli and Anna Loretoni

ABSTRACT
By applying the gender perspective to the concept of Orientalism elaborated by Edward Said, the article debates how the Orient is not only a cultural construction, but also a sexual one. This lens is able to disclose the gender rhetoric through which the Western feminist eye has framed the 'Other Woman', depicting her as bounded by cultural ties. This is well exemplified by the stereotype of the Muslim woman as veiled, victim and powerless. The deconstructive strategy and the intersectional approach will fruitfully interact with the vivid experience of some Italian and British Muslim women activists, to show that the agency of Muslim women emerges in different contexts, thus breaking the Western mainstream essentialist perspective. The concept of fluid identity is proposed to make sense of the processes of identity formation with a focus on the intertwining of religious, gender and political dimensions vis-à-vis controversial practices such as the veil and arranged marriages. It is the voices of these women that challenge and re-signify fundamental principles such as democratic citizenship and personal autonomy, creating the basis for a transnational feminism that, from the recognition of women's specificities and global inequalities, proves able to devise shared, more equitable and empowering pathways.

The 'deconstructive strategy'

Within Western thought, the 'deconstructive strategy' that gender studies has proposed to the disciplinary perspective of social sciences represents one of the most significant contributions of theoretical reflection of the twentieth century.[1] This new perspective has challenged the presumed neutral configuration of the salient aspects of modernity, starting from a very crucial aspect, the concept of identity. Reinforcing the awareness that in modernity the configuration of identity should have an elective character, that is relative to an autonomous identity-making project, the studies which have taken gender as a central category of their analysis have brought to an end the strict association between autonomy and construction of identity which defines the genealogical features of the modern subject. Within a theoretical project that challenges the ascribable dimension of the identity-making contents offered by tradition, gender studies have added a critical appeal towards liberalism.

They underlined that socially constructed ambit of the female identity which, paradoxically, seems to represent an almost solitary bridge between *ancien régime* and modern phase. Modernity, in fact, re-proposes a definition of the female identity that emphasizes in the first place an essential and natural function within the private space, effectively leaving women very little freedom to construct in an autonomous and dissenting manner their own identity-making experience. Notwithstanding the dynamic character with which gender studies, through the perspective of social constructivism, have investigated the concept of identity and belonging, it has not always appeared coherent. In particular, when Western feminism was about to deal with other, minority cultures, the overall philosophy underpinning this approach appeared embedded in an uncritical and imperialistic framework. Critical points of view have been expressed by non-Western feminism, which has accused European and North American feminism of ethnically charged paternalism towards other cultures, judged to be incapable of internal dynamism. Differently from Western culture, where the principle of equality has progressively asserted itself, other cultures have been relegated to an unchanging and homogenous space, without internal conflicts and dissenting voices. The representation of other cultures proposed by Susan Moller Okin, for example, does not seem to include local traditions of protest, or autochthonous feminist movements or independent sources of political contestation.[2] The risk we run is that of observing non-Western cultures from afar and from above, which itself reiterates the less edifying aspects of liberal patriarchalism. Distinguishing in a monolithic and simplistic way the liberal West and the rest of the world presupposes a static conception of minority cultures, which confines them to a space without time, according to a hypothesis that effectively attributes them a substantial incapacity for internal transformation and modernization. Here we meet some relevant limits of the liberal feminist approach.

Gendering Orientalism

The traditional way in which the West has looked upon the non-Western cultures, in particular the East and the Arab world, simply confirms a series of stereotypes. It sees the West as typically individualistic and democratic and the East as always despotic and collectivist. The habit of the West to look down upon cultural otherness tends to give an interpretation which is essentialist and non-dynamic. Whilst it is recognized that our culture has progressed historically towards the affirmation of new liberties vis-à-vis political, cultural and religious power, it seems almost that other cultures' opportunities for success in this respect are barred. According to this perspective, modernity is a product of the European and North American world, to be spread throughout the rest of the world. In this perspective, the seminal interpretation elaborated four decades ago by Edward Said on the concept of Orientalism remains relevant to understanding the ways in which the world is constructed along a binary logic.[3] Interpreted as a tool for establishing Western imperial hegemony, the concept of Orientalism has contributed to demystifying the contrast between a monolithic West and an equally monolithic East. The two poles have been defined not only with completely divergent internal characteristics, but on opposed axiological levels, thus dividing the world into two halves on the basis of an ontological and epistemological distinction. This becomes clear in the colonial language of the West, which reflects the concept of being a *parens patriae* that carefully looks after its children, by 'othering' the East. After 9/11 the representation of separate and incomparable civilizations, always on the verge of possible conflict, was growing and contributed to defining the dominant rhetoric regarding Islam and Muslims. An example of scholarship that in recent times restates this Orientalist approach is Samuel Huntington's *Clash of Civilizations* thesis, especially in the binary logic this work proposes.[4] The Islamophobic drift feeds on the conviction that Islam is incompatible with modernity, secularism and democracy. It is a kind of representation that defines and naturalizes the others, making us unable to understand any new subjectivities that can emerge in the Islamic world.[5] Orientalism is in fact the expression of a dualistic thinking which uses hierarchical oppositions constructed around a very simplified 'Us/Them' notion. Within the Oriental discourse 'Islam', and by extension Arabs, are seen as irrational, menacing and anti-Western, also by implying that violence, corruption and dishonesty are embedded in 'other' cultures. The idea of 'new barbarism' is one of the contemporary expressions of Orientalism, reinforced by the 'war on terror' and the 'liberating missions' by the West.[6] In addition, we believe that the topic of reciprocal views between Islam and the West should be fruitfully read also by means of the gender lens. In this way, we understand that just as the view of the Orient is not only that of the Western subject, but is also that of a male one, the East is not only a cultural construct, but also a sexual one. Today more than ever before there is a need to unveil the hidden gender rhetoric of Orientalism, attempting to understand Orientalism as shaped by gender and sexuality. The image of the veil is at the basis of an essentialist interpretation of the Orient as a land of oppression and barbarism, which is incapable of bringing to light the changes which have been introduced within a juridical context by the new family codes and through which women's role has been reinforced. Starting from these premises, we can make two important considerations. Above all, Islamic feminism is no longer an expression with an oxymoronic flavour and, according to Ruba Salih, it represents a framework within which the rights of women are claimed by means of a re-reading of the sacred scriptures.[7] This implies that it is not so much Islam, as Fatima Mernissi says, which puts forward the concept of intrinsic female inferiority, but this state is rather the result of social and cultural institutions attempting to legally subordinate and segregate women within the family structure.[8] In this way, the very same commitment to the defence of women's rights assumes an independent and original connotation separated from the Western context, also in opposition to a secular feminism of an elitist kind, judged to be a slave of Western modernity. In the Islamic world, there has been a progressive movement towards a debate on feminism and women's rights which is based on indigenous roots. This is intended to break away from the idea of feminism as a form of cultural imperialism. Even if not all Muslim women agree with this definition, to speak of Islamic feminism therefore means maintaining a cross-cultural perspective, able to emphasize the agency of a subject who performs multiple roles, of believer and of promoter of rights at the same time.[9] Adopting the gender lens immediately brings out the inadequacy of the approach that that the West—including white feminism—has always supported on the basis of a substantial essentialism. On the one hand, there is the more traditional stereotype of the dominated and passive Muslim woman, incapable of any agency. On the other hand, we have the image of the menacing fighter who subverts the Western order, its norms and values, such as the new outcome nurtured by recent events related to international terrorism. Both stereotypes represent two faces of the same coin. The primary symbol of this stereotype is the veil, to which the Muslim social system has often been reduced. The recent move in France to ban the veil from public schools, supported also by some feminists, confirms the binary opposition between the West and the Islamic world. The underpinning mentality expressed in the idea that 'we-know-better-what-is-good-for-them' is at stake here, in condemning as pure domination the act of veiling. On the contrary, the voice of Muslim women offers a different interpretation, confirming the idea that the veil, as a symbol, is open to a variety of meanings that people attribute to it. 'The presumption that Muslim women robotically suffer silently under the hijab homogenizes them and ignores the strong voice of many educated and progressive Muslim women who wear it due to a strong moral and ideological principle and who consider it a symbol of liberation'.[10] Assuming the perspective of a multiple and liberally redefined belonging, the equation 'veil equals submission' is no longer so clear. The veil itself assumes a particularly meaningful symbolic value in the definition of a modernity that is alternative to that of Western society. Recent studies have shown how wearing the hijab is not necessarily a symbol of modesty and submission, but is a visible link of identification with a transnational community of young, well-educated and fashionable Muslim women. In the opinion of one of the most attentive interpreters of this phenomenon, Seyla Benhabib, the young Muslim women who live in liberal democratic contexts are tenaciously trying to exploit the principle of equality offered by this tradition and are attempting to re-signify the act of wearing the veil.[11] If we assume that the significance of wearing the veil is merely a religious challenge to the Western secular state, or that it is a clear act of submission, we mortify the capacity of these women to set down the sense of their own actions. We risk confining them again to that patriarchal world from which they are attempting to escape, putting into effect an agency able to bargain with that tradition. Stigmatizing the behaviours of these young Muslim women seems to bring out the very contradictions of Western culture, which on the one hand emphasizes the universal dimension of rights and values, and on the other hand raises boundaries in order to define political communities from within.

The limits of Western feminist eyes

By interiorizing the notion of Western superiority and Eastern inferiority, Orientalist discourse constructs some essential differences between the liberal West and the subjugated East that foster the idea of civilizing and saving that part of the world by rescuing it from a subaltern status. This narrative includes the same Western feminist perspective which in some cases reinforces the Manichean polarity between a Western/European woman and an Islamic/Eastern woman. The first is emancipated and free, the second subaltern and slave. This approach brings in itself the inability, disclosed by postcolonial studies, on the part of the European theory to deal adequately with the complexities of colonized society. Essentializing eastern women means there is no appreciation of the cultural and historical differences, the specific realities, within eastern women's experiences. In this way, Western feminism has been scrutinized by non-Western feminism, as confirmed by the analytical work of Chandra Mohanty on Western feminist writings.[12] The Orientalist model of representing other cultures seems to be deeply rooted in the Western feminist way of building the image of the so called 'third world woman' as a singular monolithic subject. At stake here is an interpretation of colonization in terms of discursive attitude, based on a certain mode of codification and on some particular analytic categories that arise from the implicit assumption that a primary and unique referent both in theory and in practice is at work. This approach discursively colonizes the material and historical heterogeneities of the life experience of women in the third world, their fundamental complexities and conflicts which characterize women's condition in the different countries. The power related to such a process of homogenization and systematization should be discovered and named, as embedded in the Western attitude to think itself as universal. The first mistake in this approach is the assumption of women as an already constituted, coherent group with identical interests, regardless of class, ethnicity or religion. The notion implied in this framework is that of gender or sexual difference, and also patriarchy, to be applied universally and cross-culturally. According to Western eyes, as suggested in much of Western feminist discourse, the third world woman is a victim of political and religious power, interpreted only through the lens of oppression and discrimination. To Mohanty, the third world woman is represented as ignorant, poor, uneducated, tradition-bound, domestic, family-oriented and victimized, while on the contrary the implicit Western version is shaped in terms of an educated woman, modern, with freedom in her decisions and in her body and sexuality. The fact that this homogeneous group is produced not on the basis of biological essentials, but of some sociological universals that define the concept of a cross-cultural oppression, beyond race and class, is irrelevant for the critical analysis proposed by Mohanty. With the same flavour, within subaltern studies, G. Spivak has stressed the image of the subaltern woman, whose identity, starting from her inability to speak, has been defined by both local patriarchal societies and Western imperialism alike, and also by feminism in a similar way.[13] So embedded is she in this double bind that the subaltern woman becomes invisible and 'ventriloquized' as if she did not have the possibility to speak for herself.

Following this perspective, the very concept of 'sisterhood', proposed in terms of essentialist universalism, based upon the fact of being women, of being oppressed and discriminated at the same level, should be revisited with a different view. This view can rebuild it not as a perspective of departure but of arrival, able to take into account not only the category of gender but also that of race and class, as suggested by intersectionalism.[14] From a methodological point of view, in this approach the relevance of the comparative model of studying becomes clear, which tries to read jointly phenomena and events which occur somewhere in the world according to a horizontal and multi-focused analysis, able to avoid the paramount risk of using a distant, superior and top-down viewpoint on the part of the West. In so doing, we are able to assume a more sophisticated diversity perspective, in which internal transformation and original modernization are opportunities belonging to all cultures. In this way, Western feminism can avoid retracing the least edifying aspects of the colonial and patriarchal attitude of that very same liberal culture from which it attempts to distance itself. If feminist research, then, is about challenging existing power relations to generate transformative and empowering dynamics, how can it actually and concretely fulfil this fundamental, albeit ambitious, objective?

A counter-Orientalist machinery: what kind of feminist research?[15]

Methodologies and methods adopted by feminist research represent the *conditio* sine qua non to keep faith with the abovementioned mission. In this sense, the choice of deconstructing Orientalism from a gender point of view, showing the strategic role that Muslim women have played in this essentialist rhetoric, as examined in the first part of the essay, goes hand in hand with the choice of embarking on a journey into Muslim women's manifold experiences. More precisely, taking seriously the feminist credo of the need to listen to women's voices, this second part draws from the vivid narratives of 26 Muslim women activists[16] interviewed in Italy and the UK between 2009 and 2011.[17] They reflected the variegated Muslim presence in the two states not only in terms of ethnicity but, according to intersectionalism, of age, origin, class and education. Some of them were converts and some wore the veil, since adopting the headscarf represents a crucial factor when dealing with the process of external labelling and public self-definition of Muslim women. Since the ascribed label 'Muslim' hampers their capacity for self-definition, and since these women decide nevertheless to assume it, how do they manage to work inside this categorization? According to what motives and with what outcomes? Their strategic positioning at the crossroads of different worlds is a vantage point to analyse the intertwining of the religious and gender dimensions in the process of identity formation, thus paving the way for the consolidation of a counter-essentialist discourse. Adopting semi-structured interviews then allowed the research to be conducted on the participants' terms as much as possible, thus complying with the feminist attitude to carrying out a study with sensitivity, empathy and care for participants. This is a fundamental tool to expose theoretical categories such as autonomy, choice, constraint and agency to a continual process of questioning, broadening and clarification of its own assumptions according to the concrete ways in which these concepts are translated into people's everyday lives. Moreover, asking for informed consent, acting in an open and respectful manner, explaining the aims of the study to the interviewees, making them part of the process through their revision of the interviews and sharing the results with them are all fundamental tools of this paradigm.

Positionality and power

Within feminist methodology, the issue of the researcher's positionality represents a crucial aspect: her own experiences profoundly influence the form and contents of the analysis. Personal and global events forge one's perspective in a more or less conscious way, so that the researcher always ends up in a position of partial otherness. Being an Italian and a non-Muslim researcher within a European climate of mounting Islamophobia and of increasing perception of Islam as a threat may have sparked a defensive reaction in the participants since they were questioned, once again, about their Muslimness, the main source of attacks and stigmatization. Moreover, by virtue of their respective characteristics, researcher and participants were differently located in relation to one another, sharing some features while being divided for others.[18] In reporting the visions of the interviewees, however, there is the awareness of tracing only one of many possible paths through such a diverse panorama. For this reason, the research does not claim to be scientific in the sense of representing the experience of all Muslim women activists, let alone Muslim women in general. Any research, in fact, pays the price of being a mere glimpse, a specifically selected route. When analysing the data, what emerges is a broad variety of positions: differences and contradictions are the real fabric of the study. The aim is to bring out precisely heterogeneity, fluidity and blended margins. Despite the recognition of these limits, this research nevertheless represents a 'true' trajectory in the sense of reflecting and retracing the life-path of some women who found themselves enmeshed in pressing and constraining circumstances. Far from conceiving this sort of contextuality as a fatal limit, according to the feminist credo, it represents the *conditio* sine qua non for rendering and interpreting the complexity of real life and each and every person's manifold responses. Even in this contextually sensitive and self-reflexive framework, however, there is the persistent risk of overlooking the issue of power. Any research, in fact, brings with it a certain degree of objectification and exploitation, since the researcher, if anything, takes advantage of what she is studying to promote her own career. However, in order to avoid a sense of moral and ideological paralysis it is important to make this risk transparent and 'to work empirically with the permission of informants and accept that one will end up being in a partially ethical position'.[19] This is particularly important to tackle the risks of further objectification of the other implied in the profound, fluid and ongoing relationship between researcher and participants, one where 'Knowledge of the other and knowledge of the self are mutually informing because self and other share a common condition of being women'.[20] More interestingly, while the researcher discovers her own power to define, to emphasize or to omit, she is also faced with the fact that people do have the power to refuse to participate, to divert questions, to strategically exercise their position in order to address or avoid certain issues. The researcher's self and the self of the participants constitute an inseparable unit with the general context, itself permeated by power relations. The entire research, in other words, is informed by a 'contextual approach to reflexivity',[21] one that acknowledges how our position as researchers gives us a unique and deep perspective on social life and suggests how to use this privileged position to make clear the social, political and cultural forces that generally constrain and discriminate against women in their everyday lives. This is a fundamental toolkit for any feminist research that is aimed at deconstructing Orientalist discourses and pursuing women's recognition and empowerment in a fairer society.

The difficult relationship with secular feminists

The difficulties identified in the first part of the essay regarding Western feminism vis-à-vis the third world woman, especially if she happens to be a Muslim, find a strong confirmation in the narratives, where establishing a relationship with secular feminists was recognized as a critical point. According to the British interviewees, in fact, secular feminists nurture stereotypes against Muslim women: the veil is for them a sign of submissiveness that justifies the adoption of a liberating, missionary approach. Cassandra Balchin[22] explains the reaction of her feminist colleagues when they discovered that she was Muslim: 'people's behaviour changed overnight toward me. It seemed to overlook decades of my working on human rights; people presumed I had dropped that. Everything was conflated, identity and political position'. According to her colleagues, religion is irreconcilable with feminism and with a commitment to women's rights. How is that different, Cassandra continues,

> from claiming a feminist identity or an Asian identity? They say that we need to have black women's movements: how is that different from saying that Muslim women need to come together in order to have a safe space so that they can articulate their specific concerns, get the confidence and then go out and be part of a broader movement? It is not isolating.

Denying someone the right to claim their religious identity means for Cassandra denying the same right for all other possible identifications. That this reaction was coming from women who had developed a deep knowledge about identity politics, a sophisticated postmodernist, anti-essentialist sociological analysis, was the thing that struck her the most. After all, they contradicted what they were criticizing in theory. According to Cassandra, the atheist presumption inherent in this approach, which considers religion as bad per se, ends up by discarding the majority of world women who have religious beliefs, judging them as stupid or opportunistic. Moreover, in the UK many non-religious feminists have seen the increasing number of Muslim women's organizations as a ploy to drain resources away from secular spaces. This harsh accusation, however, ends up further weakening and dividing the women's movement itself. Against these attacks my interviewees defend the presence of Muslim women's organizations as positive and inspiring for British society. More specifically, stemming from grassroots demands, these spaces are the physical arena where important and controversial aspects of their cultural and religious identity can be safely discussed and properly tackled. Supporting these circles would be fundamental for Muslim women, who are a particularly disadvantaged group. In this sense, the anti-religious stance expressed by secular women betrays the feminist emancipative and liberating vocation, thus preventing it from becoming a mass movement. According to the interviewees, only when acknowledging women's right to see religion either as a problem or as a crucial resource in their life will feminism fulfil its promise. This problem does not emerge with the same urgency in Italy, where the emergency-oriented approach of the Italian government, by pushing Muslim activists to adopt fast and stop-gap measures, retards the emergence of an organic course of action. The fragmented and 'karstic' nature of Italian feminism has done the rest, blocking the process of consolidation and self-awareness of Muslim activism and resulting in the absence of a gender-sensitive orientation, also at the governmental level. This feature has prevented Italian feminism from becoming a mainstream force in the public and political debate. Paradoxically, however, while in the UK the strong and widespread nature of secular feminism nurtures hostile attitudes toward religious expressions, in Italy the role and power of the Catholic Church makes the public sphere more porous toward the recognition of religious identities and the creation of interfaith initiatives.

Unveiling Muslim women

Especially after 9/11 and the following terrorist attacks, the headscarf has played a crucial role in the Western debate on Muslims. As stated by the interviewees, the image of the veiled, submissive and subjugated Muslim woman has been instrumental in fostering the process of otherization and condemnation of Islam and Muslims. The twofold stereotype of the veiled voiceless on the one hand and the radical and frightening Islamist on the other de facto obscures the internal heterogeneity and complexity of this category, hampering women's self-expression and delegitimizing those who choose not to veil, relying on a modest dress-code rather than on covering up. Also in response to this general mistrust many women, especially the so-called daughters of migrations, have chosen to use the veil in a more proactive and emancipatory way. This is not only as a symbol of their religious identity, but also because

> I was constantly told that a Muslim woman is segregated, but I saw my mother who is not segregated at all, and the same applies to my neighbours. They say that veiled women can't study or drive a car: I study, work and drive a car as well. The problem is that people think that the freedom that I have is only a covering. They can't believe, for instance, that I travel a lot, in daylight and at night, even alone. They tend to generalize the small realities where veiled women suffer violence from their husbands.[23]

This is to say that the richness of their identities cannot be reduced to a piece of fabric: the veil, in this regard, is a badge of honour, an expression of agency rather than a passive acceptance of traditions or male impositions. From their narratives, the polysemic meaning of the headscarf emerges as religious, identitarian and even political. All these dimensions are not fixed but subjected to a continual process of redefinition according to different moments in their personal lives and in response to national and global events. They veil, un-veil and re-veil, being involved in a continual process of questioning traditions and religious precepts, searching for a creative balance between legacies and new belongings. The rise of Islamic fashion is a telling example of this search for a new balance that combines in a unique way the instances stemming from families and communities with those of the country where they live. Moreover, the choice to use the veil or to adopt a modest though trendy and modern dress code represents an act of individuation which, while taking a critical stance toward both communities of origin and the broader society, does not end up as a form of self-segregation. As exemplified by the title of one of the interviewees' books—*I wear the veil and listen to Queen*—these young women want to be recognized in their uniqueness and to make a significant contribution to the spheres they participate in. The headscarf, in other words, implies a profound redefinition of religious belonging, marking a substantial difference with tradition; it is a badge of honour against multiple discriminations and Islamophobia, a non-violent political act to assert a recognized and unique place within communities of origin and the broader society.

Bargaining with Muslim communities

Conforming to certain ideas of being a Muslim woman is widely recognized as a source of pressure within male-dominated communities, with men attempting to restrict their freedom to marry whomever they want or to get divorced, to inherit, to access the public sphere, to get a job, to create or lead Muslim organizations, to perform an advisory role within mosques, etc. The pressures to conform to the mainstream image of the mohajabeh, Sabin Khan[24] admits, de facto silences the British debate on the increasing number of women who choose not to wear the veil, believing that the Islamic headscarf does not represent the best way of expressing their Muslim identity. Shaista specifies[25]:

> If you are a woman you are an easy target. Muslim men, especially those in power, don't mind if you bring reasoned arguments in the discussion, they do not answer back with counter arguments: they just state that you are not a good Muslim. And even if you were covered they would say that you are a woman, or that you don't know Arabic, or that you come from the UK. They will always find an excuse.

Cassandra Balchin, a white, British, non-veiled convert, criticizes the use of a piece of fabric to measure the credibility of women as good Muslims and to exclude them from the religious community. For converts who do not abide by the traditional image, the need to be recognized as insiders and to be legitimate voices is even stronger than for veiled women. Men, in other words, tend to experience female assertiveness as an attempt to overcome their role and power. This has also emerged in Italy with Meriem Finti[26] revealing that male leaders tend to see young people's willingness to assert a new identity that is both Muslim and Italian as an attempt to subvert traditional values, sexual roles and hierarchies of power, thus undermining the respect that is supposedly due to adults. Some of my interviewees, like Amra Bone,[27] appeal to religious arguments to demonstrate that at the time of the Prophet women were very powerful in society, fulfilling leading roles: this strategy enables them to challenge misogynist stereotypes and to achieve a prestigious position within the Muslim community. In Italy, more specifically, women adopt various approaches, combining confrontational measures with, especially for first generations, a more gradual attitude based on cultural commitment. Some of them urge for a twofold project to be pursued within communities: not only with men but also with women: 'because women are their own worst enemies. Who has raised and educated these men in such a misogynous way? Mothers forge those who will be their enemies!'[28] Some, especially in the UK, have also warned against fundamentalist groups which, while advocating women's rights, actually take advantage of them to gain power and prestige in the public and political arena. They promote a specific idea of what a Muslim woman should be, ostracizing and even repudiating those who do not comply with it. According to my interviewees, the government's tendency to engage primarily with self-appointed male Muslim representatives makes the risk of succumbing to these male leaders even greater. The combination of all the factors mentioned above jeopardizes the survival of women's organizations. However, despite these obstacles, they regard the results achieved so far as a source of inspiration for the future. All in all, what seems more challenging and interesting is the way they internally transform traditional practices to enhance their own position. Although in certain cases they abide by controversial practices such as arranged marriages, they combine it with political activism, with husbands supporting their engagement, sharing family responsibilities and helping with children and domestic duties. The adoption of traditional practices, in other words, hardly ever results in a mere passive acceptance, quite the opposite. It implies a complex game of bargaining and compromise whereby, while reassuring community desiderata, it is nonetheless able to subvert and redefine traditional gender roles, opening up new opportunities for Muslim women as active subjects within the public sphere.

My Muslim identity, my fluid identity

In response to essentialist and stereotypical attacks, the essay asks whether asserting a Muslim identity proudly in the public sphere at a time when claiming a cultural or a religious identity is regarded as suspicious and alarming merely represents a passive acceptance of certain pre-defined labels. What, then, is the space for manoeuvre when people find themselves burdened by a label that concretely restricts their choices and the capacity for self-definition? By exploring this challenging field, the present contribution

> tries to disrupt the negative stereotype of the 'veiled Muslim woman', the one who is supposed to be silently suffering due to her religion or the one who is portrayed as a radical believer, totally absorbed by her religious identity. What better way to do this than to invite activist Muslim women to speak about themselves and tell their own stories?[29]

In particular, these women's unique struggles, problems, challenges and successes are fundamental to understanding the complex and never-ending process of negotiation, bargaining, compromise, critique and self-assertion that is part of their lives. Since the very first question, namely 'What does your Muslim identity mean for you and why did you choose to assert it in the public sphere?', Islam is portrayed as a natural way of being, a guide that gives a sense of direction and of understanding the world. Islam enables them to pursue a balance among the possible tensions that may arise from their manifold affiliations. This is particularly important because, despite the general mistrust toward Muslims, they chose to use their strategic positioning for the sake of mutual understanding and dialogue between communities and cultures. Especially in the UK, it is their confidence as Muslim as well as British that allows them to work for inclusion, equality and justice within society. This strategy, therefore, does not break down to a self-centred defence of Muslim women's rights: according to them, in fact, the promotion of gender equality and justice within their communities will benefit the entire society. In Britain the women are more self-confident vis-à-vis their status as citizens and from this stance criticize both communities of origin and British society. On the other hand, Italy reflects a more variegated panorama, with first generations adopting a low profile to make Muslims accepted in the host country, as if they still considered themselves guests, while converts and the so-called 'second generations'[30] appear more confident and combative in their role of bridging different communities: being born or raised in Italy makes them feel naturally part of the country. What emerges is that despite the differences, Islam represents for all of them an empowering element, a bridging identification, a journey that draws from personal and global events and that continues into the present. In Italy, again, this is particularly true for the youngsters who creatively combine the language of Islam with that of human rights and at times of Western feminism to promote their role and to pursue their inner aspirations. Despite the bureaucratic obstacles to being recognized as full citizens, these young women are paving new ways: 'I am a new Italian. I see myself as a tree which has its roots elsewhere but branches out and releases its seeds in this country. These seeds will bear fruits that all people can enjoy'.[31] More interestingly, for all of them Islam plays an important though not exclusive role, as Haleh Asfhar points out:

> we have fluid identities and we work across them all of the time. I don't see it as a problem. Fluid identity is not a conscious thing; it is not that you say, now I am being a mother, now a grandmother, now a teacher. It is part of you, is there, because of the women's multitask. People move from identities and even out of particular classifications. Some use it strategically, others live them more naturally.[32]

These paragraphs represent an in-depth, though not exhaustive examination of the main potentials and constraints of this daily and complex exercise of bargaining and compromising in some crucial areas of Muslim women's lives.

Conclusions

The topic related to the feminization of the Orient and the essentialization of its women by Orientalists and feminists alike is a wide area of potential discussion, provoked by the seminal interpretation of Orientalism pointed out by Edward Said. Starting from this perspective, the relationship between 'woman', as a cultural construction based on diverse representational, hegemonic discourses, and 'women', as real, bodily and material subjects, is one of the central questions that feminism has to deal with also when approaching the new citizenship of foreign women in the European context. As suggested by Judith Butler, we need a shift in the understanding of identity categories, by moving towards a reconceptualization of identity as an effect, as produced or generated. This approach opens up possibilities of agency that are insidiously denied by positions that take identity categories as foundational and fixed.[33] Seeing identity as a dimension that is produced and generated gives greater access to agency. If identity were fixed, in fact, a person who does not conform to this specific idea of identity would have their agency or choices and freedoms limited. On the contrary, even when identities are not chosen by but imposed on women, they nonetheless develop fluid identities in order to overcome the negative impact of those ascriptions which hinder their access to the political sphere as well as to socio-economic resources. Many are the strategies, the daily negotiations adopted by women in order to balance the private with the public dimension of their lives and to fulfil their needs. As Haleh Afshar notes,[34] the boundaries of the self are always historically and culturally constructed within unique socio-economic contexts. Women, more specifically, construct and reconstruct the notion of self according to their lifecycle: different ages, places, the issue of generation produce new priorities, needs, aspirations and responsibilities. While political, economic and cultural factors push women to retain certain identities or to function with different and at times conflicting identities, they strive and strategize to move across them, maintaining the sense of their self and belonging. The Muslim activists interviewed interpret the ascribed identity 'Muslim woman' as a label that severely restricts their freedom, and they re-signify it from within, with empowering outcomes. By critically choosing to adopt this controversial definition, in fact, they break stereotypes and prejudices. A case in point is the issue of the Islamic headscarf: if we regarded a veiled woman as not conforming to the Western notion of what an autonomous woman should be, that veiled woman would be seen as self-limiting and unable to access the same freedoms of Western women. However, as explained by some interviewees, veiling can also be used as a way to express identity and in some communities it even becomes a political reaction to Islamophobia. At stake here is a sort of 'agency in resistance', according to which different identities are forming, also in order to create an alternative community of belonging. As suggested by some interviewees, the tension between personal autonomy and cultural traditions is a challenging field for feminist theory. The idealized, strong conception of autonomy as independence seems inadequate for exploring what is at stake within the complex framework of the so-called 'bargaining with patriarchy'. In dealing with traditional culture, 'in which customs may represent more complex social dynamics between community and family pressures and individual reflection', the idea that autonomous lives are completely detached from the cultural norms is highly problematic.[35] To frame and understand the responses elaborated by individuals vis-à-vis specific controversial customs we need a more adequate interpretation of agency, able to recognize expressions of reflexivity, as implied in the idea of subverting cultural traditions from within. With this thinner conception of autonomy in our hands, we can draw attention to the manifold ways in which women challenge and revise some traditional cultural practices, by legitimizing at the same time some controversial practices such as veiling or arranged marriage. In other words, in order to apply this approach it is crucial to reduce the centrality of the category of autonomy and place it within a broader concept of agency based on the idea, as Deveaux points out, that 'to count as an expression of agency, actions need to be reflexive to the extent that they reflect or help to secure something that a person has cause to value'.[36] Individual agency may be exercised within contexts characterized by social constraints and pressures, in which women negotiate and bargain with oppressive patriarchal structures.[37] The same European public space, characterized by the rising visibility of Muslim women, can represent the main dimension in which the condition of women belonging to minority cultures can be empowered through participation and deliberative democratic processes. Nevertheless, the outcomes of these processes are not totally predictable and a wide range of possible scenarios are at stake. If, on the one hand, we cannot take for granted the capacity of our democracies to be hospitable and inclusive towards differences *tout court*, and to reshape the borders of 'we, the people' endlessly and without certain limitations, at the same time there is not an alternative way beyond giving voice to those women who inhabit and share our political spaces. In opposition to the clash of civilizations theory, it seems necessary to reformulate the hypothesis of a complex dialogue among cultures, whose background is the acoustic image of a continual interaction, and therefore creation and re-creation, between 'us' and the 'other', beyond the same perspective of traditional versions of multiculturalism.[38] Both cultures and individuals are in constant, potential conversation, and the model of identity formation that is a setting for these reflections is essentially a dynamic model, characterized by a voluntary membership, encouraged by the public space and institutions. The feminist approach to cultural diversity should proceed by substituting a top-down approach based on the mechanical application of the presumed universal principles to the particular case and context, drawing a line between what could be tolerated and what could not. In the place of it, it is necessary to embrace a perspective of cultural change and transformation, an experience of continuous border crossing, in which principles, rights and values are constantly negotiated, while at the same time they are translated into multifaceted and controversial practices. The difference between the two Kantian concepts, *Anwendung* as mechanic application of principles to reality and, on the other hand, *Ausübung* as a specific sensitivity in putting into practice the general rules, can help us to frame this challenging field.[39] This special sensitivity here is the commitment of politics, which in establishing the contents of the public policies should measure and evaluate the complex intersection of discrimination and potentialities, submission and agency, asymmetries and empowering processes. Furthermore, the combination of different languages, from the language of human rights to that of religion, from the liberal principles of gender equality to the specificity of cultures, shown by the interviewees, illustrates the productive internal dynamic of transforming the self. In this case, Muslim women seemed to reshape all these different perspectives by re-proposing a new intersectional language, able to combine the culture of the community of origin and a new assessment of agency and freedom. Only a point of view from afar and from above can deny the intrinsic value of this experience. What is at stake now is the creation of an inclusive approach, one that through the recognition of differences among women proves nonetheless able to create synergies and to find common empowering pathways. In this respect, there are two promising directions that emerge from the essay which need to be pursued and sustained with greater determination if we want to achieve the ambitious goal mentioned above. On the one hand, we must enforce the deconstructive attitude developed by Western feminists towards a more demanding decolonization process of their mind and recognition of their privileged position and point of view, while on the other hand we need to strengthen the commitment of those among non-Western women who seek to mainstream feminism, fighting discrimination against women. This would enforce a transnational kind of feminism, one that draws from the intersections among nationhood, race, gender, sexuality and economic exploitation within the risks implied in emergent global capitalism. This kind of feminism that is aware of the legacies of colonialism and nationalism questions the very social, political and economic factors comprising imperialism and looks at the role of gender, race, class, and sexuality in organizing the various forms of women's resistance to hegemonies. Exactly in this way, by striving for more equitable social relations among women, new strategies and practices can be identified and developed which can go far beyond the roots of 'Eurocentrism'[40] and cross-border and cross-cultural contexts.

Disclosure statement

No potential conflict of interest was reported by the authors.

Notes

1. On the role of deconstruction within gender studies see A. Loretoni, 'Identity and belonging. Gender criticism of the liberal tradition', in A. Loretoni, J. Pauchard and A. Pirni (eds), *Questioning Universalism. Western and New Confucianist Conceptions*, ETS, Pisa, 2013, pp. 97–114.
2. S. Moller Okin, *Is Multiculturalism Bad for Women?*, Princeton University Press, Princeton, 1999.
3. E. Said, *Orientalism. Western Conceptions of the Orient*, Penguin, London, 1978.
4. S. Huntington, *The Clash of Civilizations and the Remaking of World Order*, Touchstone, New York, 1997.
5. Challenging the Orientalist approach, in the recent past the Arab Spring confirmed that the capacity to include dissenting and critical views on traditional values no longer belongs exclusively to the northern part of the world, by showing a new agency for women. See Olivier Roy, 'The transformation of the Arab world', *Journal of Democracy*, 23(2), 2012, pp. 5–18.
6. In relation to the topic of the 'war on terror' see M. Khalid, 'Gendering Orientalism. Gender, sexuality, and race in post 9/11 global politics', *Critical Race and Whiteness Studies*, 10(1), 2014, pp. 1–18.
7. R. Salih, *Musulmane Rivelate. Donne, Islam, Modernità* [Muslim Women Revealed. Gender, Islam and Modernity], Carocci, Roma, 2008.
8. F. Mernissi, *Beyond the Veil. Male–Female Dynamics in Muslim Society*, Saqi, London, 2011.
9. On Islamic feminism see B. Henry's article in this special issue, B. Henry, 'Islamic Feminism(s) in the Mediterranean Area: a Hermeneutical Approach', *Journal of Balkan and Near Eastern Studies*, 19(5), 2017. doi: 10.1080/19448953.2017.1296254
10. M. M. Hasan, 'The Orientalization of gender', *The American Journal of Islamic Social Sciences*, 22(4), p. 48.
11. S. Benhabib, *The Rights of Other. Aliens, Residents and Citizens*, Cambridge University Press, Cambridge, 2004.
12. See C. T. Mohanty, 'Under Western eyes', in C. T. Mohanty, *Feminism without Borders. Decolonizing Theory, Practicing Solidarity*, Duke University Press, Durham, NC, 2003, pp. 17–42.
13. G. Spivak, 'Can the subaltern speak?', in C. Nelson and L. Grossberg (eds), *Marxism and the Interpretation of Culture*, University of Illinois Press, Urbana, 1988, pp. 271–313.
14. For the critical concern of 'sisterhood' see C. T. Mohanty, *Under Western Eyes*, op. cit. On intersectionality see K. Crenshaw, 'Demarginalizing the intersection of race and sex. A black feminist critique of anti-discrimination doctrine, feminist theory, and anti-racist politics', in *University of Chicago Legal Forum. Feminism in the Law: Theory, Practice and Criticism*, 1989, pp. 139–167.
15. The part of the essay which analyses the vivid experiences of some Muslim women living in Italy and the UK relies on the qualitative research conducted by A. Belli between 2009 and 2011 as part of her PhD dissertation titled 'Progressive multiculturalism and fluid identities:

the case of Muslim women activists in Italy and the United Kingdom', discussed on 19 December 2011 at the Scuola Superiore Sant'Anna, Pisa, Italy.

16. Following Katherine Bullock's definition, activists are understood as 'people committed to a "cause", to something they believe will benefit humanity and that requires struggle and self-sacrifice (of time and resources). I see activism as doing something concrete for the sake of a social good'. This definition is flexible enough to include women involved in associations, movements, NGOs, scholars and intellectuals and also those linked to the political sphere. Katherine Bullock, *Muslim Women Activists in North America. Speaking for Ourselves*, University of Texas Press, Austin, 2005, p. xv.

17. This part draws from A. Belli's abovementioned PhD dissertation. The choice to focus on the UK and Italy, the former an example of the multicultural approach, the latter a case of 'absent model', stems from the fact that both countries represent interesting settings, although for opposite reasons, in which to analyse the dynamics of identity formation in situations where people find themselves in the crossfire of multiple manipulative dynamics.

18. P. Hill Collins, *Black Feminist Thought: Knowledge, Consciousness, and the Politics of Empowerment*, Routledge, New York, 2000.

19. M. Franks, *Women and Revivalism in the West. Choosing 'Fundamentalism' in a Liberal Democracy*, Palgrave, Basingstoke, 2001, pp. 37–48.

20. M. Westkott, 'Feminist criticism of the social sciences', *Harvard Educational Review*, 49(4), pp. 422–430.

21. L. Haney, 'Negotiating power and expertise in the field', in Tim May (ed.), *Qualitative Research in Action*, Sage Publications, London, 2002, pp. 286–299; S. Harding, 'Introduction: is there a feminist method?', in S. Harding (ed.), *Feminism and Methodology: Social Science Issues*, Indiana University Press, Bloomington, 1987, pp. 1–14.

22. Cassandra Balchin, a non-veiled British convert who worked as a freelance researcher, writer and human rights advocacy trainer. I interviewed her twice in London, in April 2008 and in November 2009.

23. Meriem Finti in September 2009 was a 25-year-old Italian woman of Moroccan origin living in Bologna, part of the national managing board of GMI (Giovani Musulmani d'Italia/Young Italian Muslims) and head of the GMI's sections in Emilia Romagna.

24. Sabin Khan, community adviser at the British Home Office for Security and Counter Terrorism; met at the Home Office in London in February 2010.

25. When I interviewed Shaista Gohir, in November 2009, she was a journalist and the executive director of the Muslim Women's Network UK.

26. Meriem Finti in September 2009 was a 25-year-old Italian woman of Moroccan origin living in Bologna, part of the national managing board of GMI (Giovani Musulmani d'Italia/Young Italian Muslims) and head of the GMI's sections in Emilia Romagna.

27. In December 2009 Amra Bone was a lecturer in Islamic Studies at Warwick University, community activist in Coventry and member of the Birmingham Sharia Council.

28. Latifa Bouamoul, co-President of the association Life onlus, based in Ravenna. The author met her in 2009.

29. Bullock, op. cit., p. xvi; K. Bullock, *Rethinking Muslim Women and the Veil. Challenging Historical & Modern Stereotypes*, The International Institute of Islamic Thought, Richmond, 2002; S. Silvestri, 'La questione del burqa in Europa' <http://www.ispionline.it/it/documents/Commentary_Silvestri_13.5.10.pdf> (accessed June 2010); S. Silvestri , 'Europe's Muslims: burqa laws, women's lives' <http://www.opendemocracy.net/sara-silvestri/french-burqa-and-%E2%80%9Cmuslim-integration%E2%80%9D-in-europe> (accessed July 2010).

30. This expression raised lots of disagreement among my interviewees, who pointed out its exclusionary dimension. For them it reinforces, in fact, and perpetuates the idea of a presumed insurmountable otherness: being a 'second generation' means being relegated to a distinct category that is excluded from citizenship. Many preferred the expression 'second generation of immigration': <http://www.secondegenerazioni.it/about/> (accessed September 2010).

31. Interview to Sumaya Abdel Qader, young Italian activist, writer and columnist of Jordanian origin, conducted in July 2010.

32. Haleh Afshar, British academic and peer in the House of Lords, interviewed in York in autumn/winter 2009 and in spring 2010. H. Afshar (ed.), *Women and Fluid Identities. Strategic and Practical Pathways Selected by Women*, Palgrave Macmillan, Basingstoke, 2012.
33. J. Butler, *Gender Trouble. Feminism and the Subversion of Identity*, Routledge, New York, 1990, p. 187.
34. Haleh Afshar interview 2009.
35. M. Deveaux, *Gender and Justice in Multicultural Liberal States*, Oxford University Press, Oxford, 2006, p. 162.
36. Ibid., p. 177.
37. On the specific issue of the 'arranged marriage' see U. Narayan, 'Minds of their own. Choices, autonomy, cultural practices and other women', in L. M. Antony and C. Witt (eds), *A Mind of One's Own. Feminist Essays on Reason and Objectivity*, West View Press, Boulder, CO, 2002, p. 429.
38. Anne Phillips, *Multiculturalism without Culture*, Princeton University Press, Princeton and Oxford, 2007.
39. I. Kant, 'Perpetual peace. A philosophical essay', in *Political Writings*, Cambridge University Press, Cambridge, 1991.
40. R. Braidotti, *Nomadic Subjects. Embodiment and Sexual Difference in Feminist Theory*, Columbia University Press, New York, 1994.

Women, Globalization and Civil Society in the MENA Area: Between Marginalization and Radicalization

Leila Simona Talani

ABSTRACT
This article analyses the condition of women in the MENA area in the light of the challenges faced by those countries within the context of globalization. It argues that, if the position of the MENA countries in the global political economy is increasingly marginalized, this is even truer for women, who are left behind in the process of up-skilling necessary to catch up with the increasing technological demands imposed by globalization. Moreover, the crisis of the Arab state within globalization seems to produce an increasing radicalization of society, with all that this means in terms of further marginalization of women. In this article a transnationalist conceptualization of globalization is adopted.

Introduction

This article analyses the condition of women in the Middle East and Northern Africa (MENA) area in the light of the challenges faced by those countries within the context of globalization. It will argue that, if the position of the MENA countries in the global political economy is increasingly marginalized, this is even truer for women, who are left behind in the process of up-skilling necessary to catch up with the increasing technological demands imposed by globalization. Moreover, the crisis of the Arab state within globalization seems to produce an increasing radicalization of society, with all that this means in terms of further marginalization of women. In this article a transnationalist conceptualization of globalization is adopted.

This is particularly relevant if we consider that the definition of globalization adopted here implies that it is a dynamic process, a sort of virtuous circle that once activated produces more and more integration. Indeed, a conceptualization of globalization resting on the central role played by technological development entails the need of a constant updating and re-qualification of skills for societies to keep up with scientific progress.[1]

Societies failing to embark on this constant updating, although in absolute terms they may gain some skills, are doomed to be progressively more and more marginalized from globalization and therefore be increasingly worse off.

Table 1. Core indicators on access to, and use of, ICT by households and individuals 2010–2011.

Core indicators on access to and use of ICT by households and individuals, latest available data

	Year of latest data	Proportion of households with (HH4) computer	Proportion of households with (HH6) Internet access at home	Proportion of individuals who used ICTs in the last 12 months (HH5) Computer	(HH7) Internet
Egypt	2011	36.4	30.5	32.4	-
Libya	-	-	-	-	-
Tunisia	2010	19.1	11.4	24.9*	17.1*
United Kingdom	2011	84.6	85.1	-	86.8**
United States	2010	75.5	71.1	-	71.7***

*Population age 10+; **Population age 16–74; ***Population age 3+; - data not available.
Source: ITU World Telecommunication/ICT Indicators Database.

This poses the problem of the polarization of wealth in both social and geographical terms. Those societies and societal strata that already have access to educational and vocational systems and have the economic possibility of remaining in education for longer, if not staying in education forever (the so-called concept of the 'knowledge society'), are in a much better position in the global political economy. On the contrary, the lower strata of society, as well as the weakest ones, like the elders or the women, and especially those living in marginalized countries, will be increasingly left behind by the fast-moving world of the new skills necessary to keep up with globalization. It follows that the social and geographical wealth gap is expected to increase, leading to the paradox of 'marginalization within globalization'. Indeed, as Mittleman puts it: 'The further away populations are from the global economy, whether in rich or poor countries, the worse they fare in terms of well-being, wealth and social protection. These divisions exist not only between states but also within states'.[2]

In light of this, the first section of this article is devoted to verifying the level of technological integration (or marginalization) of the Arab world and the MENA countries in general, and of women within them in particular, and their capacity to catch up with the skills necessary to gather the full benefits of globalization.

However, in the transnationalist perspective, the restructuring of production leading to flexible specialization does not rely only on a change in the techno-economic structure of a specific territory, but also implies cultural transformations affecting civil society.[3] Indeed, in the transnationalist conceptualization, globalization is a dialectical, dynamic process affecting civil society, transforming societal institutions and conducing to the establishment of the new social relations.[4] Thus, as Mittleman puts it: 'In so far as the flexible specialisation model as a productive system requires strong relations with civil society, socio-cultural institutions may represent either a constraining or a potentially enabling factor'.[5]

It is therefore necessary to analyse also the evolution of civil society institutions and social capital in the MENA area to see how they have been modified by globalization-induced economic restructuring and how women are integrated within them. This is the subject of the second section of this article.

Technological marginalization

Technological innovation is integral to globalization, especially new information technologies, transportation and communication. Although these are becoming spread around the globe, this does not happen evenly among regions and nations and therefore the scope for broadening global inequalities increases, instead of decreasing.[6] Furthermore, technological development has not been taking place completely by chance, but is itself a socially and institutionally embedded process which is much more likely to happen in those societies fostering it; it is therefore less likely to take place in countries that are already lagging behind.[7] Finally, the weaker strata of society are likely to be progressively weaker if they are unable to be integrated in the technological revolution implied by globalization. This is a typical self-reinforcing dynamic which leaves the losers further and further behind.

This is particularly true in the case of the Arab world where technological integration has been very weak in the last decades, especially with respect to women. For some scholars: 'The Arabs can be said to be suffering from technological anorexia; and they are disheartened because they are powerless. Arab analysts point to a state of paralysis on both the national and regional levels'.[8]

Also according to the conclusions of the second Arab Human Development Report, dedicated to building a knowledge society, the situation regarding Arab technological production and expertise was dire.[9]

In order to substantiate these considerations, this section will first look at the technological sources of globalization and then assess to what extent they have been achieved in the Arab world and, more specifically, by women.

The qualitative definition of globalization adopted in this article relies on the assumption that the current phase of capitalist development is defined by some technological achievements that make it different from any other stages in the development of the world economy. In particular, scholars refer to the current phase as the early stages of the fifth Kondratiev wave (K-wave); a digital, information and communication technology one.[10] Each K-wave is characterized by various dimensions: the main 'carrier' branches, the infrastructure, the solutions offered to previous problems by the new techno-economic paradigms, the organization of firms and forms of cooperation and competition, and, most importantly for our purposes, the geographical focus, which clearly does not include the MENA area.[11] In Dicken's conceptualization, in the current wave of technological innovations, the above dimensions are substantiated as in Figure 1.

This scheme allows us to recognize the technological innovations which are progressively more significant as sources of integration in the global political economy and to define the indicators used in the literature to establish the degree of integration of a country or region within it. There is a generalized consensus in the literature[12] that the telecommunications revolution and the widespread use of internet and digital resources that facilitate not only generic communication, but also learning and production processes, are the most significant technological innovations of the current phase of capitalist development.

However, the spread of the use of ICT technologies is extremely uneven around the globe and amongst societal groups. Instead of producing a general time-space shrinking, technological innovations have exacerbated, in relative terms, the peripherization of some parts of the world. The digital divide is therefore increasingly privileging certain countries and certain social groups over others, especially urban spaces and big cities in the developed world.[13] Moreover, as access to communication technologies is, nowadays, fundamental to acquire vital information and knowledge, its increasingly uneven distribution poses increasingly serious developmental problems.[14]

The figures released by International Telecommunication Union (ITU)[15] confirm the existence of a clear technological divide between developing and developed countries.[16]

Main "carrier" branches	Infrastructure	Solutions offered to previous problems by the new techno-economic paradigms	Organisation of firms and forms of cooperation and competition,	Geographical focus
Computers Digital Information technology Internet Software Telecommunication Optical Fibers Robotics Ceramics Biotechnology	Digital networks Satellites	Flexible manufacturing systems Networking Economies of scope Electronic control systems and components Systematisation Integration of design, production and marketing	Networks of large and small firms based increasingly on computer networks and close co-operation technology, quality control, training, investment planning and production planning (just-in-time).	Japan, USA, Germany, Other Europe, Sweden, Taiwan, Korea, Canada, Australia

Figure 1. Kondratiev fifth long wave: late 1990s onwards. Source: Adapted from P. Dicken, *Global Shift: Mapping the Changing Contours of the World Economy*, 6th ed., Guilford Press, London, 2011, p. 79.

Within the developing world, Asia is the region improving the most in terms of access to ICT technologies, accounting for more than half of all mobile subscriptions in 2013. As far as the internet is concerned, ITU estimated that 2.7 billion people, which is 39% of the world's population, would be using the internet by the end of 2013. Access to the internet would, however, remain limited in the developing world with no more that 31% of the population forecast to be able to be online at the end of 2013, compared with 77% in the developed world. Europe would remain the most connected region in the world with 75% internet penetration, while Asia-Pacific would have a 32% rate of penetration and Africa only 16%.[17]

Also, household internet penetration, which is often considered the most important measure of internet access, was forecast grow, with 41% of the world's households connected to the internet by the end of 2013. However, notwithstanding the generally positive outlook, 90% of the 1.1 billion households around the world that are still unconnected are in the developing world. In 2013 two-thirds of the world's population, around 4.5 billion people, were still offline and they were overwhelmingly in the developing world, especially Africa.[18]

Moreover, although the cost of fixed-broadband services dropped enormously between 2008 and 2013, decreasing by 82% if measured as a share of Gross National Income (GNI) per capita, in developing countries residential fixed-broadband services remained very expensive, accounting for over 30% of average monthly GNI per capita compared to just

1.7% of average national income in wealthy countries. In some developing countries, that figure rises to well over 50%.[19]

Also, differences in high-speed broadband internet access persist. The best performers in terms of access speeds were in Asia: the Republic of Korea, Hong Kong (China) and Japan. In Africa, in contrast, less than 10% of fixed-broadband subscriptions offered speeds of at least 2Mb.[20]

Finally, in developing countries the gender divide was still very significant, with 16% less women than men using the internet, compared with only 2% less women than men in the developed world (Figure 2).[21]

As far as the MENA region is concerned, data on the use of the internet by gender are very revealing. Indeed, not only MENA countries have by far fewer individuals using the internet, but also the gender gap is much bigger. For example, in Egypt only 36.6% of men ever use the internet, but the proportion of women who use the internet is 31.1%. In Turkey almost 20% less women than men use the internet, and this can be compared to the US where more women than men use internet.

Hence, the analysis of indicators relating to the usage of telecommunications and internet or digital resources (so-called Information and Communication Technology, ICT indicators) can help in establishing whether or not a country and/or a region is catching up with the globalization process.

The UN identifies 41 core ICT indicators, divided into four groups[22]:

(1) ICT infrastructure and access (12 indicators).
(2) Access to, and use of, ICT by households and individuals (13 indicators).
(3) Use of ICT by businesses (12 indicators).

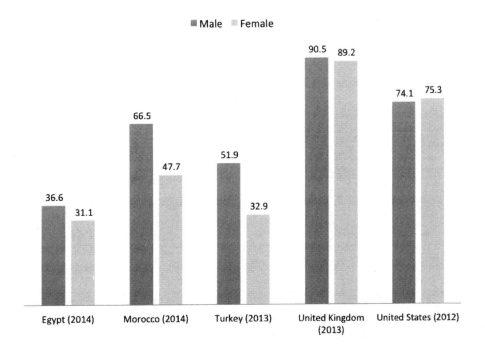

Figure 2. Individuals using the internet (from any location) by gender. Source: ITU database (http://www.itu.int/en/ITU-T/publications/Pages/dbase.aspx, accessed 7 March 2017).

WOMEN IN THE MEDITERRANEAN

(4) The ICT sector and trade in ICT goods (4 indicators).

Reference is made below to some such indicators in the Arab world in general and in Egypt, Libya and Tunisia in particular. It is worth noting, however, that the author does not consider these indicators the only relevant ones for assessing marginalization, as symptoms of lack of integration via ICT indicators do not appear totally reliable. Indeed, if we look at indicators of access to technology for countries such as China, these are still relatively low (although they have been improving at a faster rate than anywhere else), but this cannot and does not mean that the country is not being increasingly integrated into the global economy.

Given these considerations, the Arab region[23] and the countries considered in this study are, without doubt, lagging behind in terms of access to the new technologies.

With respect to the first category of indicators, ICT infrastructure and access, for example, the position of Egypt, Libya and Tunisia is very negative, with Tunisia and Egypt not reaching even five internet subscriptions per 100 inhabitants in 2011 (Figure 3).

Even worse is the situation regarding the number of fixed broadband subscriptions per 100 inhabitants in the three countries considered, with Egypt recording less than two in 2010, Libya around one, and Tunisia not reaching five (Figure 4).

In terms of access to, and use of, ICT by households and individuals, the latest data do not portray a particularly positive picture. The proportion of households with a computer in Egypt in 2011 was around 36% and the number of individuals who used a computer was only 32%. Only 30% of the Egyptian population had access to the internet at home, as opposed, for example, to 85% of the British population. In Tunisia the situation was even worse, with only 19% of households having a computer and only 11% of the population having access to the internet at home. In the last 12 months of 2011 the proportion of individuals who used a computer in Tunisia was only 24% and even less, 17%, used the internet,

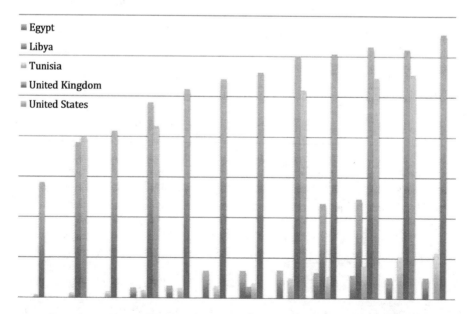

Figure 3. Fixed (wired) internet subscriptions per 100 inhabitants (A4). Source: ITU statistics (http://www.itu.int/en/ITU-T/publications/Pages/dbase.aspx, accessed 7 March 2017).

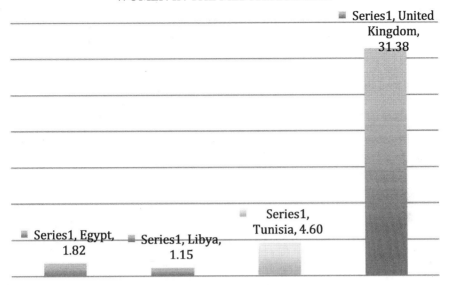

Figure 4. Fixed (wired) broadband subscriptions per 100 inhabitants 2010 (A5). Source: ITU statistics.

whereas in the UK this figure was 87%. In Libya, the percentage of estimated internet users in 2010 was 14%.[24]

Concerning the use of ICT by businesses, data on regions outside Europe and excluding Organisation for Economic Co-operation and Development (OECD) member countries are fairly scattered. Until 2003, hardly any developing economy was collecting ICT usage statistics from businesses. In the last few years, more and more developing and transition economies started producing these statistics, yet they are mainly located in the Latin American and Caribbean region.

The data provided by UN and Eurostat show a very similar picture for the use of ICT by businesses to that found with households; widespread use of computers and the internet is present only in developed economies. Moreover, in developing and transition economies the proportion of employees using a computer or the internet is much lower than the proportion of businesses using a computer or the internet. This means that within businesses with ICT, not many employees regularly use it.[25]

In the MENA region, some country statistics are available only for Egypt. In Egypt, the proportion of businesses having internet was 53% at the end of 2007, as opposed to 93% in the EU 25. The proportion of employees using computers was 18% and only 10% was using internet, whereas for the EU 25 these figures were 49% and 37% respectively.[26]

In terms of core indicators for the ICT sector and trade in ICT goods, there is no data available for the region and for the countries considered. However, World Bank indicators for science and technology can help an understanding of the situation in these countries with respect to the technological content of their economies.[27]

Indeed, the percentage of high technology exports—products with high R&D intensity, such as aerospace, computers, pharmaceuticals, scientific instruments and electrical machinery—is very low in the MENA developing countries, recorded at only 3.2%. In Egypt it is almost inexistent at 0.9% of manufacturing exports while in Tunisia it is around 5%. For

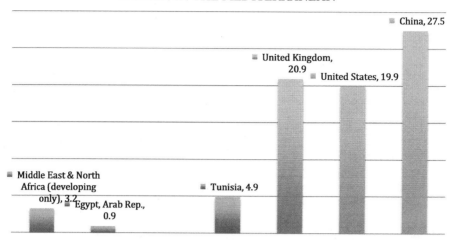

Figure 5. High technology exports (percentage of manufacturing exports) in 2010. Source: Elaboration by the author of data from the World Bank website <http://web.worldbank.org/WBSITE/EXTERNAL/DATASTATISTICS/0,,menuPK:232599~pagePK:64133170~piPK:64133498~theSitePK:239419,00.html> (accessed 15 March 2013).

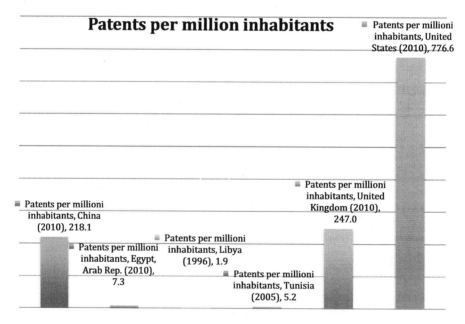

Figure 6. Number of patents by residents per million inhabitants-last available data. Source: Elaboration by the author of data from the World Bank website <http://web.worldbank.org/WBSITE/EXTERNAL/DATASTATISTICS/0,,menuPK:232599~pagePK:64133170~piPK:64133498~theSitePK:239419,00.html> (accessed 15 March 2013).

the sake of comparison, China high technology exports are 27.5% of the total, Britain's are around 21% and those of the US are 19% (Figure 5).

Even more relevant to ascertain the level of technological starvation of the MENA countries are figures relating to the number of patents per million inhabitants. As Figure 6 shows,

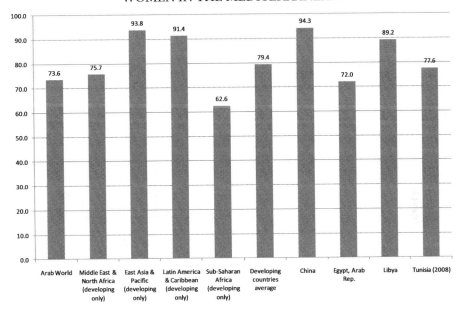

Figure 7. Adult literacy year 2010 (percentage age 15 and above). Source: Elaboration by the author of data from the World Bank website <http://web.worldbank.org/WBSITE/EXTERNAL/DATASTATISTICS/0,,menuPK:232599~pagePK:64133170~piPK:64133498~theSitePK:239419,00.html> (accessed 15 March 2013).

Egypt, Libya and Tunisia are basically producing no new patents at all and are therefore not contributing to technological progress in any significant way.

If knowledge and information are key to keeping up with the process of globalization and avoiding further marginalization, it is worth looking also at basic education indicators as well as indicators of the use of ICT in education. In the words of the Arab Human Development Report: 'A knowledge-based society is one where knowledge diffusion, production and application become the organising principle in all aspects of human activity: culture, society, the economy, politics, and private life'.[28]

In Arab countries, key knowledge dissemination processes, such as education and socialization, are profoundly constrained by social, economic, institutional and political impediments.[29] In particular, dwindling economic resources limit the possibility for individuals, families and institutions to acquire the epistemological and societal skills necessary for knowledge production.

Despite some gains in the quantitative expansion of education in Arab countries in the last decades, these are still modest in comparison with other developing countries and do not allow the countries to meet the requirements of a knowledge society.[30]

For example, in 2010, the Arab World and the MENA area still had lower literacy levels in the total adult population than the developing countries' average (Figure 7).

The situation is clearly worse for women, whose literacy rates in the MENA countries are 15% less than men, 16% less in the Arab world and almost 17% in Egypt, where the literacy rate for adult women was only 63.5% in 2010 (Figure 8).

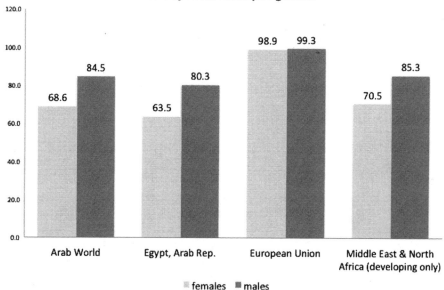

Figure 8. Literacy rates 2010 per gender. Source: World Bank <http://databank.worldbank.org/data/reports.aspx?source=Gender%20Statistics> (accessed 9 February 2016).

Moreover, many children still do not have access to basic education, and public spending on education has actually declined in the MENA area from around 22% of government expenditure in 2002 to 16% in 2008.[31]

Looking at some indicators of the use of ICT in education, the situation of MENA countries is not particularly positive. In Tunisia, for example, in 2008 only 40% of schools had a telephone and around the same percentage had access to the internet. Data for Egypt and Libya are not available.[32]

In all cases, nevertheless, the most important challenge facing Arab education is its deteriorating quality.[33] In Egypt, for example, a wide field survey revealed that mastery of the basic skills of reading, writing and mathematics, which should be obtained in primary school, was exceptionally low, recorded at about 40% and 30% respectively.[34]

In 2010/11, all of the Arab countries which took part in the Trends in Mathematics and Science Study (TIMSS), a competition in mathematics and science for year 5 pupils, ended up at the bottom of the table. In mathematics, Tunisia was ranked fourth from last with 359 points. As a point of comparison, Singapore was first with 606 points, followed by Korea with 605, Hong Kong with 602 and Chinese Taipei with 591.[35]

Overall the data confirm that the MENA region is lagging behind in terms of the technological and educational requirements of entire sections of its society, especially women, to catch up with the process of globalization.

As in the literature the development of civil society is often associated with the level of education, especially of women, and the use of modern technologi,es[36] this might point to a certain underdevelopment of civil society and social capital in these countries. However this conclusion is far too superficial and a closer attention to all the factors influencing the evolution and characteristics of civil society is needed. To this we turn our attention in the next section.

Women, civil society and social capital in the MENA area

The notion of civil society adopted by transnationalists is mainly a Gramscian one. Gramsci conceptualized civil society as the primary political realm, where socio-economic groups acquire consciousness of their interests and expectations, ideologies are produced and spread, and alliances formed.[37]

It is in the context of civil society that the battle for the conquest of true hegemonic power takes place, thanks also to the fundamental role played by intellectuals. This means that any socio-economic group aspiring to take the lead of the state needs to gain consensus in the context of civil society by both taking care of the economic needs of the other socio-economic strata and convincing them through ideological means that the interests of the historically dominant socio-economic bloc coincide with the interests of society as a whole.[38]

On the other hand, the idea of civil society has also been associated with the notion of social capital as developed a century ago. In the tradition influenced by the work of Bourdieu, social capital is defined as resources embedded in civil society and accessed and used by actors for action.[39] The broadly used conception from Coleman of social capital emphasizes its impact at the level of community.[40] This conception has acquired a substantial heuristic value thanks to the contribution of Robert Putnam.[41] The core idea of social capital is that a person's social assets, family, friends, associates, are not irrelevant in a person's life. On the contrary, they are crucial to solve situations of crisis or to obtain economic or other advantages. This is not only true for individuals but for communities too, to the extent that the density of social capital in a given community can bring about material advantages and avoid or limit the impact of crises. Civil society matters, or, in Putnam's words: 'civil society affects the health of our democracies, our communities and ourselves'.[42]

The link between social policy and social capital lies in the amount and quality of mutual welfare delivered informally by friends, mutual support groups and community (neighbourhood or identity/religion-based) associations, which adds to and reinforces the social service nets provided by law. Social capital represents communal assets produced and reproduced by interpersonal relations based on trust and reciprocity and sustained by solidarity norms and values, including religious ones, as well as (in some contexts such as family and friendship networks) by emotional investment. Social capital relations are by their nature inclusive rather than exclusive.

Three interrelated and cumulative dimensions of social capital are important. These are: bonding social capital (relationships at the basic level of the family, built on identity and sense of belonging), bridging social capital (relationships that tie together different families and neighbourhoods into a larger civic community able to pursue common goods and outcomes) and linking social capital (relationships that connect the civic community and political/policy-making institutions).

Importantly, the amount of social capital in a community is not given; it varies across time and space which makes it imperative to study this notion in different societies and different historical periods.

How do social networks and relations matter? They matter first of all for the people who belong to them, providing for psychological and social comfort, but also for simple economic returns. This is what the economists would call 'the internal value' of social capital and it defines social capital as a private good. One classic example is the case of employment opportunities created by the intervention of friends or relatives or, more generally, 'social connections'.

However there is also an external value of social capital, as its existence provides benefits also for those who do not belong to the social networks in question. In the economists' jargon, there are some positive externalities from social capital. For example, a neighbourhood watch programme against local crime also produces a safer environment for those who do not take part in it. From this point of view, social capital also represents a public good. Even more importantly, it helps to solve collective action problems as it produces trustworthy relations. In other words, the existence of a social interaction based on trust can help people to act for the collective good without coercion or immediate reciprocation.

In operative terms, scholars distinguish between a narrow and a wider definition of social capital.[43] In a narrow sense, social capital refers only to the networks and groups joined voluntarily by individuals and involving regular face-to-face meetings. This could be cultural associations, religious groups or even sport clubs. In a broader sense, individuals can belong to social groups by chance, or birth, or constraint, as in the case of a family or a social class or a neighbourhood. Finally, in the widest meaning, social capital refers to situations where meetings are irregular and casual, like groups of commuters, or participants in a public demonstration.

Consequently, the social cohesion of civil society can be measured at various levels:

(1) Within each group and community.
(2) Between different groups and communities.

This distinction, as well as the distinction between the narrow and the wider definition of social capital, is especially relevant when dealing with social capital in Muslim-majority countries. Indeed, as further elaborated below, the most relevant form of social capital in these countries is narrow social capital, especially religious social capital (RSC). Moreover the recent evolution of civil society and social capital in MENA countries, especially resource-poor ones, substantiates the hypothesis that new forms of social cohesion have been created both horizontally, within social classes, and vertically, between social classes.

Finally what is most relevant is whether social capital is created through public intervention or is a completely private venture. Indeed, the relations between state and civil society are very complex. The state is shaped by society, but society is also shaped by the state and its political institutions and legislation, as becomes very clear when studying MENA countries' civil societies. Indeed, the state can also hinder the formation of social capital through repressive policies, as in the case of Tunisia.

As far as religious organizations are concerned, these are generally considered in the literature about social capital as just another form of voluntary association.[44] Evidence shows, however, that RSC, as represented for example by faith-based organizations active in civil society, plays a distinctive role not only in building social capital but also with respect to its wider implications, including political ones.[45] In addition, as we will see below, the Arab world is peculiar in the extent to which social capital is generated mainly through religious institutions, also due in part to the distinctive characteristics of Islam.

Following Gramsci,[46] it is possible to hypothesize that the impact of globalization on the Arab states considered, especially its impact in terms of the crisis of the nation state, produced the conditions for the emergence of a new hegemonic historic bloc. This was based on alternative ideologies such as Islam and underpinned by different socio-economic alliances, namely a new alliance between the 'discontented' middle class(es) and the 'dispossessed' lower ones,[47] what Harvey[48] calls the discontented and the dispossessed.[49]. According to the relevant literature,[50] in the Middle East, the bulk of the middle class would be represented by civil servants, which are, by definition, discontented by the retreat of statist regimes.[51] This is compounded by professionals and a very limited group of small and medium-sized entrepreneurs, sometimes explicitly Islamic businesses.[52] Indeed, most of the very small entrepreneurs would belong to the category of the 'dispossessed' lower classes. With respect to the business component of the middle class, both in Egypt and in Tunisia, state capital tended to ally more with international capital than with local small and medium capital, which was generally weak, according to Ayubi's conceptualization.[53]

As noted by Ayubi: 'The private business bourgeoisie, insofar as it was allowed to exist, became subservient to the State and to the requirements of state capitalism.'[54]

Even the intensive liberalization policies adopted in both countries as a consequence of globalization-induced economic restructuring seem to have failed to incorporate local private small and medium-sized entrepreneurs not connected to the regimes.[55]

On the other hand, the dispossessed are the poor— that is, those who do not have possessions and therefore are unable to access the marketplace to meet their basic needs.[56]

Both strata have been increasingly marginalized by the statist regimes in Middle East, from the political sphere as well as from the socio-economic and cultural ones.[57] Indeed, the latest batch of economic restructuring measures mainly affected the lower and middle classes[58]. In the words of Ayubi: 'Marginalisation is an important phenomenon in many Third world countries, not only because of the large size of the lumpenproletariat but also because of the dangerous phenomenon of the unemployment (or underemployment) of the educated'. Such marginalization is a very important breeder of protest movements, such as 'Political Islam'.[59]

What it is hypothesized here is that in the Arab world, especially in the Middle East, Islam progressively became the point of reference of those strata of civil society marginalized by the existing regimes: the discontented middle classes and the lower classes. This means that in practical terms, Islam increasingly came to represent their only ideology, as well as the basis of their identity and, wherever possible, of their social relations and networks. In other words, it became the source of their social capital. This might have been favoured by the ideological weakness of the existing power bloc, which limited its capacity to gain hegemony in civil society.[60] Thus, in this context, the impact of globalization on civil society would be the creation of a new socio-economic alliance between the marginalized strata of civil society cemented by a common ideology, Islam. How this took place is the subject of the next section.

Islam and civil society

The purpose of this section is to discover whether the crisis of the nation state as a consequence of globalization and the lack of a regional integration project in the MENA area has been accompanied by a progressive re-Islamization of civil society, particularly the middle and lower classes, and whether this is reflected in the emergence of a distinct Islamic social capital within those socio-economic groups.[61] The idea is to ascertain to what extent

Islamic social capital and Islamic social institutions favoured the decline of previously well-established political solutions, or whether they have been constrained by repressive policy-making.[62]

Already before the Arab Spring, commentators and experts of Arab politics had noticed how from the 1990s Arab societies had undergone fundamental changes.[63] In Egypt, for example, economic crises, economic restructuring and globalization had progressively undermined the statist order created during the Nasserist rule. In line with our transnationalist perspective, these changes brought about a weakening of state control over the economy and society, especially the withdrawal of the public sector and the progressive demise of the system of subsidies.[64] Rutherford notes how these transformations also eroded the already weak political ideology legitimating the regime, whose liberal conception of law within the judiciary was increasingly challenged by the Islamic conception of governance proposed by the Muslim brotherhood and political Islam. In a word, the declining statism of the regime, which was no longer sustainable given the constraints imposed on the state by globalization, was increasingly challenged by an alternative political ideology based on Islam.[65] It is outside the scope of this very short section to discuss the economic ideology of Islam or rather the complex and contradictory relationship between Islam and capitalism, which has been addressed exhaustively elsewhere.[66]

The role of Islam in society and politics is a highly debated question, not only between scholars, but also within Islam itself.[67] With respect to its basic principles, Islam can be considered a unified whole.[68] However, countless interpretations exist relating to secondary prescriptions as well as to the objectives of the Islamic texts, to the extent that experts of Muslim-majority societies generally speak about 'Islams' to underline the diversity of Islamic social and cultural contexts.[69] As Ramadan puts it: 'What is meant by the concept of "Islamic Civilisation" is precisely this: One single Islam, a diversity of interpretations and a plurality of cultures'.[70]

Political Islam does not come in a single, unified version either, although its origins can be traced back to the late nineteenth century reformers who were both pan-Islamic and anti-colonial and had a great impact on twentieth century Islamic thought.[71] According to them, Muslims had to go back to their religious teachings, acquire consciousness of their subordination and free themselves from the chains of colonialism. From this perspective, Islam as a religion was invoked and played a fundamental role in the liberation from colonialism as well as in the future political, economic and cultural organization of Muslim-majority states. It was however only with the creation of the Muslim Brotherhood by Hassan al-Banna (1906–1949) that what is known now as 'political Islam' or 'Islamism' acquired a much clearer definition. Relying heavily on the thoughts of the first generation of reformers, al-Banna proposed early on a programme of re-Islamization of Egypt.[72]

Currently, Islamist movements are divided mainly on the following issues: (1) the definition of who is a Muslim and what are their prerogatives; (2) the use of violence; (3) the application of the sharia as a closed legal system or as open to foreign references such as democracy; (4) whether it is acceptable to create an Islamist political party or it is preferable to retain the status of a religious and social organization; (5) the role of women in Muslim-majority societies; (6) the relationship with people of other religion or no religion in society; (7) the relationship with the West.[73]

To understand the capacity of Islamism to conquer the realm of civil society, it is extremely important to underline that not only did it originate as a legalistic, societal movement, but it also never lost its original strategy of reforming society from the bottom up, by educating the masses in order to change society as a whole and restructure the state into an Islamic state.[74]

Indeed, the relationship between religion and sovereignty has always been a contested one in the Arab state. Even in the most advanced Islamic constitutions, such as the Tunisian one, moving away from the sharia to a legal system devoid of theological–political influence proved extremely difficult; the legislature stipulated that Islam is the religion of the state. Consequently, citizens were not free to choose their beliefs, or lack thereof.[75]

In Egypt, the re-Islamization of society and the American alliance went hand in hand, constituting another paradox, which is known in the literature as the Egyptian paradox.[76] The explanation might be found in the need of the regime to protect itself from the violent sections of the Muslim Brotherhood which attempted to assassinate Nasser in 1954, successfully managed to eliminate Sadat in 1981,[77] almost killed Mubarak in 1995 and were increasingly gaining support in civil society.[78] Indeed, although politically the Islamists had not yet won power, they were increasingly taking control of society. As Meddeb puts it:

> In the war of words, the state thought it had to take away from the fundamentalists the argument denouncing the non-conformity of their society to Islamic norms. To defuse this criticism, the state decided to entrust to Al-Azhar the governance of souls, provided it would minimize the reach of political Islam. After such a tacit agreement, society found itself metamorphosed.[79]

What remains to be ascertained now is how Islamism was successful in its endeavour to gain cultural hegemony in Muslim-majority countries, to what extent and why.[80]

A prominent source for identifying the role of Islamists in civil society, their level of penetration and their capacity to substitute the state in the provision of public goods is represented by the Arab Human Development Reports (AHDR), prepared by a team of prominent Arab intellectuals under the auspices of the United Nations Development Programme (UNDP) between 2002 and 2009. These reports argued that throughout the Middle East Islamist groups had increasingly obtained broad popular support, had provided effective service networks and developed a formidable capacity to mobilize followers.

As underlined in the AHDR of 2002, the Arab world has a well-established tradition of religious civil society organizations based on the 'waqf' system.[81] Since the end of the nineteenth century this has led to the creation of Islamic cultural associations and charities which, in line with the programme of political Islam, were heavily involved in education, provision of health care and other social and religious matters. These organizations, whose activities within civil society were limited if not prohibited by the state in the past, witnessed a strong revival later on, especially in more recent decades as a consequence of the increasing difficulty of the state to provide similar services, or, in the words of the report, 'more or less encouraged by public authorities needing their assistance in times of difficulty'.[82]

On the contrary, non-religious civil society organizations encountered several external constraints in playing their role effectively, such as the imposition of bureaucratic constraints in the form of control of civic associations by public authorities.[83] Moreover, non-religious civic associations were considered by the AHDR to be dysfunctional in various ways. They lacked internal democracy, as demonstrated by the low participation of women and youth and the concentration of power in the hands of a single individual, usually the founder of the organization.[84] This usually led to conflicts and often splits. Moreover, they were seen as lacking transparency in their decision-making processes and incapable of settling disputes peacefully through debates. In administrative terms they were considered unable to respect clear-cut rules of management and accountability. All these shortcomings contributed to non-religious NGOs encountering many problems in financing their activities. On the contrary, civil associations with a religious background were much more successful at maintaining financial independence. This was the case because they enjoyed credibility and legitimacy in society as their actions accorded with traditional Arab and Muslim norms of civic action, associating such activities with welfare and charity work. Moreover, their missions were clear and their social impact immediate as they satisfied pressing needs of the population.[85] Finally they could rely on donations from the private sector under Zakat[86] as well as providing certain services for a fee.

As underlined by the reports, this was clearly not the case with other, more advocacy-oriented kinds of civil society organizations which provided for functions or services alien to, or at least not appreciated by, society at large. They provoked distrust amongst private donors, entering into antagonistic relations both with civil society and with the authorities and having to rely heavily on finances coming from international donors.[87] This, in turn deepened public hostility towards their activities and increased their incapacity to communicate with domestic societal actors who did not contribute to their activities either through voluntary work or through financial help.[88]

Thus, throughout the Middle East, it is almost exclusively Islamist charities and social welfare organizations that have played a major role in addressing the socio-economic needs of Muslim societies.

In some resource-poor Muslim-majority societies, this role has been increasing with the crisis of the nation state and has not only affected the poorer strata of society.[89] In fact, Clark demonstrates through case studies of Islamic medical clinics in Egypt that the Islamic Center Charity Society in Jordan, and the Islam Women's Charitable Society in Yemen,[90] also served the interests of the middle classes.[91] Hence, Islamic social institutions (ISIs) were not only a means to influence the lower classes, as often underlined in the literature,[92] but have clearly been playing an increasingly essential role in providing social networks that strengthened the ties of solidarity amongst the different components of the middle class, as well as between the middle and lower classes.

As clearly underlined by Clark: 'Then, as now, the middle class established nongovernmental organisations in reaction to state weakness'.[93]

This also allowed for the diffusion of Islamic ideas amongst these classes, which produced as its outcome new social and political movements based on Islam as opposed to other, more secular, ideologies:

> ISIs are more than just a challenge to the State's ability to do its job; they are a challenge to the secular state itself. They represent an alternative organization of state and society—a potentially revolutionary one—based on Islam.[94]

In the case of Egypt, the Muslim Brotherhood represented by far the most important religious civil society organization and no doubt also the most successful one.[95]

The Muslim Brotherhood was created in 1928, just a few years after the demise of the spiritual caliphate controlled by the Ottoman Empire. The objectives of the Brotherhood were quite specific from the beginning and included a return to Islam which had to be achieved through a bottom-up strategy based on programmes of mass education, social and economic reform and progressive implementation of Islamic legislation. The final aim was to set up an 'Islamic state'.[96] To achieve this new moral, social and legal order, the programme conceived by al-Banna required a complete transformation of the educational system, asking, for example, for primary schools to be attached to mosques. The formation of political parties was forbidden and civil servants were required to have religious training.[97] It seems clear that, from its establishment, political Islam, especially as embodied by the Muslim Brotherhood, had a clear agenda of conquering civil society before establishing an Islamic state. It defined itself not as a political party, but as solidarity-based social and educational organization alternative to the state.[98] Eventually, al-Banna's ideas transcended national boundaries and gained millions of supporters all over the Arab world.[99]

Thus, the Muslim Brotherhood was from its origins a civil society organization building religious social capital especially amongst the strata of society that did not have full access to the public goods provided by the state. A more violent component came to the forefront in Egypt in the early 1960s as a reaction to the consolidation of power by Colonel Gamal Abdel Nasser (1918–1970). The Brotherhood then started to include different trends, ranging from its mainly societal and legalistic origins to more radicalized and violent elements following Nasser's repression in the 1950s and 1960s.[100] With the retreat of the state and the progressive reduction of its services to the middle classes, the reach of the Muslim Brotherhood as a social solidarity system has substantially increased.[101] This societal dimension, therefore, has become all the more important. If the strategy of the Muslim Brotherhood during the regimes of Nasser and Sadat was divided between violent opposition to the regime and a grassroots programme of conquest of civil society by focusing particularly on education, in the course of Mubarak's regime, especially from the early 1990s, its reach became more web-like.[102] By 1992 the Muslim Brotherhood led all of the major professional associations, apart from that of journalists, and all of the university students' unions. The more that the regime faced difficulties in maintaining control over the economy and guaranteeing even the most basic services in some deprived areas, the more the Muslim Brotherhood stepped in and substituted the state by establishing Islamic schools, health clinics based on Islamic rules and values and credit unions.[103] Moreover, this alternative network of schools, hospitals and social services was heavily supported by the so-called 'Islamic business sector'.[104] It is outside the scope of this discussion to identify foreign sources of financing of Islamic social institutions.[105]

It might be true that the Islamists and the Muslim Brotherhood abstained from taking the lead in the events of Midan Tahir between 25 and the 28 January 2011. However, as rightly explained by Hamid: 'For the members of Egypt's Muslim Brotherhood—the oldest and most influential Islamist political party—the Arab Spring may not have been entirely of their making, but it surely was the answer to their prayers'.[106]

Indeed, the leaders of the Muslim Brotherhood were careful to instruct their militants not to shout explicit Islamist slogans in Tahir Square, to avoid the US or other Western countries intervening to crack down on the Islamist threat. However, the Brotherhood made its presence felt during the revolts, providing vital medical services to the protesters, protecting them from violent repression and keeping order.[107]

In contrast to Egypt, in Tunisia the retrenchment of the state in terms of welfare provision was not so marked and, because of the control of the regime over civil society and its repressive policies, civic groups, including Islamic groups, did not manage to be active on social issues.[108]

In Tunisia, the Islamic political opposition, Al Nahda, was a direct product of the regime. In response to the growing relevance of secular civil society organizations such as labour unions, student movements and other secular political groupings in the early 1970s, Bourguiba allowed the formation of a religious association for the Preservation of the Koran.[109] This organization later became the Jamma Islamiyya and initially limited its activities to questions of faith and morality. However, with the economic crisis of the late 1970s, the Islamists started to propose a more socio-economic project, appealing to unions and workers.[110] Political concerns followed in 1980 with the establishment of the Islamic Tendency Movement (MTI), an Islamist political movement which was refused recognition by the government and heavily repressed.[111] The change of regime in 1987, with Ben Ali freeing thousands of Islamists, including the leader Rachid Ghanoushi, led the MTI to change its name to Hizb' Al Nahda (the Renaissance Party), looking for government recognition that never arrived. Instead, after the Islamists' independent list won 14% of the vote as opposed to 5% by all other opposition groups combined, Al Nahda was brutally repressed Ben Ali's regime of, and any other form of independent civil society activity was frozen.[112]

Therefore, given the incredibly repressive nature of the Tunisian regime in more recent years, the Islamist movements could not be actively involved in social and charity activities on the ground as had been the case for the Muslim Brotherhood in Egypt. Despite this, the re-Islamization of the Tunisian society was a reality for at least a decade before the uprising of 2011.[113] As the human rights activist Ilhem Abdelkifi pointed out: 'Tunisians are religious. [Al Nahda] will attract those who do not know where to go'.[114]

Furthermore, interviews with Islamist leaders indicated globalization and economic restructuring as relevant factors in producing a return to Islam. In particular, Rachid Ghanoushi explicitly condemned economic restructuring brought about by globalization for 'marginalizing the most vulnerable and favouring the most powerful'.[115]

Thus, even in the case of Tunisia, where ruthless repression made it impossible for Islamist movements to take control of civil society and build religious social capital, economic reforms and globalization are generally recognized as the sources of the re-Islamization of society in recent times.[116]

As noted by Noueihed:

> Arab leaders demonstrated a knack for 'upgrading authoritarianism' to survive the challenges posed not only by globalisation ... One of several tactics they employed was to curtail, co-opt, compete with and therefore undermine efforts to build a strong civil society through the creation of non-governmental organisations.[117]

This was certainly the case of Libya, where soon after taking power Gaddafi started a policy of complete eradication of any sort of civil society structure.[118] Granted, this was somehow easier in this country than anywhere else. The literature indeed agrees on tracing back the origins of the fragmentation of the Libyan civil society to the legacy of the Italian colonization.[119] The Italians were ruthless in their colonization efforts and tore Libyan society apart, leaving little in exchange.[120] Given the way in which the Italian colonization process was carried on and concluded, Libyan society did not benefit from the establishment of solid political institutions, an effective legal system or an educational infrastructure.[121] However, if some elements of civil society are to be identified in the Libyan case, these are related to the spread of Islam. Already under King Idris, immediately after the independence, the Muslim Brotherhood managed to penetrate Libya from neighbouring Egypt. Despite the harsh repression of its members carried on by Gaddafi, the Muslim Brotherhood remained active into the 1980s and 1990s. Although clearly a small group of mainly educated people and intellectuals, it did represent one of the few instances of civil society organizations in the country. When Gaddafi finally decided to destroy it completely, at the end of the 1990s, the Brotherhood's presence in Libya was much reduced, but the consequence was, as in other countries, the radicalization of Islam and its deeper penetration into the minds of Libyan people[122] as the only possibility of resistance to the dictator.[123] This happened, however, after Libya had been politically and economically isolated by the West, a political-economic isolation which brought economic marginalization.[124] No doubt these dynamics will play a role in the post-Gaddafi Libyan political and social order, although the situation is much complicated by other elements such as tribal rivalries and, above all, the question of the control of oil.[125]

In conclusion, globalization-induced economic restructuring, by either restricting the ability of the state to protect the poor and the middle classes or by causing a profound identity crisis in civil society through state repression, strengthened the hand of political Islam and undermined the legitimacy of the regimes in the resource-poor countries of the MENA area, including Egypt and Tunisia.[126]

Such a process did not occur suddenly on the eve of the Arab Spring. In Egypt this was clearly the consequence of a systemic penetration of Islam into civil society thanks to its capacity to foster social capital and establish solidarity networks between lower and middle classes as well as within them (binding and bridging social capital, in the classification of the relevant literature)[127].

Thus, in Egypt, as well as in other resource-poor MENA countries such as Jordan,[128] and Yemen, the Islamic social institutions, which were adding to the creation of social capital, also created horizontal and vertical social networks of solidarity among the discontented middle classes and the dispossessed poor ones. However, these prevailing forms of social capital were based on an Islamic view of society and the state; they were therefore alternative to both the status quo and to more secular social movements. In these cases, civil society was indeed empowered by globalization, as proposed by transnationalists. However, this happened through the creation of a distinct Islamic social capital, binding the middle classes and the poorer strata of society more closely in the name of a vision of the state and society alternative to both the existing regimes and a more secular project. Islamism, as an ideology, permeated the middle and poorer strata of society, cementing a new socio-economic alliance, or, as Gramsci would put it, a new socio-economic historic bloc.[129]

Similarly, in Tunisia Islamism came to penetrate deeply into civil society and to represent a strong cohesive factor between the middle and lower classes. Given the repressive nature of the state, which tightly controlled civil society as well as the welfare state, this could not happen through faith-based welfare provision and religious social capital. However, by negating an evolution of civil society towards a model already prevailing in other Arab states, it widened the sources of discontent, especially amongst the marginalized strata of society, thus creating a vacuum which Islam increasingly filled. In a way, the development of the Egyptian and Tunisian civil society (or lack of it) are the two sides of the same coin: by adopting de facto opposite attitudes towards the development of Islamic social institutions and social capital, the two regimes obtained exactly the same result, the empowerment of the Islamic ideology in opposition to both the status quo and any other alternative ideological/political projects.

Thus, as the corrupt nationalistic regimes in Egypt and Tunisia failed to guarantee prosperity to their societies, so these same societies turned to Islamism as the only alternative to the status quo. These new approaches to constitutional order based on political Islam progressively grew into meaningful alternatives to the declining statism of the regimes.[130]

To a certain extent, this analysis of the radicalization and penetration of Islam in society can also be applied to the case of Libya. However, the case of Libya, as an oil-producing country, requires a more detailed analysis of the political economy of oil.

Conclusion

Although some progress has been achieved in terms of increasing the educational attainments of women in the MENA area, their marginalization seem to be further warranted by the two phenomena identified in this article. On the one side, the lack of integration of most of MENA countries in the global political economy seems to be a consequence of their incapacity to catch up with the technological skills necessary to upgrade their productive and economic systems. If this is true for the general population, as clearly demonstrated in this article, it is even truer for women, who represent a social group increasingly lagging behind in the process of up-skilling and in the acquisition of the technological expertise necessary to integrate in the new global economy.

On the other hand, as a consequence of the retreat of the Middle Eastern and Arab states from the provision of jobs and public services, Arab societies seem to have undergone a process of Islamization which penalizes especially women.

This is related both to the need for women to provide those services previously offered by the state and also to the role that women are perceived to have in a more radicalized context, which limits women's possibility to gain centre stage in economic and public life.

Neither of these two developments looks good for the future of women in the MENA area.

Disclosure statement

No potential conflict of interest was reported by the author.

Notes

1. J. H. Mittleman, The Globalization *Syndrome: Transformation and Resistance*, Princeton University Press, Princeton, NJ, 2000; W. Robinson, *A Theory of Global Capitalism: Transnational Production, Transnational Capitalists, and the Transnational State*, Johns Hopkins University Press, Baltimore, MD, 2004.
2. Mittleman, op. cit., p. 122.
3. Ibid., pp. 122–123.
4. Ibid.; similarly S. Sassen, *The Global City*, Princeton University Press, Princeton, NJ, 1991.
5. Mittleman, op. cit., pp. 122–123.
6. Ibid., p. 226; L. S. Talani, A. Clarkson and R. Pacheco-Pardo, *Dirty Cities*, Palgrave, London, 2013.
7. P. Dicken, *Global Shift: Mapping the Changing Contours of the World Economy*, 6th ed., Guilford Press, London, 2011, p. 76.

8. N. Shafik, 'Technology: a disintegrative factor in the Arab world', in C. M. Hudson (ed.), *The Middle East Dilemma*, Tauris, London, 1999, p. 212.
9. Arab Human Development Report (AHDR), *Building a Knowledge Society*, 2003 <http://www.arab-hdr.org/contents/index.aspx?rid=2> (accessed 5 April 2013).
10. Dicken, op cit., p. 77.
11. Ibid., p. 79.
12. Ibid.; S. Strange, *Mad Money*, Manchester University Press, Manchester, 1998.
13. Sassen, op. cit.; Talani et al., op. cit.
14. Dicken, op. cit., p. 95.
15. ITU, *ICT Facts and Figures*, 2013 <http://www.itu.int/ITU-D/ict/facts/material/ICTFactsFigures2013.pdf> (accessed 7 March 2013).
16. The list of the countries belonging to each region as well as to the developing/developed world is based on the UN classification and is available at the ITU site <http://www.itu.int/ITU-D/ict/definitions/regions/index.htm> (accessed 7 March 2013).
17. ITU, *ICT Facts and Figures*.
18. Ibid.
19. Ibid.
20. Ibid.
21. Ibid.
22. UN (United Nations), *The Global Information Society: A Statistical View – Partnership on Measuring ICT for Development*, April 2008, LC/W.190 <http://www.itu.int/ITU-D/ict/material/LCW190_en.pdf> (accessed 7 March 2013).
23. According to the ITU classification, Egypt, Libya and Tunisia belong to the Arab world. See <http://www.itu.int/ITU-D/ict/definitions/regions/index.htm> (accessed 7 March 2013).
24. ITU, *ICT Facts and Figures*.
25. UN, op. cit., p. 55.
26. Ibid.
27. World Bank Statistics <http://data.worldbank.org/indicator/SE.XPD.TOTL.GB.ZS?page=1> (accessed 22 March 2013).
28. Arab Human Development Report, op. cit., p. 2.
29. Ibid., p. 2.
30. Ibid., p. 3.
31. World Bank Statistics, op. cit.
32. UN, op. cit.
33. Arab Human Development Report (AHDR), *Creating Opportunities for Future Generations*, 2002<http://www.arab-hdr.org/contents/index.aspx?rid=1> (accessed 5 April 2013), pp. 47–51; AHDR, *Building a Knowledge Society*, op. cit., pp. 51–56.
34. AHDR, *Building a Knowledge Society*, op. cit., p. 55.
35. See <http://www.educationcounts.govt.nz/__data/assets/pdf_file/0011/114995/Key-Findings-NZ-Participation-in-TIMSS-and-PIRLS-2010-2011.pdf>, (accessed 16 September 2016), p. 11.
36. AHDR, *Building a Knowledge Society*, op. cit., p. 38; Mittleman, op. cit.
37. A. Gramsci, *Selections from the Prison Notebooks of Antonio Gramsci*, Elecbook, electronic books, London, 1999; A. Gramsci, *Quaderni dal carcere* [Prison Notebooks], Einaudi, Torino, 1975.
38. Gramsci, *Quaderni dal carcere*, op. cit.; Gramsci, *Selections from the Prison Notebooks*, op. cit.
39. P Bourdieu, 'Le capital social: notes provisoires', *Actes de la Recherche in Sciences Sociales*, 31, 1980, pp. 2–3.
40. J. Coleman, 'Social capital in the creation of human capital', *American Journal of Sociology*, 94, 1988, pp. 95–120.
41. R. Putnam, *Democracies in Flux*, Oxford Scholarship online, 2002, p. 3 <http://www.oxfordscholarship.com> (accessed 19 February 2007).
42. Ibid., p. 6.

43. J. Worms, 'France: old and new civic and social ties in France', in R. D. Putnam (ed.), *Democracies in Flux: The Evolution of Social Capital in Contemporary Society*, Oxford University Press, New York, 2002, p. 138.
44. Putnam, *Bowling Alone*, op. cit.
45. J. Harrigan and H. El Said , *Economic Liberalisation, Social Capital and Islamic Welfare Provision*, Palgrave, London, 2009, p. 13.
46. Gramsci, *Quaderni dal carcere*, op. cit.; Gramsci, *Selections from the Prison Notebooks*, op. cit.
47. R. Roccu, 'Of middle classes, economic reforms and popular revolts', in S. Panebianco and R. Rossi (eds), *Winds of Democratic Change in the Mediterranean?*, Rubbettino, Palermo, 2012, pp. 61–82.
48. D. Harvey, 'The right to the city', *New Left Review*, 53, 2008, pp. 23–40; D. Harvey, *The Enigma of Capital and the Crises of Capitalism*, Profile Books, London, 2010.
49. For a very good account of the definition of middle class in the Middle East see G. Luciani, 'Linking Economic and Political Reform n the Middle East: The Role of the Bourgeoisie', in O. Schlumberger (ed), *Debating Arab Authoritarianism: Dunamics and Durability in Nondemocratic Regimes*, Stanford University Press, Stanford CA, 2007, p. 163: '[t]he middle class per se has no other distinguishing feature except that it finds itself between a top class, comprising the elite, and a lower class, comprising the masses'. See also Roccu, op. cit.; J. Clark, *Islam, Charity and Activism*, Indiana University Press, Bloomington, 2004; N. Ayubi, *Over-stating the Arab State: Politics and Society in the Middle East*, London: I. B. Tauris, 2008; N. Ayubi, *Political Islam: Religion and Politics in the Arab World*, Routledge, London, 1991
50. Ayubi, *Over-stating the Arab State*, op. cit., p. 343; Clark, op. cit.; Roccu, op. cit.
51. M. Said, 'The fall and rise in wage inequality in Egypt: new evidence from the ELMPS, 2006', ERF Working Paper Series, WP 0708, Economic Research Forum, Cairo, 2007, p. 6.
52. Oliver Schlumberger (ed.), *Debating Arab Authoritarianism: Dynamics and Durability in Nondemocratic Regimes*, Stanford University Press, Stanford, CA, 2007.
53. Ayubi, *Over-stating the Arab State*, op. cit., pp. 180–181.
54. Ibid., p. 181.
55. Roccu, op. cit.; Ayubi, *Over-stating the Arab State*, op. cit., pp. 329–357.
56. Clark op. cit., p. 11; 'Morti di Fame', in Ayubi, *Over-stating the Arab State*, op. cit., p. 179.
57. Roccu, op. cit.; Ayubi, *Over-stating the Arab State*, op. cit., p. 181.
58. Ayubi, *Over-stating the Arab State*, op. cit., p. 352; S. Heydemann (ed.), *Networks of Privilege in the Middle East: The Politics of Economic Reforms Revisited*, Palgrave Macmillan, Basingstoke, 2004; Roccu, op. cit.
59. Ayubi, *Over-stating the Arab State*, op. cit., pp. 181–182.
60. Ibid., p. 399.
61. Similarly Clark, op. cit.; Harrigan and El-Said, op. cit.
62. A. Jamal., *Barriers to Democracy: The Other Side of Social Capital in Palestine and the Arab World*, Princeton University Press, Princeton, NJ, 2007.
63. Ayubi, *Over-stating the Arab State*, op. cit.; Clark, op. cit.; B. Rutherford, *Egypt after Mubarak: Liberalism, Islam, and Democracy in the Arab World*, Princeton University Press, Princeton, NJ, 2008, p. 2; Harrigan and El-Said, op. cit..
64. Ayubi, *Over-stating the Arab State*, op. cit.
65. Rutherford, op. cit., p. 2.
66. C. Tripp, *Islam and the Moral Economy: The Challenge of Capitalism*, Cambridge University Press, Cambridge, 2004; M. Rodinson, Islam and Capitalism, Saqi, London, [1987] 2007.
67. T. Ramadan, *The Arab Awakening: Islam and the New Middle East*, Penguin, London, 2012.
68. Ibid., p. 72.
69. Ibid., p. 72.
70. Ibid., p. 74.
71. Ibid., p. 75; similarly Clark, op. cit., pp. 13–14; Ayubi, Political Islam, op. cit.
72. Ramadan, op. cit., p. 75.

73. Ibid., p. 79; L. Snider, 'The clash of mental models in the Middle East: neoliberal vs. Islamic ideas', in R. Roy, K. Denzau and T. Willett (eds), Neoliberalism: National and Regional Experiments with Global Ideas, Routledge, London, 2007, pp. 206–228.
74. C. Tripp, Islam and the Moral Economy: the Challenge of Capitalism, Cambridge University Press, Cambridge, 2006; Clark, op. cit., pp. 11–12.
75. H. Meddeb, Ambivalence de la politique migratoire en Tunisie, FASOPO, Paris, mimeo, 2008.
76. Ibid.
77. Sadat was killed in 1981 by a member of the Jihad, a militant Islamic group that had split from the MB in the early 1970s. Rutherford, op. cit., p. 83.
78. Ibid., p. 20.
79. Meddeb, op. cit.
80. A different issue is the discussion of the role of civil society in promoting democracy in general and in the Middle East in particular. For this see H. Blair, 'Donors, democratisation, and civil society: relating theory to practice', in D. Hulme and M. Edwards (eds), Too Close for Comfort? NGOs, States and Donors, Macmillan, Basingstoke, and St Martins' Press, New York, 1997; S. E. Finkel, 'Can democracy be taught?', Journal of Democracy, 14(4), October 2003, pp. 137–151; J. Hearn, 'Aiding democracy? Donors and civil society in South Africa' Third World Quarterly, 21(5), 2000, pp. 815–830; C. Henry and R. Springborg (eds), Globalisation and the Politics of Development in the Middle East, Cambridge University Press, Cambridge, 2001; M. Hoogh and D. Stolle, Generating Social Capital, Palgrave, London, 2003; S. E. Ibrahim, 'Crises, elites, and democratisation in the Arab world', Middle East Journal, 47(2), 1993, pp. 292–305; S. Huntington, The Third Wave: Democratisation in the Late Twentieth Century, University of Oklahoma Press, Norman, OK, 1991; A. Krishna, 'Enhancing political participation in democracies: what is the role of social capital?', Comparative Political Studies, 35(4), 2002, pp. 437–460; N. Letki, 'Socialisation for participation?', Political Research Quarterly, 57(4), 2004, pp. 665–679; K. Newton, 'Trust, social capital, civil society and democracy', International Political Science Review, 22(2), 2001, pp. 201–214; A. R. Norton, 'The future of civil society in the Middle East', Middle East Journal, 47(2), 1993, pp. 205–216; M. Ottaway, and T. Carothers, Funding Virtue, Carnegie Endowment for Intl Peace, 2000.
81. This is a system of donations to Islamic charitable trusts.
82. AHDR, Creating Opportunities for Future Generations, op. cit., p. 109.
83. Arab Human Development Report (AHDR), Challenges to Human Security in the Arab Countries, 2009 <http://www.arab-hdr.org/contents/index.aspx?rid=2> (accessed 5 April 2013).
84. AHDR, Creating Opportunities for Future Generations, op. cit., p. 110.
85. Ibid., p. 110.
86. Charity.
87. AHDR, Challenges to Human Security in the Arab Countries, op. cit., p. 71.
88. AHDR, Creating Opportunities for Future Generations, op. cit., p. 110.
89. Ibid., p. 110.
90. For a thorough analysis of the middle classes in the Middle East see Clark, op. cit.; Ayubi, Over-stating the Arab State, op. cit.; Roccu, op. cit.
91. Clark, op. cit.; similarly Rutherford, op. cit.,
92. Harringan and El-said, op. cit., p. 2; S. Zubaida, 'Islam, the state and democracy', Middle East Report 179, 1992, p. 9; A. Roussillon, 'Entre Al Jihad et al. Rayyan', Modernisation et nouvelles forms de mobilisation sociale, Dossiers du centre d'etudes et the documentation economiques, Cairo, 1991, p. 45; M. Al Sayyid, 'A civil society in Egypt?', Middle East Journal, 47(2), 1993, p. 45.
93. Clark, op. cit., p. 5.
94. Ibid., pp. 5–6.
95. Ibid.
96. Ramadan, op. cit., p. 75.
97. Meddeb, op. cit.

98. Rutherford, op. cit., p. 78; B. Lia, The Society of the Muslim Brothers in Egypt: The Rise of an Islamic Mass Movement 1928–1942, Ithaca Press, Reading, 1998, p. 37; R. Mitchell, The Society of the Muslim Brothers, Oxford University Press, Oxford, 1993, pp. 214–216.
99. Ramadan, op. cit., p. 75.
100. Ibid., p. 78.
101. Clark, op. cit., pp. 11–12.
102. Jamal, op. cit.
103. Clark, op. cit., pp. 14–18, 42–81; Rutherford, op. cit.
104. Ayubi. Over-stating the Arab State, op. cit., p. 408.
105. Ramadan, op. cit.; recently the *Financial Times* stressed the intervention of Qatar.
106. S. Hamid, 'Islamists and the Brotherhood: political Islam and the Arab Spring', in K. Pollack (ed.), *The Arab Awakening*, The Brookings Institution, Washington, DC, 2011, p. 29.
107. Hamid, 'Islamists and the Brotherhood', pp. 29–39; S. Hamid, 'Tunisia', in Pollack, op. cit., pp. 111–117.
108. Harrigan and El-Said, op. cit., pp. 2–4; B. Hibou, *The Force of Obedience: The Political Economy of Repression in Tunisia*, Polity Press, Cambridge, 2011.
109. C. Alexander, 'Back from the democratic brink: authoritarianism and civil society in Tunisia', Middle East Report 205, October–December 1997, p. 35; Harrigan and El-Said, op. cit.
110. Alexander, op. cit.
111. Harrigan and El-Said, op. cit., p. 169.
112. Hibou, op. cit.
113. Harrigan and El Said, op. cit., p. 171.
114. Hamid, 'Tunisia', op. cit., p. 114.
115. Harrigan and El-Said, op. cit., p. 173.
116. Ibid., p. 174; Ayubi, Over-stating the Arab State, op. cit., p. 420; F. Halliday, 'The Middle East and the politics of differential integration', in T. Dodge and R. Higgott (eds), *Globalisation and the Middle East: Islam, Economy, Society and Politics*, Royal Institute of International Affairs, London, 2002, pp. 42–45; Henry and Springborg, op. cit.
117. L. Noueihed, *The Battle for the Arab Spring*, Yale University Press, Newhaven, 2012, p. 15.
118. D. Kawczynski, *Seeking Gaddafi: Libya, the West and the Arab Spring*, Biteback Publishing, London, 2011.
119. Ibid.; G. Simons, *Libya and the West, Centre for Libyan Studies*, 2003, Chapter 1; D. Vanderwalle, A History of Modern Libya, Cambridge University Press, Cambridge, 2006; World Bank, World Bank website <http://web.worldbank.org/WBSITE/ EXTERNAL/ DATASTATISTICS/0,,menuPK:232599~pagePK:64133170~piPK:64133498~the SitePK:239419,00.html> (accessed 15 March 2013), p. 40; J. K. Marshall, *Libya: A Look into History*, Thomas R. Mann (ed.), Kindle edition, 2011.
120. Marshall, op. cit.
121. Vandewalle, op. cit., p. 33.
122. Gaddafi was successful in quashing the two most prominent Islamist factions in the country, the Libyan Islamic Group (the Libyan branch of the Muslim Brotherhood) and the Libyan Islamic Fighting Group (LIFG). The latter was formed in the early 1990s by Libyan jihadists who had fought in Afghanistan against the Soviet Union. In the mid-1990s, the regime launched ground and air attacks against LIFG bases and arrested suspected sympathizers, quickly disrupting the group's cohesiveness and capabilities. In 1996, in Abu Salim, Tripoli's main political prison, guards killed 1270 prisoners, many of them Islamists. This incident, more than any other during Gaddafi's rule, would become one of the main rallying cries for the opposition movement that would eventually bring down the regime. See A. Al-Turk, 'Libya from revolt to state-building', in K. Pollack (ed.), *The Arab Awakaning*, The Brookings Institution Washington, DC, 2011, pp. 111–117.
123. Kawczynski, op. cit.
124. Simons, op. cit.; Marshall, op. cit.
125. Marshall, op. cit.

126. Harrigan and El-Said, op. cit., pp. 1–2; Clark, op. cit., pp. 11–12; H. Hakimian and Z. Moshaver (eds), *The State and Global Change: The Political Economy of Transition in the Middle East and North Africa*, Curzon, London, 2000.
127. Similarly A. Richards and J. Waterbury, *A Political Economy of the Middle East*, Westview Press, Boulder, 1998, pp. 348–350.
128. W. Knowles, *Jordan since 1989: A Study in Political Economy*, I. B. Tauris, London, 2005.
129. For a convincing account of the role played by the Islamists in the events of 25 January 2011 in Egypt see Hamid, Tunisia, 2011.
130. Rutherford, op. cit., p. 2.

Gender Mainstreaming towards the Mediterranean: the Case of the ENP

Serena Giusti

ABSTRACT
This article explores how the European Neighbourhood Policy (ENP) has supported policies promoting the improvement of women's conditions in Mediterranean countries. It points out the evolution of the European Union's gender mainstreaming in the various manifestations of its external policies directed to the region. Gender mainstreaming has been pursued through the usual practice, largely used in recent enlargements: norm diffusion. This method does not allow for a reconceptualization of the policies issued: partners only have the possibility of deciding the pace of implementation of a set of goals selected among those recommended by the EU. The 2011 wave of turmoil on the southern shores of the Mediterranean has contributed to refocusing the EU's actions on women. The new framework for Gender Equality and Women's Empowerment delivered in 2016 has established that gender equality will be mainstreamed through all the EU's external policies. Although efforts have been made to appraise it, the EU's gender strategy has mostly failed to confront the structural causes of inequality. It has mainly focused on the external aspects of the question while underestimating cultural, domestic and familial impediments and neglecting national debates or the contributions of local feminists. The EU's gender mainstreaming remains a unidirectional policy.

Introduction

European Union politics and the feminist literature have so far mainly concentrated on the way the EU deals with gender issues internally while there are still few studies on how the EU promotes gender equality beyond its borders. Even in the case of the 2004–2007 enlargement, considered the most efficacious action of the EU's foreign policy, gender mainstreaming has not been intensively examined. This is not only because the EU has treated that policy as part of the ordinary process of Europeanization but also because the topic has been dealt with by narrow perspectives.[1] Hopefully, a new strand of literature handling the question of gender through a multidisciplinary approach and blending different theoretical perspectives is emerging.[2]

While giving an account of poignant weaknesses highlighted by feminist literature and philosophical reflections on the issue, this article will analyse gender mainstreaming from a political perspective. It will point out, in particular, the EU's modalities to promote gender equality and how the concept has been progressively understood and spelt out. It will discuss its 'elasticity' in accordance with the EU's external goals and the necessity of coping with many emergencies in the Mediterranean region, especially after the 2011 awakening. In a relatively short period of time, gender mainstreaming has turned into a comprehensive and multisectoral strategy while women have been recognized for the strategic and challenging role they play in advancing and stabilizing their societies.

The article analyses the European Neighbourhood Policy's (ENP's) features and draws attention to the limits and potentialities of this policy in terms of instruments and contents elaborated for promoting gender equality. The ENP (including its revisions), in comparison to enlargement, has been shaped as a more flexible and tailor-made policy since it gathers countries with a high level of heterogeneity. However, the ENP's flexibility is mainly intended to give the possibility of choosing a set of objectives already endorsed by the EU. As a result, the principle of 'joint ownership' inspiring the ENP offers partners the opportunity to select what is more suitable and convenient for them without letting them take part in the making of policies over which the EU holds full power. What the EU is transferring is not unbiased; on the contrary, it is a cultural and political product although 'manufactured' in an unusual way (being the result of pooling and sharing among currently 28 member states). The way it is mainstreaming gender equality replicates what the EU has achieved internally while disregarding partners' traditions, culture and history.

At the same time, the EU's conditionality, very pervasive in the accession process, becomes enfeebled as each partner benefits from a wider space for manoeuvring with regard to prioritizing the reforms. The action plans, the new contractual arrangements pioneered in the ENP, have often been abstract and not sympathetic to the EU's goals. So, on one hand, the partners are constrained by the EU's policy patterns which ignore their national background; on the other, they might end up not complying with what the EU establishes for installing democracy, stabilizing and modernizing the Mediterranean region. However, the Union for the Mediterranean (2008), designed to make the EU and the Mediterranean countries more concrete and visible through additional regional and sub-regional projects relevant to the citizens of the region, has encountered various political obstacles. The 2011 wave of turbulence in the region has, in effect, interrupted and neutralized the EU's efforts to engage the Mediterranean countries. Furthermore, after 2011, the status of women has tended to worsen (fewer rights and less freedom, consistent irregular migration, conflicts).

The 2015 ENP review has tried to make the policy more effective and consistent. The review has furthered the principle of differentiation and joint ownership and lightened the whole monitoring process. This move is not likely to open a dialectical process when dealing with the neighbouring states but simply to better adjust to each partner's needs and expectations. The relaxing of control by Brussels is also due to the EU's plummeting appeal in the neighbourhood and to the concomitant necessity of keeping all the partners on board. As for gender mainstreaming, more emphasis has been placed on the role of women in society and in the political realm, including in the fight against terrorism.

It is, however, the new framework for Gender Equality and Women's Empowerment: Transforming the Lives of Girls and Women through EU External Relations (2016–2020), seeking to promote gender equality in all the EU's external actions, that will drive the ENP's gender mainstreaming. The new framework creates the undertaking of concrete measures and tangible results at different levels as gender mainstreaming is increasingly seen as a multi-policy and multi-level challenge. The role of women is valued not simply for its impact on economic and social fields but also because women are seen as important agents in the spreading of democracy and in the counterinsurgency and counterterrorism strategies.

Although the EU has progressively elaborated an encompassing policy strategy for supporting gender equality, it has nevertheless failed on two main fronts: (1) the elaboration of gender mainstreaming has largely neglected domestic debates and cultural peculiarities as the EU has maintained a unidirectional approach; (2) the private dimensions of gender equality, so dramatically relevant in the Mediterranean countries, have not been pondered. The EU has not advanced policies caring for all the gender nuances, from private to public life, which are determined by culture, values, history identity, religion and beliefs. The EU has treated gender mainstreaming merely as a matter of Europeanization. The strategy has been slightly modified in the case of unexpected intervening factors such as political instability, conflicts and terrorism.

The article is based on a textual analysis. The main ENP documents (strategy, progress reports, action plans, reviews) and other documents on gender equality connected to the ENP have been analysed to discover how gender mainstreaming has been understood and managed. The assessment has been conducted diachronically in order to capture any revision regarding the conceptualization of gender inequality and any change of the strategy and the tools used for reducing the gender gap on the southern shores of the Mediterranean.

Gender: insideoutside

The development of gender equality within the EU has followed the classic path of integration, from removing obstacles (negative integration) to actions helping women reach equality (positive integration). As far back as 1957, Article 119 of the Treaty of Rome stated that 'each Member State shall ensure that the principle of equal pay for male and female workers for equal work or work of equal value is applied'.

In the Treaty of Amsterdam (1997), the promotion of equality between women and men was recognized as one of the EU's fundamental tasks. It introduced the elimination of inequalities and discrimination and the promotion of equality between women and men in all activities. It strengthened the European commitment to gender equality and extended the equality principle of Article 141 beyond the workplace. As a result, the EU itself has a general obligation in all of its actions not only to remove inequalities but also to support equality between men and women. This obligation of gender mainstreaming means that both the Community and the member states shall actively take into account the objective of equality between men and women when formulating and implementing laws, regulations, administrative provisions, policies and activities.[3]

The Lisbon Treaty (2009) emphasizes even further the importance of the principles of non-discrimination and equality as fundamental principles of EU law. Article 2 of the Treaty of the European Union (TEU) affirms that

> the Union is founded on the values of respect for human dignity, freedom, democracy, equality, the rule of law and respect for human rights, including the rights of persons belonging to minorities. These values are common to the Member States in a society in which pluralism, non-discrimination, tolerance, justice, solidarity and equality between women and men prevail.

According to Article 3(3) of the TEU, one of the aims of the EU is to 'combat social exclusion and discrimination, and … promote social justice and protection, equality between women and men, solidarity between generations and protection of the rights of the child'. Furthermore, Article 8 of the Treaty on the Functioning of the European Union (TFEU) provides that 'in all its activities, the Union shall aim to eliminate inequalities, and to promote equality, between men and women'.

The adoption of the Charter of Fundamental Rights of the European Union, representing another important advancement in gender equality, states that equality between men and women must be ensured in all areas, including employment, work and pay (Article 23) and reaffirms the ban on discrimination on a wide number of grounds, including sex (Article 21).[4] The Charter states the right to gender equality in all areas, thus not only in employment, and the possibility of positive action for its promotion (Article 23). It also defines rights related to family protection and gender equality. It recognizes the importance of reconciliation of family/private life with work and guarantees the 'right to paid maternity leave and to parental leave' (Article 33).[5]

On the basis of the principles stated in the Treaties, the EU has produced a consistent body of legislation on gender equality while the Court of Justice has contributed to widening the scope of application of the Treaties and the Charter's principles. Gender equality has been extended to all areas, and positive measures to achieve it have been advocated—with the focus encompassing work, family and private spheres.

Nevertheless, the 2015 Gender Equality Index, produced by the European Institute for Gender Equality, has evidenced (using data from 2005 to 2012), that women are only halfway to equality with men and that progress has stagnated since 2005. In 2010, women were 52.4% equal compared with 52.9% in 2012. The picture varies greatly across the EU, with Sweden reaching an overall score of 74.2% while Romania is at 33.7%. The index also indicates that women's rights have been backsliding in eight countries, including the United Kingdom and Austria.[6]

With regard to power, the index shows that men are still largely over-represented in political and economic decision-making: more than 75% of parliamentarians and 84% of corporate board members in Europe are men. There have been some minor improvements on pay and work, significant because these areas have been the focus of most strategic action at the EU level. The gender gap in monthly earnings has decreased from 22% to 20%, and women's full-time employment rate has increased slightly.

These data prove that the EU must still work to make gender policies more effective and to fill the gap between countries oriented toward gender equality and those countries still struggling for equality between the sexes. Existing differences at the European level also testify to the fact that the initial EU gender regime does not secure a parallel 'Europeanisation' of gender order that concerns a hierarchy of relations and social practices.[7] The EU's normative power clashes in this field, in particular with national hindrances, partly due to countries' structural differences in terms of economic and social opportunities but also rooted in culture, history, tradition and educational diversity.

The way the EU regulates and supports gender policies impacts on its external action. The transfer of principled policies beyond the EU's perimeter refers to the widely debated conception of the EU as a normative power. From this perspective, the EU is seen as a peculiar power, different from pre-existing political forms and inclined to act in a normative way.[8] The determinants of the EU's normative power are genetic and are identified by Manners as the EU's historical context, its characteristic as a hybrid polity and its political–legal constitution.[9] Manners intends to move beyond the debate over state-like features through an understanding of the EU's identity: effectively a series of principles and shared beliefs that the member states adhere to and set an example with.[10] These principles and norms (including the centrality of peace, liberty, democracy, supranational rule of law and human rights) are enshrined in the *acquis communautaire* and regarded as legally binding commitments by member states. The EU's normative set is widening and includes also social solidarity, anti-discrimination, sustainable development and good governance.[11]

The EU has placed universal norms and principles not only at the centre of its member states but also of the world.[12] As noted by Tocci,

> After centuries of warfare, members of the European family appreciate that cooperation and integration are the only route to shared security, peace and prosperity. This internal Kantian logic has been extended to the realm of foreign policy, engendering a normative European foreign policy.[13]

The EU, when dealing with third countries, requires conditionality clauses that bind the recipients to practise ethical human rights, as stipulated in the European Convention on Human Rights. In addition, the EU includes human rights clauses with trade partners or when offering technical assistance.[14] The Lisbon Treaty (2009) has further clarified that in international affairs the EU would be guided by and would seek to promote the values on which the Union is founded, including democracy, human rights, fundamental freedoms and the rule of law.[15]

The EU's most powerful instrument for the externalization of its normative apparatus is attraction. Attraction is a mutable source of power depending on internal (status, cohesiveness, economic performance, capacity to deliver) and external variables (European identity of third countries, economic expectations, available alternatives besides the EU, perceived legitimacy of the EU). The more the EU is capable of offering both material and symbolic rewards (and is willing to do so), the more it can attract and influence other countries. On the basis of its offering potential (in a range from cooperation and partnership to membership), the EU has established a set of conditions the other countries are required to fulfil. Each partner's disposition to comply with those conditions is contingent on its desire to intensify the relationship. Although the relationship between the EU and third countries is clearly uneven, it is not founded on coercion but on the latter's willingness to strengthen links with Brussels.

It is a result of the EU's 2004–2007 enlargement that the diffusion of norms beyond the EU's legal boundaries became systematic and framed. In the context of the Eastern enlargement, the EU had in fact a deep 'impact on domestic policies, institutions and expectations of the societies emerging from communism after 1989, working through social norms and the construction of identity as well as material incentives'.[16]

Enlargement has clearly shown that playing the role of a normative power entails exerting a pervasive influence. The EU has progressively engaged in what Keukeleire defines as structural foreign policy,[17]

> a foreign policy which, conducted over the long-term, aims at sustainably influencing or shaping political, legal, economic, social, security or other structures in a given space. Structural foreign policy seeks to promote and support structural changes and structural reforms, tackle structural problems and constraints, or support and sustain existing structures.

A structural foreign policy relies on both material and immaterial factors. The immaterial factors are related to history, identity, values and legitimacy, and contribute to the 'internalization' of the structures that an actor is willing to endorse. The degree of internalization can vary from structures not internalized at all (for instance, adopted in a purely declaratory way) to structures that are deeply ingrained in the belief system. Therefore, the success of a structural foreign policy depends not only on the way it is managed but also on what is being channelled.

As Manners has correctly pointed out, the way the EU promotes its norms is as important as what it is promoting.[18] What the EU is transferring is not unbiased; on the contrary, it is a cultural and political product although forged by a post-modern entity that has broken down national borders and rejected force as a method of resolving disputes. As the process of norm diffusion is rooted in an unequal distribution of power, third countries are just absorbing what the EU transmits without having the possibility of affecting the content of norms and policies. It is as if the EU presumes to operate in a tabula rasa environment. On the contrary, as Börzel and Risse have remarked, 'European efforts to diffuse values, norms, and rules—both internally as well as externally—have to cope with heterogeneity and diversity'.[19] The absorption of the EU's normative apparatus can therefore significantly vary from one partner to another, hardly bringing about the adoption of structural reforms.

Other articles in this Special Issue have discussed the importance of national context, cultural milieu and religious beliefs when dealing with the promotion of gender equality. But the ENP procedures do not consent to modifying policies according to national peculiarities. So, as David and Guerrina have rightly pointed out,

> the *acquis communautaire* connected to gender equality is neither negotiable nor adaptable to the domestic setting of the ENP's partners. Instead the gender framing in the ENP is a complex process as it affects the issue of culture, dominant values and hegemonic structures.[20]

The European Neighbourhood Policy and gender mainstreaming

The EU's first attempts to promote gender equality beyond its borders dates back to the 1990s when the EC started to work on the inclusion of gender equality in development policy. The 2001 'Programme of Action for the mainstreaming of gender equality in Community Development Co-operation' is a formalization of those attempts. During the process of enlargement that brought 12 new members between 2004 and 2007, gender equality has been conveyed mainly as a part of the *acquis communautaire* on employment and social policy.[21]

The EU supported various programmes promoting gender equality without, however, putting forward an ad hoc strategy. As Bretherton underlined, in the course of accession negotiations, the governments of the candidates were mainly required to fulfil the requests of the Directorate General Employment and Social Affairs. Although not very rich, the literature on gender and enlargement tends to agree that gender equality had only a low priority during the accession negotiations and that the EU failed to increase gender awareness in candidate countries.[22]

The ENP was designed to build up strong relations—everything but the institutions[23]—with both southern and eastern neighbours, and with no or just long-term prospect of accession, can also be considered part and parcel of a structural foreign policy. Because in this case the incentives are less advantageous in comparison to enlargement, the EU's capacity to influence the partners is lower. As for the southern neighbours, not only are they excluded from membership—on the basis of Article 49, only a European state can apply to become a member of the Union—but they also have a weaker European identity. The relationship with the EU has been for most of these countries led by pragmatic and utilitarian considerations while some of the countries (e.g. Libya, Syria) have deemed that relationship undesirable.

The EU asks for respect of basic criteria, essentially the Copenhagen criteria, but the concrete requirements for deepening the bilateral relationship are to be set in an action plan as a result of a give-and-take bargaining process. Within the ENP, the EU, together with partner countries, defines a set of priorities which are to be incorporated in the action plans jointly agreed upon, covering a number of key areas for specific action. The action plans draw on common principles but are differentiated, reflecting the existing state of relations with each country, its needs and its capacities, as well as common interests. The level of ambition of the EU's relationships with its partners considers the extent to which these values are effectively shared. The Commission periodically assesses the progress accomplished and, together with partner countries, reviews the content of the action plans and decides on their adaptation and renewal.[24]

The introduction of the principles of 'joint ownership' and differentiation as the cornerstones of the action plans has not changed the substance of the process. The grade of flexibility of the ENP is restricted to quantity (how much to adopt) and to phasing (at what pace to implement) while it excludes quality and what is being implementing. Therefore, 'reflexivity', intended as consistency between the internal and external dimension of EU policy, is very high, as deviation is not contemplated for the recipient countries. A significant inconsistency would simply signal a very poor interest on the part of the recipient country to strengthen its partnership with the EU. To generate a truly 'joint policy', this would need to be the product of a dialectical process involving both sides. This new policy would thus derive from 'bringing the outside world back in' and would imply the establishment of a symmetrical relationship.[25]

Cremona and Hillion have underlined that the 'joint ownership' could be characterized as one of 'solidarity (as well as equality)'.[26] The ENP deals with 'concrete actions which build trust'; a relationship built on 'doing together what can be done together' rather than on fulfilling conditions.[27] Nevertheless, the joint ownership does not entail a rebalancing of the relationship. This in fact would presume 'joint ownership of both the process (learning about each other and adjusting to each other's needs and behaviour) and the outcome (of mutual goals and gains)'.[28] The EU does not renounce the imposition of conditionality that is ingrained in the inherent asymmetry of the relationship.

From that perspective, the principle of differentiation results are ambiguous. On one hand, differentiation might apply to the very limited freedom recognized for a partner when selecting its priorities within an already established range of options; on the other hand, it is conditionality that regulates differentiation. Differentiation would then depend on progress made in meeting conditions, as judged by the EU. If the EU, however, allows too much freedom of choice, partners may end up not sticking to the organization's policy targets or follow them in a very loose way. In other words, the ENP risks being a weak strategy that allows for the behaviour of 'free riders'. In the case of gender, given a policy that might easily encounter national reservations and suspicions, a defection justified on the basis of differentiation is quite predictable.

Although often mentioned in the related documents, the question of gender equality has not been a top priority in the ENP. In the early action plans concluded by the EU and the Mediterranean countries, gender issues have been treated moderately and differently across countries. In Tunisia's action plan (2005), gender equality is dealt with as part of the social and employment package.[29] In the action plan for Morocco (2005), the stress is on gender equality in the context of employment policy and on the role of women in promoting social and economic progress. The country is also invited to apply the UN Convention on the Elimination of All Forms of Discrimination against Women.[30] In the case of the action plan for Egypt (2007), support for women covers various aspects, ranging from the economic sphere to violence and education (participation in political, economic and social life; fighting against discrimination and gender-based violence; female genital mutilation; trafficking in human beings; women's literacy and education; Small and Medium Enterprises (SMEs); entrepreneurship of youth and women; productivity and competitiveness are all quoted).[31]

Since action plans did not recognize gender issues as pressing, the ENP monitoring reports have not been so alert to highlighting them. In the Communication on the Implementation of the ENP (2007), for instance, it is simply affirmed that progress has been made on *gender issues* in a number of countries and for each country the achievement is listed (for example, in Egypt, female genital mutilation has been formally prohibited; in Morocco, an amendment to the Nationality Code allows the transmission of nationality through the mother; and in Tunisia, the procedure to ratify the Optional Protocol to the Convention on the Elimination of All Forms of Discrimination against Women has been initiated).

In the 2011 report, gender issues are clearly related to education as well as participation in economic and political life. It is the 2013 report that openly considers the activation of civil society as beneficial for advancing women's rights and recognizes the role played by women in the 2011 revolutions.[32] The Commission indicates that 'the transition process and constitutional reform do not hinder progress on, or undermine the equality of women before the law and in society'. However, as revolt turned into hiatus and stalemate, Arab women found it difficult to advance their requests. The 2014 report denounces persistent signs of social divisions, reflecting discrimination against women and minorities. Besides reporting gender-based violence, it also points out discrimination on grounds of sexual orientation against the lesbian, gay, bisexual, transgender and intersex (LGBTI) community.[33]

The ENP documents (strategies, action plans, reports) need to be interpreted in the light of the activities and documents produced in the framework of the Barcelona Process, launched in November 1995 by the Ministers of Foreign Affairs of the 15 EU members and 12 Mediterranean partners (the numbers of each at that time) as the framework to manage both bilateral and regional relations, and re-launched in 2008 as the Union for the Mediterranean (UfM).[34] The content of the guidelines for the improvement of women's status and situation in the Euro-Mediterranean region, adopted at the Barcelona Summit of Heads of State and Government in November 2005, are aligned with those promoted within the ENP (gender equality, fighting against discrimination and protection of the rights of women). In the framework of the UfM, two ministerial conferences addressing women's equality were held in Istanbul (2006) and in Marrakesh (2009). They both reiterate the UfM commitment to promote de jure and de facto equality between women and men and to respect the civil, political, economic, social and cultural rights of women as well as men, as defined in the international human rights instruments to which they are parties—in particular, the UN Convention on the Elimination of All Forms of Discrimination against Women (CEDAW), the Programme of Action of the International Conference on Population and Development (ICPD), and the Beijing Platform for Action, the Millennium Declaration and the Millennium Development Goals (MDG).

WOMEN IN THE MEDITERRANEAN

The Marrakesh Conference enabled the partners of the UfM to evaluate progress achieved since its founding and to learn the lessons of this first experience. Ministers also reviewed common actions initiated since the First Ministerial Conference and exchanged views on the ways and means of implementation of their common political will through actions at national, sub-regional and regional levels, targeted towards improving women's status; strengthening the role of women in political, civil, social, economic and cultural life; and combating all forms of discrimination against women and girls. The path towards democracy and respect for human rights is clearly correlated with women's full enjoyment of human rights.[35] The conclusions summarized the negative impact of the financial crisis and the global economic slowdown on women's lives and gender equality and advocated promoting cultural and social rights, combatting all forms of gender stereotyping and ensuring equal access to education and vocational training—including new information technologies.

It also stressed the importance of dialogue between cultures and the inclusion of a gender dimension in education and training and in health policies. Ministers have called attention to migrant women who play a positive role in the development of their host societies while they need to be protected from discrimination and xenophobia and integrated into the societies in which they live. The UfM, committed to the promotion of concrete projects of cooperation, currently supports over 20 projects with 200,000 beneficiaries in the field of youth employability and gender equality.[36]

The ENP has been exposed to various revisions. The backdrop of the 2011 awakening in many of the Northern Mediterranean countries forced the EU to rethink the whole strategy, putting more emphasis on differentiation and democratization. The communication 'A New Response to a Changing Neighbourhood', presented by the Commission together with the High Representative of the Union for Foreign Affairs and Security Policy (May 2011), following a consultation with the governments and the civil society representatives of the EU and the 16 partners in Southern and Eastern Europe, was meant to produce a more consistent impact on the neighbourhood. The communication launched a whole review of the ENP with the aim of creating a 'deep and sustainable democracy'. The EU committed itself to promoting the political and institutional reforms necessary to complete the democratic transition in the 'Arab Spring' countries. This would have implied the involvement in the political game of all the actors who for a long time remained outside, including women, youth and non-governmental organizations (NGOs), among others. For this reason, the communication included the creation of a new financial instrument, the Civil Society Facility (CSF), providing €48 million for the period 2011–2013.

The EU started to complement its pressure on resistant political elites with a strategy for engaging civil society. The CSF is, in fact, designated to help identify and analyse the needs and capacities of civil society actors in the region, as well as the way in which these actors could contribute to specific sector policy dialogues. It also sought to strengthen the role of civil society actors in the policy-making process, and to promote a more favourable attitude of governments and local authorities towards them, through participatory approaches and consultations'.[37] In this perspective, women came to be seen as powerful agents for fostering bottom-up changes in societies where they were usually marginalized from power.

The focus on civil society and women is not entirely new. However, past initiatives were criticized for their excessive reliance on structured, pro-active, Western-style NGOs, at the expense of grassroots movements and other groups with a more marked political profile. The 2011 communication also launched a new institution, the European Endowment for

Democracy (EED), a private law foundation autonomous from the EU, designated to bolster 'the likely actors of change', thus involving both a wider spectrum of potential actors and stricter selection criteria. The foundation's main purpose is direct grant-making towards pro-democracy activists and/or organizations struggling for democratic transition in the European Neighbourhood and beyond.[38]

The EED's theoretical background is inspired by an actor-centred approach as far as democracy promotion is concerned. This means putting more trust in actors, including women, than in structural measures in order to produce deep modifications in the economic, social and political structure of a country. Indeed, the EED is mainly designed for short-term interventions, but this risks overlooking long-term processes and dynamics. Only when included in a wider strategy and in long-term dynamics can short-term, targeted actions bring lasting results in terms of regime change or sustainable democratization processes. Furthermore, the emphasis on the role of actors may be misleading, especially in complex situations where different groups are struggling for power and the direction of change may not be clearly defined (e.g. Libya, Syria, Egypt and Ukraine).[39]

Finally, the 2015 ENP review inaugurated a more tailored approach with the scope of adjusting the EU's neighbourhood policies to the high level of heterogeneity of the partners and to their peculiar national needs and expectations. The review recognizes that 'not all partners aspire to comply with EU rules and standards' and reflects 'the wishes of each country concerning the nature and scope of its partnership with the EU'.[40] The EU's former single set of progress reports issued for all the partners at the same time will be replaced by a new form of assessment, focusing specifically on meeting the goals agreed with partners. These reports will be timed to provide the basis for a political exchange of views in the relevant high-level meetings with partner countries. Reporting might be further adjusted for those countries committing to just a small number of strategic priorities. In addition to country-specific reporting, regular thematic reports will track developments in the neighbourhood, for instance concerning the rule of law, fundamental rights and gender equality. The review therefore reinforces differentiation in relations with neighbouring countries and privileges shared interests while promoting the EU's values. Since the ENP did not tackle the root causes of the protracted conflicts in the region (poverty, lack of education, unemployment) and was unable to settle frozen conflicts, the review places more emphasis on overcoming economic and social unbalances as a way to stabilize the region.

The ENP review presents gender equality as a topic that needs to be tackled not only as such, but also as a component of all the other policies. Emphasis will be given to ensuring girls' and women's physical and psychological integrity; promoting their social and economic rights and empowerment; promoting their access to justice, education, health care and other social services; strengthening their voice and political participation; and shifting the institutional culture to deliver on these commitments.

The review, in fact, recalls the EU Gender Action Plan 2016–2020 that mirrors the targets endorsed in the universal 2030 Agenda and backs the implementation of United Nations Security Council Resolution (UNSCR) 1325 on women, peace and security.[41] This resolution has certainly opened a sort of 'securitization of women' that is further elaborated in the ENP review in which the question of the fight against terrorism is clearly connected with that of gender equality and women's empowerment.[42] The ENP's review, in fact, presents gender mainstreaming as a stretchable concept encompassing a number of new challenges facing the EU. Gender mainstreaming seems to intersect a number of issues: stabilization (security, conflict prevention, border protection/management, counter-terrorism and anti-radicalization policies); economic and social development; greater crisis-response capacities; and safe and legal mobility. This implies that any policy action seeking to promote gender equality should result in a collection of measures across various sectors, but also that women are seen as a vanguard of the Mediterranean societies. Although this new approach greatly values the role of women, it only addresses the public sphere without looking at the obstacles women face in the private sphere. The EU's policies dedicated to women appear segmented since they are only directed at some aspects of the question of inequality.

The analysis of the ENP documents reveals two main narratives on gender equality that portray women either as an economic potential for growth and development or as active political participants and civil society activists contributing to the transformation of their countries. Especially since the Arab uprisings, women are considered key democracy promoters and agents of change, valuable in the fight against terrorism and radicalization. The ENP vision on women seems a bit resilient to the view that gender equality can only be achieved if gender policies are designed to influence all the components of gender regimes— paid work, care, income, time and voice— since gender equality in the labour market alone is unachievable.[43] This all-encompassing understanding theorizes the gender regime's concept as a crystallized order composed of production relations, power hierarchies, emotional relations (sexuality) and symbolic relations.[44] Gender mainstreaming therefore requires a number of interventions at different levels—individual, household, civil society and state.

Gender equality and women's empowerment in EU's external relations

The EU's prioritization in terms of gender targets and the framing of congruent policies have also been greatly oriented by policy choices set up by international actors like the UN. The twentieth anniversary of the UN Beijing Platform for Action (1995)[45] induced governments to elaborate a post-2015 framework aimed at linking gender equality and women's empowerment with the goals of the 2030 Agenda for Sustainable Development that dedicates section five to gender equality and the empowerment of all women and girls.[46] By aligning with the UN targets, the European Commission and the European External Action Service have elaborated a new framework for the EU's activities on gender equality entitled *New Framework for Gender Equality and Women's Empowerment: Transforming the Lives of Girls and Women through EU External Relations (2016–2020)*.[47]

The new framework, built on the achievements and lessons drawn from the implementation of the Gender Action Plan in Development 2010–2015, states that gender mainstreaming will affect all the external policies of the Union. Besides specific bilateral or regional development support programmes, the EU will finance gender policies through other thematic actions like food, security, rural development, private sector development. Some gender-specific actions were to be developed under the climate change programme for the years 2014–2016 (estimated €16 million, DCI).[48] As for the financing, a variety of EU external action instruments (such as the Development and Cooperation Instrument) and aid modalities (for instance, budget support or assistance to civil society organizations) will be available. About €100 million has already been allocated to concrete measures specifically targeted at improving women's and girls' rights.

The new framework revolves around four pillars:

(1) Fighting violence of any kind against women and girls, including protecting women against violence in situations of conflict and the prevention of trafficking of girls and women, but also fighting harmful practices, such as female genital mutilation and cutting, and empowering women to have control over their sexual and reproductive life.

(2) Economic and social empowerment—by increasing the access of women and girls to quality education and training (including for entrepreneurship), as well as facilitating their access to financial services, to decent jobs and to basic services like energy or clean water.

(3) Strengthening the voice and participation of women, allowing their participation in policy- and decision-making at all levels, enhancing their role as peace-builders, and supporting them in changing social and cultural norms through grassroots organizations or the media.

(4) Shifting institutional culture, which should better enable achievement of the goals set. The fourth pillar seems to hint to a cultural approach when dealing with gender topics. Nevertheless, not unlike the logic of joint ownership, third countries are merely left with the possibility of influencing prioritization within a range of options already decided in Brussels.

As for the implementation of the new framework, all the actors involved are expected to contribute to achieving the targets and assessing its overall implementation. The document notes that measuring and quantifying financial investment and results is not easy as they often take the form of mainstreaming gender equality in many types of different interventions across sectors. It also points to a gap between the EU's level of commitment to gender equality and its internal institutional capacities to implement it. Although the EU's financial commitment to gender equality has been quite significant, the Commission has not been prepared to face up to the increasing volume of work required to meet the EU's ambitions.

Gender equality has been quite absent from programme and project monitoring systems, while the use of gender analysis to advise recipient countries how to improve and progress with gender mainstreaming has been limited. An innovative aspect of the framework is that gender analysis will be done systematically for all new external actions undertaken, such as in projects and in bilateral and regional programming. The Commission will use sex-disaggregated data wherever available. Concerted efforts will be made to generate data when needed. The EU is willing to accurately assess the effects produced by this new framework, and it requires every new EU-funded project to incorporate measurable targets and objectives on gender. With the scope of assuring substantial improvements to the strategy, the Commission recommends creating a gender advisory board that includes leading experts from partner countries. This does not necessarily mean that those experts can also influence the content of gender mainstreaming, but rather that they should suggest ways to improve the performance of policies already shaped within the EU.

The new framework introduces a results-driven approach; sets standards for reporting, evaluation and accountability mechanisms,[49] and promotes evidence-based decision-making.[50] Although depicted as effective and more results-oriented, with a robust system of monitoring and accountability, the framework is weak because of the very nature of the document endorsing it. The framework is not an official communication of the EU but rather is relegated to a Joint Staff Working Document, which can hardly be seen as generating cases of soft law. It simply has the merit of unifying within the EU the gender mainstreaming efforts and making it a priority for all the policies reverberating outside the EU's borders. For the partners, the framework is a sort of memo for improving gender equality in a more effective and comprehensive way.

Conclusion

Gender mainstreaming has not been considered a top priority in the case of either the 2004–2007 enlargements or the ENP. The promotion of gender equality beyond the EU's borders has been accomplished through the traditional process of exporting what has been achieved inside to the outside, without bringing the outside in. Within the ENP framework, the EU's conditionality power is lower than in the process of enlargement and so is its 'transformative' power. The inclusion of the principle of joint ownership allows the reform agenda to be shared with the partners without, however, advancing a dialectical method for forging policies jointly. Not unlike other policies, gender equality promotion is agreed between the contracting parties within a set of choices already formulated by the EU, in line with the 'reflexivity' practice. Differentiation simply concerns the share of what is applicable and the pace of its implementation by the partners.

The 2015 ENP review is injecting more differentiation, giving the partners the possibility of picking and choosing among a set of goals established at the European level. The method of assessing agreed-upon goals is more tailored to adjusting to national contexts. While the recognition of national peculiarities gives the partner more autonomy in programming the reforms, it might, in practice, induce it to avoid sensitive issues which are part of what the EU considers its normative background. In other words, 'free riders' would find a favourable terrain, in consideration also of a worsening political climate and a tendency to autocracy in some countries in the region.

The EU's idea of gender equality might conflict with partners' cultures, identities and values, which vary from country to country. As the negotiations for the conclusion of action plans are not public, it is difficult to intercept any episode of norm resistance. It is quite likely that where incompatibilities with norms emerge, these are suspended and put on hold. At the moment, it is also difficult to assess the degree of internalization of gender policies by the ENP partners.

The ENP remains an elite-driven process although the EU has supported and incentivized grassroots movements, especially after the 2011 tumults and dramatic changes in the Northern Mediterranean countries. Civil society has been targeted as a key factor in accelerating and diffusing gender equality. The EU increasingly sees gender mainstreaming as a two-way process in which inputs from the top (Europeanization) blend with incentives from below. However, it is not clear to what extent top-down instructions and bottom-up initiatives can work in a complementary and efficacious way since the two dynamics are often set in motion by different institutional actors without coordination. Gender mainstreaming has traditionally suffered from an institutional dispersion, lack of synchronization, sporadic actions and poor instruments for evaluating policies implemented in the region after the EU's commitment.

Furthermore, it seems contradictory to call for a broader involvement of civil society in gender mainstreaming while ignoring the indigenous debate on feminism and women's rights, corroborating the Eurocentric approach leading the EU's external policies. The EU has treated gender mainstreaming in its neighbourhood by placing it in an ahistorical and decontextualized dimension. Being a normative power rather than a change entrepreneur, the EU has concentrated its efforts on women's equality in the public sphere. The domestic sphere remains impenetrable not only because it is a traditional national domain but also because the EU has put forward a standardized strategy that disregards countries' diversity.

Similar to gender policies developed within the EU, the emancipation of women is very much embedded in the economic and social sphere. According to the new framework for Gender Equality and Women's Empowerment, women's economic empowerment is considered a driver of development that addresses poverty, reduces inequalities and improves development outcomes. Since the 2011 awakening, the role of women has been tightly connected with the promotion of democracy and good governance. Strengthening women's roles and participation at all levels of society is seen as a way to facilitate peace and further reconstruction and state-building processes. Women are also deemed crucial for fighting terrorism and radicalization. The political discourse on security increasingly involves women as an antidote to complexity and instability so that women in the Mediterranean are subject to a phenomenon of 'securitization' intended as a response to threats. The enhancement of women as a societal vanguard might also mirror the idea that human agency can prevail over determinants of social structure or cultural habits on which the EU has a poor position. An actor-centred strategy, however, needs to be complemented by structural interventions.

The great novelty introduced by the new framework for Gender Equality and Women's Empowerment is that gender equality is being mainstreamed in all other goals and policies. The framework places much attention on the phase of evaluating the policies adopted in order to bridge the gap between the EU's level of commitment and its capacity to implement it. Embracing a clear, results-driven approach does not substantively correct the EU's focus on the output phase rather than on the way the policy is framed. The EU's self-referential tendency is not yet overcome while national views and, in particular, feminist voices from the Mediterranean are not properly accounted for.

Acknowledgements

This article was published thanks to support from the Jean Monnet Module 'The EU's Responses to the Challenges of its Neighbourhood', Sant'Anna School of Advanced Studies, Pisa.

Disclosure statement

No potential conflict of interest was reported by the author.

Funding

This work was supported by European Commission [grant number 553495-EPP-1-2014-1-IT-EPPJMO-MODULE].

Notes

1. The concept of Europeanization elaborated within the EU ('Processes of (a) construction (b) diffusion and (c) institutionalisation of formal and informal rules, procedures, policy paradigms, styles, "ways of doing things" and shared beliefs and norms which are first defined and consolidated in the making of EU decisions and then incorporated in the logic of domestic discourse, identities, political structures and public policies', R. Radaelli, 'The Europeanization of public policy', in K. Featherstone and C. Radaelli (eds), *The Politics of Europeanization*, Oxford University Press, Oxford, 2003, p. 30) is being used also to indicate the EU's diffusion of legislation and norms beyond its borders.
2. See G. Allwood, R. Guerrina and H. MacRae, 'Unintended consequences of EU policies: reintegrating gender in European studies', *Women's Studies International Forum*, 39, 2013, pp. 1–2; M. David and R. Guerrina, 'Gender and European external relations: dominant discourses and unintended consequences of gender mainstreaming', *Women's Studies International Forum*, 39, 2013, pp. 53–62; R. Kunz and J. Maisenbacher, 'Women in the neighbourhood: reinstating the European Union's civilising mission on the back of gender equality promotion?', *European Journal of International Relations*, 11 December 2015, doi: 10.1177/1354066115621120.
3. Article 29 of Directive 2006/54.
4. OJ C 2010, C 83/02.
5. For a general overview of gender equality law at the EU level, see S. Burri and S. Prechal, 'EU gender equality law: update 2013', European Commission, 2014 <http://ec.europa.eu/justice/gender-equality/files/your_rights/eu_gender_equality_law_update2013_en.pdf> (accessed 24 April 2016).
6. EIGE, 'Gender Equality Index 2015—Measuring gender equality in the European Union 2005–2012: Report' <http://eige.europa.eu/rdc/eige-publications/gender-equality-index-2015-measuring-gender-equality-european-union-2005-2012-report> (accessed 24 April 2016).
7. A gender regime refers to the state of play of gender relations in a given institution (e.g. state regulation or workplace organization) while the gender order refers to the relationship between different gender regimes or 'the current state of play in the macro-politics of gender'; see R. W. Connell, *Gender and Power*, Polity Press, Cambridge, UK, 1987, p. 20.
8. I. Manners, 'Normative power Europe: a contradiction in terms?', *Journal of Common Market Studies*, 40(2), 2002, p. 242.
9. Ibid., p. 240.
10. Ibid., p. 239.
11. See T. Dunne, 'Good citizen Europe', *International Affairs*, 84(1), 2008, p. 22.
12. I. Manners, 'The European Union as a normative power: a response to Thomas Diez', *Millennium*, 35(1), 2006, p. 176.
13. N. Tocci, *Who is a Normative Foreign Policy Actor? The European Union and its Global Partners*, Centre for European Policy Studies, Brussels, 2008, p. 3.
14. I. Manners, 'Normative power Europe', op. cit., p. 245.
15. Article III-193(1), Article I-2 and I-3.
16. H. Grabbe, 'Lessons of enlargement ten years on: the EU's transformative power in retrospect and prospect', *Journal of Common Market Studies*, 52, 2014, p. 41.
17. S. Keukeleire, T. Delreux, The Foreign Policy of the European Union, London, Palgrave, 2014.
18. I. Manners, 'The normative ethics of the European Union', *International Affairs*, 84(1), 2008, p. 55.
19. T. A. Börzel and T. Risse, 'The transformative power of Europe: the European Union and the diffusion of ideas', *KFG Working Paper* No. 1, May 2009 <http://www.polsoz.fu-berlin.

de/en/v/transformeurope/publications/working_paper/WP_01_Juni_Boerzel_Risse.pdf> (accessed 3 May 2016).
20. David and Guerrina, op. cit., p. 59.
21. See S. Steinhilber, 'Women's rights and gender equality in the EU enlargement: an opportunity for progress', WIDE, October 2002, p. 2, <http://www.eurosur.org/wide/EU/Enlargement/EU%20_Enlargement_Steinhilber_Oct.2002.htm> (accesssed 24 April 2016).
22. C. Bretherton, 'Gender mainstreaming and EU enlargement: swimming against the tide?', *Journal of European Public Policy*, 8(1), 2001, p. 75.
23. R. Prodi, 'A wider Europe—a proximity policy as the key to stability', Speech at the Sixth ECSA-World Conference, Brussels, 5–6 December 2002 <http://europa.eu/rapid/press-release_SPEECH-02-619_en.htm> (accessed 22 February 2016).
24. Commission Communication, *European Neighbourhood Policy Strategy Paper*, COM(2004) 373 final, 12 May 2004 <http://trade.ec.europa.eu/doclib/docs/2004/july/tradoc_117717.pdf> (accessed 31 March 2016).
25. K. Nicolaïdis and R. Howse, '"This is my EUtopia …": narrative as power', *Journal of Common Market Studies*, 40(4), 2002, p. 769.
26. M. Cremona and C. Hillion, 'L'Union fait la force? Potential and limitations of the European Neighbourhood Policy as an integrated EU foreign and security policy', *EUI Working Papers*, Law No. 2006/39, p. 19.
27. Ibid., p. 21.
28. E. Korosteeleva, *The European Union and its Eastern Neighbours*, Routledge, London, 2012, p. 33.
29. <http://eeas.europa.eu/enp/pdf/pdf/action_plans/tunisia_enp_ap_final_en.pdf> (accessed 31 March 2016).
30. <http://eeas.europa.eu/enp/pdf/pdf/action_plans/morocco_enp_ap_final_en.pdf>.
31. <http://eeas.europa.eu/enp/pdf/pdf/action_plans/egypt_enp_ap_final_en.pdf> (accessed 31 March 2016).
32. European Commission and HR, 'A new response to a changing neighbourhood: a review of European Neighbourhood Policy', COM(2011) 303 final, Brussels, 25 May 2011 <http://eeas.europa.eu/enp/pdf/pdf/ com_11_303_en.pdf> (accessed 31 March 2016).
33. European Commission and HR, 'Implementation of the European Neighbourhood Policy Partnership for Democracy and Shared Prosperity with the Southern Mediterranean Partners Report', SWD(2015) 75 final, Brussels, 25 March 2015 <http://eeas.europa.eu/enp/pdf/2015/enp-regional-report-southern-mediterranean_en.pdf> (accessed 31 March 2016).
34. On the basis of the Barcelona Declaration, the Euro-Mediterranean Partnership was launched as an innovative alliance based on the principles of joint ownership, dialogue and cooperation, seeking to create a Mediterranean region of peace, security and shared prosperity. The partnership revolved around three main dimensions: Political and Security Dialogue, Economic and Financial Partnership, Social, Cultural and Human Partnership.
35. Union for the Mediterranean, 'Conclusions', Second Ministerial Conference on Strengthening the Role of Women in Society, Marrakesh, 11 and 12 November 2009 <http://www.eeas.europa.eu/euromed/women/docs/ 2009_11_conference_en.pdf> (accessed 31 March 2016).
36. To learn more on the projects see <http://ufmsecretariat.org/projects/> (accessed 31 March 2016).
37. 'Neighbourhood Civil Society Facility', EU Neighbourhood Info Centre <http://www.enpi-info.eu/mainmed.php?id=393&id_type=10> (accessed 31 March 2016).
38. European Council, 'European Endowment for Democracy—additional support for democratic change', Press Release A 5/13, 9 January 2013 <http://www.consilium.europa.eu/uedocs/cms_data/docs/pressdata/EN/foraff/134628.pdf> (accessed 31 March 2016).
39. S. Giusti and E. Fassi, 'The European Endowment for Democracy and democracy promotion in the EU Neighbourhood', *International Spectator*, 49(4), 2014, pp. 112–129.
40. European Commission and HR, 'Review of the European Neighbourhood Policy', Join(2015) 50 final <http://eeas.europa.eu/enp/documents/2015/151118_joint-communication_review-of-the-enp_en.pdf> (accessed 31 March 2016).

41. The Security Council adopted resolution S/RES/1325 on women and peace and security on 31 October 2000. The resolution reaffirms the important role of women in the prevention and resolution of conflicts, peace negotiations, peace-building, peacekeeping, humanitarian response and post-conflict reconstruction, and stresses the importance of their equal participation and full involvement in all efforts for the maintenance and promotion of peace and security. Resolution 1325 urges all actors to increase the participation of women and incorporate gender perspectives in all United Nations peace and security efforts. It also calls on all parties in conflict to take special measures to protect women and girls from gender-based violence, particularly rape and other forms of sexual abuse, in situations of armed conflict. The resolution provides a number of important operational mandates, with implications for member states and the entities of the United Nations system <http://www.un.org/en/ga/search/view_doc.asp?symbol=S/RES/1325(2000)> (accessed 31 March 2016).
42. The concept of securitization is generally associated with the Copenhagen school that developed it to contribute to the debate between those who claimed that threats are objective (i.e. what really constitutes a threat to international security) on the one hand, and those who maintained that security is subjective (what is perceived to be a threat) on the other. The Copenhagen school maintains that security should be considered a speech act, in which the central issue is not whether or not threats are real but the ways in which a certain issue (environmental questions, migration, culture heritage) can be socially constructed as a threat. By women's securitization, we hint here to the fact that women are increasingly mentioned in relation to the necessity of stabilizing Mediterranean countries and of combatting radicalization. On the Copenhagen school, see for instance: B. Buzan, O. Wæver and J. de Wilde, *Security: A New Framework for Analysis*, Lynne Rienner, Boulder, CO, 1998.
43. G. Pascall, J. Lewis, "Emerging Gender Regimes and Policies for Gender Equality in a Wider Europe", *Journal of Social Policy*, 33 (3), 2004, p. 374]. Gender equality policies need to be built across all component parts while also considering families, citizenship and civil society peculiarities.
44. R. W. Connell, *Gender*, Polity Press, Cambridge, 2002.
45. The United Nations Fourth World Conference on Women, Beijing, China, September 1995, see <http://www.un.org/womenwatch/daw/beijing/platform/plat1.htm> (accessed 25 March 2016).
46. United Nations, 'Transforming our world: the 2030 Agenda for Sustainable Development', A/RES/70/1 <https://sustainabledevelopment.un.org/post2015/transformingourworld> (accessed 25 March 2016).
47. European Commission and HR, 'Gender equality and women's empowerment: transforming the lives of girls and women through EU external relations 2016–2020', SWD(2015) 182 final, Brussels, 21 September 2015 <https://ec.europa.eu/europeaid/sites/devco/files/staff-working-document-gender-2016-2020-20150922_en.pdf> (accessed 20 March 2016).
48. United Nations, 'Transforming our world', op. cit., goal 5, gender equality.
49. EU Plan of Action on Gender Equality and Women's Empowerment in Development 2010–2015 (SWD, SEC(2010) 265 final).
50. Council conclusions on Gender Equality and Women's Empowerment in Development Cooperation, doc. 9561/07, Council conclusions on the 2013 Report on the Implementation of the EU GAP, doc. 9360/14, 19 May 2014.

Representations of Gendered Mobility and the Tragic Border Regime in the Mediterranean

Heidrun Friese

ABSTRACT
The current media hype covering (undocumented) mobility to Europe produces powerful images. Global media, politicians, scientists, artists and activists take part in the production of the tragic border regime in the Mediterranean (Lampedusa) and the negotiation of the limits of European hospitality. In a first step, the article envisages the social imagination and its signifying processes staging mobile people as *threat*, *victim* or *hero/liberator*. These figures are related to discourses of security as well as to humanitarian or critical perspectives and are part of the political economy of the migration industry. As these figures are gendered, the representation of mobile women is addressed in a second step. Women are hardly depicted as a social threat or as political heroes/liberators. On the contrary, the entanglement of signifying processes of the social imagination brings forth the figure of mobile women as traumatized victim and/or as caring mother.

1. Mapping the Field—The Social Imagination and the Tragic Border Regime

On 15 April 2015 a heading in the online newspaper *La Repubblica* (Palermo) reads: 'Emergency landings (*sbarchi*), a new-born is being fed by a volunteer at the port of Palermo.' The caption of 17 images covering the landing of sub-Saharan people reads:

> two ships with more than 400 immigrants who have been rescued yesterday in the Channel of Sicily arrived at the port of Palermo. Amongst them women and new-born babies as well. ... The immigrants, amongst them women and children, get medical treatment and are transferred to various centres of first reception. [see Figure 1][1]

These images have a strong expressive potential and embrace a humanitarian cause. Looking straight at the viewer, the female protagonist at the centre of the next slide holds the baby covered in a huge blue blanket, in the background a mercantile ship, silos and an officer from the *Guardia di Finanza* (Figure 2). Perspective and composition suggest that she had come a long way and only the white rubber glove disturbs the protecting gesture of motherly care. Both image and text connect what has been labelled as the 'emergency' of immigration—the arrival of mobile people, the management of rescue and the ordinary procedures of first reception, which merge policing and humanitarian action.[2] But why is

Figure 1. Port of Palermo. Source: *La Repubblica Palermo*, 15 April 2015 (foto Igor Petyx) <http://palermo.repubblica.it/cronaca/2015/04/15/foto/emergenza_sbarchi_due_navi_cariche_di_migranti_al_porto_di_palermo-111998895/1/?ref=HREC1-11#1> (accessed 2 April 2016). Screenshot.

Figure 2. Port of Palermo. Source: *La Repubblica Palermo*, 15 April 2015 (foto Igor Petyx) <http://palermo.repubblica.it/cronaca/2015/04/15/foto/emergenza_sbarchi_due_navi_cariche_di_migranti_al_porto_di_palermo-111998895/1/?ref=HREC1-11#1 > (accessed 2 April 2016). Screenshot.

it mentioned twice that among the arriving people were women and babies? Why are the baby and the female volunteer at the centre of the images? Where is the black mother? Why has the black caring mother been substituted by the white caring mother? Is the black baby being handed over to the care of the nation-state, are giving birth and letting die moments of the tragic border regime? What is to be signified?

Addressing the 'missing women' in the 'media coverage of the Mediterranean', the journalist, blogger, activist and director of Women Under Siege, Lauren Wolfe, states:

> I'd begun to wonder why there so rarely seemed to be a woman's story or face in the coverage. Why are we barely hearing about these lives amid the on-going crisis? And now I knew part of the reason: Women who make the dangerous crossing from Libya to Italy by boat are being hidden away. Bureaucracy and what seems to be an attempt to conceal some of the failings of the overburdened (and corrupt) Italian infrastructure are preventing these women's stories from being heard.[3]

Indeed, women have been invisible and female mobility has long been a blind spot in migration studies, as it was considered a secondary phenomenon, a derivative of male migration.[4] It is widely taken for granted that 'reasons for leaving the origin country and the decision to migrate more generally' are related to economic circumstances: '*economic motives* largely explain the *migration of males*', whereas 'the reasons for *female migration* are more diverse. Work is increasingly important, but *family reasons* (mainly marriage and spouse reunification) still dominate female migration patterns', as Gian Carlo Blangiardo notes.[5] Second, female mobility has been envisaged in the context of welfare, care and the 'care drain'.[6] Last but not least, female mobility, the flourishing sex industries and human trafficking have been tied together and are at the centre of attention.

Generally, while female mobility is associated with images of care, and female vulnerability and victimhood, the arrival of male migrants is usually correlated with invasion, aggression, danger and threat. The dominant visual representation of current mobility in the Mediterranean is the 'overcrowded boat', a representation 'of threatening immigration to the West. In the European context this is usually a flimsy looking craft filled with black Africans', as Gilligan and Marley remark.[7] It reiterates the prevailing image of the 'assault', the racialized male migrant as aggression and menace, the catastrophe or the biblical 'flood' that has to be contained, if not stopped, by European policies of so-called border management and efficient governance of mobility.

With reference to Michel Foucault, it can be emphasized that the *gouvernementalité* of mobility and the border is made up of an ensemble of multiple actors, even contradictory practices, models and economic calculation.[8] These historically shifting constellations—which are no longer ordered by a centralized site of power—are shaped by (military) technologies of policing and surveillance, administrative acts and logics, pastoral practices and orientations, humanitarian impetus and, last but not least, scientific discourse. On one hand, therefore, the dominant discourse of security brings forth scenarios of threat, insists on the defence of sovereignty or, in a culturist version, an alleged national identity and opts for the increasing surveillance of borders, if not the shielding of national territories against an 'invasion'. On the other hand, humanitarian and critical discourse addresses either (religious) prescription, ethics and values or (antagonistic) political mobilization. The social imagination and images of mobile people are part of *gouvernementalité*, its techniques, the production of truth and power. Images are certainly not innocent, nor are they processes of signification. Mixing tragic fate with guilt and pathos, anguish and suffering, the social imagination and the production of specific images and figures of mobile people as aggressors, *threats*, *victims* or *heroes/liberators* are part of such powerful constellations.

If we follow Cornelius Castoriadis' understanding of tragedy as political drama displaying conflicts that make up the *political*,[9] then the border regime is to be considered tragic not because human beings are left to die at the borders[10] but because it reveals, elaborates and reiterates the founding tensions of democracy. The central feature of democracy is autonomy, the autonomy of a demos and the polis which is entitled to deliberate its own laws. Democracy is grounded on autonomy and is the explicit political form of an autonomous political community. As no (divine) Law is 'above' the demos as subject of legislation, it is grounded on autonomous will. Such circularity—a demos decides who is to be the demos and thus the subject of deliberation—opens up the paradox of the original and arbitrary moment of foundation which decides about membership, citizenship and borders. At the same time, therefore, the constitution of the demos is inclusive and exclusive. (Undocumented) mobility challenges democracy as it points towards the democratic paradox of the constitution of the demos, a political community that is founded on the exclusion of those who do not belong. The dynamic signifying processes of the *social imagination*, in the sense offered by Castoriadis,[11] work within this paradox and are also constitutive for the political and the tragic border regime, they organize visibility as well as invisibility and the European 'limits of hospitality'.[12]

The social imagination, therefore, is not a mere reproduction of society, a secondary or 'second order' product, but plays a decisive and vital role in the creation of social life and its reshaping and reorganization. The media hype, the pathos of the event society and the 'economy of attention'[13] make the tragic border regime work. Lampedusa has become a prominent part of the popular media spectacle, a constant backdrop of 'tragic' and 'catastrophic' events. The island became the *terra santa* of pilgrimage for the veneration of innocent victims and authentic feelings of post-humanitarian horror and catharsis. In the same vein, the Aegean islands of Kos and Lesbos have recently attracted massive media coverage. In early September 2015 the picture of Aylan al-Kurdi's drowned body washed up on the holiday beach of Kos became a media icon and 'a symbol of refugee misery'.[14] Images and the politics of indignation and pity are constantly produced, staged and replayed. They are part of dominant discourse, the 'economy of attention', the border regime and the migration industry.

Connected to the relations of (in)visibility and recognition,[15] and asking the question how indignation and political action in the face of human suffering are advanced, Luc Boltanski's *Souffrance à distance* develops a triple topic: the 'topic of denunciation', the 'topic of sentiment' and the 'aesthetic topic'.[16] One may add the topic of knowledge, as social science may contribute to political mobilization (even if individual suffering is not at the centre of attention). These topics display the tensions between universality and the particular, mass suffering and the singular case:

> In fact, while it is easier to integrate general forms of presentation into the logic of political programs ..., nonetheless it is necessary to go into particular cases, that is go into details, in order to arouse pity, involve the spectator and call on him to act without delay.[17]

Such a *dispositif* however, has been modified—not least with the day-to-day use of digital media. Whereas pity, commotion and solidarity had once been tied to religious prescription, moral-philosophical universalism, humanitarian demand[18] or *grands récits* that ordered and mediated suffering through rational insight and knowledge, today, suffering is imprinted on the subjectivity of the spectator. Universalism has been replaced by irony, the displaying of subjectivity and reason has been replaced by authenticity. Solid principles have converted into consumerism, rational judgement into subjective opinion. Solidarity converted into a feature of the lifestyle industry and its offers to identify with *celebrities*, as Lilie Chouliaraki—following Richard Rorty—characterizes the 'ironic spectator' and the 'post-humanitarian imagination'.[19] Current post-humanitarian imagination and the adjoined 'economy of attention' take up the tension between universalism and particularity. Additionally, these are characterized by further tensions: the tension between suffering and its branding, the tension between actor and victim(ization), between consumer and the political,[20] between pathos, distance and prudence.

In the following, the gendered staging of mobile people as aggressors, threats, victims or heroes-liberators will be addressed. On one hand, the signifying processes of the social imagination bring forward well-known images of the stranger. On the other hand, they are connected to the border regime, the migration industry and current governance and are to legitimize a continuum of political positions, be it populism, humanitarianism or a critical perspective (section 2). As we will see, the social imagination brings forth gendered significations and depicts women neither as threat nor hero. As women are less associated with autonomous agency, as they are less visible in the public sphere and are not associated with the realm of the political, the female hero cannot be but a vulnerable victim. In a next step, therefore, the dominant image of mobile women as traumatized and/or as caring mothers will be addressed (section 3).

2. Threat and Hero-Liberator

Mainstream representations 'reflect recurrent imagery found throughout NGO, intergovernmental and UN-reports, in popular media (including press, films and novels) and in academic literature' reproducing a 'gender dichotomy' by framing women as victims and men as aggressors.[21] Mobility associated with male aggression allows for the declaration of a state of emergency. Indeed, for decades, the Italian Civil Defence Department (*Protezione Civile*), which has to cope with natural disasters, has been present in Lampedusa and became an integral part of the tragic border regime and its economic interests. Allowing public tenders to be circumvented and clientelist networks to be promoted, the Berlusconi government declared the 'emergency migration' in July 2008. After the Tunisian revolution and the arrival of undocumented border-crossers (*harragas*) throughout 2011, the 'state of humanitarian emergency in the territory of North Africa [*sic*]' was confirmed 'in order to allow efficient measures hindering the exceptional influx of aliens on national territory'.[22] Part of the 'emergency' was a fiscal moratorium for local tourist operators and hotel owners who complained about the decline of the sector because of the migratory fluxes and extensive media coverage harming the image of an 'uncontaminated' paradise. Indeed, the dominant media gaze fostered the fear of being assaulted. The production of such images was part of a political strategy of the former minister of the interior, Maroni (*Lega Nord*), not least to press the EU for financial aid. The arriving *harraga* were not immediately transported to mainland Sicily, but had to camp in the streets of the small village. For weeks, the island resembled an open-air TV studio hosting journalists, freelance photographers, artists and anthropologists from all over the world who co-produced the 'humanitarian crisis'. The fiscal moratorium (decided by Silvio Berlusconi who visited the island during the politically produced state of emergency, promising inhabitants milk and honey) was extended by the Monti government until June 2012. In July, and referring to the measures adopted by the government in the aftermath of the devastating earthquake in Aquila, the newly elected mayor of Lampedusa—a left-wing activist—demanded yet another extension until December 2012.[23] The famous 'state of emergency' has indeed become the normality and the evocation of catastrophe promotes massive economic interests of local and national actors.[24]

The notion of catastrophe—from the Greek *kata* 'down' (*cata-*) + *strephein* 'turn', '*katastrephein* "to overturn, turn down" denotes the "reversal of what is expected" (especially a fatal turning point in a drama)'—has been extended to 'sudden disaster' and is part of the tragic border regime, the political imagination and the permanent state of exception.[25] The permanent state of emergency and the normalization of the exception are promoted by highly symbolic visualizations of undocumented mobility. '[H]ighly visible interceptions of smuggling operations tend to play out as contemporary crisis', as Alison Mountz remarks,[26] and dominant media coverage reproduces images of 'biblical exodus, the alarming human tsunami'. Images thus became a powerful resource increasingly mined in order to boost the legitimacy and authority of cross-border policies and the permanent state of emergency. The images of mobile people as sudden, abrupt catastrophe penetrate civil society, generating a public siege mentality against 'invasion', which in turn has to be calmed by efficient, well-calculated measures of border management. Dominant mass media images, policies of border management and the state of exception are interrelated: images reiterate the exception, as the exception needs its images in order to get public and political legitimacy. At the same time, they foster (local) economic interests and the migration industry.[27] However, not just the security industry refers to catastrophe. The scenario of catastrophe and tragedy is well used by humanitarian entrepreneurship.

As the Vice President of the Sicilian winery *Settesoli* and member of the Italian board of directors of Save the Children notes in a testimonial of the Non-Governmental Organization (NGO) for fundraising, connecting the arrival of mobile people, natural disaster and troops of helpers animated by humanitarian impetus:[28]

> Another aspect of Save the Children ... is its flexibility and its rapid response to emergencies like the earthquake in Aquila, in Haiti or the arrival of unaccompanied minors at Lampedusa where Save the Children promptly intervened to support children.[29]

The border regime also nurtures an expanding branch of competing Intergovernmental Organizations (IGOs) and NGOs—such as International Catholic Migration Committee (ICMC), the International Organization for Migration (IOM), Save the Children, Médecins sans Frontières—public-private enterprises, research institutes generating knowledge, infrastructures that are to manage mobility and make up a dense transnational fabric of actors, practices and policies, and powerful images of undocumented mobility.[30] Images of flows, invasion, crisis or emergency are an integral part of such an industry, as the media gaze produces and disseminates dominant views of undocumented mobility. This dense fabric of organizations, the security and military industry, the European border agency (Frontex) make up the highly dynamic postcolonial border regime that connects policing, surveillance, the state of exception and the imagination of threat that has to be kept under control. The constantly repeated image of invasion reverses the postcolonial situation—it relies on forgetting, withholding, repression of European colonialism and installs historical revisionism. They invoke the invasion of black masses, which threaten to take what has been taken from them; they show the phantasms of colonialism and the ghastly return of the colonized on the shores of the colonizer—the threat of a revenant.

Georg Simmel has noted that the wanderer provokes 'latent or open antagonism (*Gegnerschaft*)' and becomes a 'irreconcilable enemy', a 'parasite of the sedentary elements of society'.[31] The provocation, the affront is the other who menaces pollution, an intruding heterogeneity that contaminates, infects the sane body of the people, the interior of the nation and its welfare. The intruder, the parasite, is to be detected at the borders, he is to be neutralized, eliminated symbolically or physically by 'letting him die',[32] and therefore modern biopolitics—which is not to govern a territory but one's 'own' population—is to be employed. '[T]erritorial borders are superimposed on the boundaries of the body; migration appears at the same time as an assault upon the integrity of one's own body and that of Europe', and a 'discursive and iconic connection between infection and immigration' is established.[33] (Indeed, the black baby is handed over to the white mother and the nation-state.)

Dominant media representations evoke catastrophe and contamination. They also repeat juridical classifications and distinguish between different categories of mobile people. At one pole there is the miserable refugee who escapes from war and annihilation; at the other pole there is the one who escapes economic circumstances (economic migrant)—the one who flees on the grounds of autonomous decision and will. It seems that the demonstration of individual decision and autonomy cannot be pardoned; it is exactly such a demonstration that distinguishes the figure of the victim—who is not responsible for his decisions—from the enemy, the figure of threatening autonomy, decision and will. Threatening agency, the power of autonomy, it seems, cannot be pardoned. The migrant is not only a parasite on the nation's body and welfare but an autonomous agent. Paradoxically, autonomy and will both characterize the modern subject. A helpless, needy and dependent person can be pardoned for that which in reverse marks the other as threat: namely autonomy, choice and decision.

Next to the imagination of threat, the image of mobile people as *heroes* and/or liberators is produced. The refugee as hero is acknowledged and legitimized by his dangerous, heroic voyage. Compassion converts into solidarity with refugees and, even more, the just fight of refugees. However, the symbolism of critical discourse demanding indignation and protest is in no way autonomous but well integrated into the current 'economy of attention'. It has to produce spectacular and tragic images in order to incite emotion, subjectivity, identification and solidarity.

The image of the refugee mobilizes. Compassion, in Hannah Arendt's sense, has been elevated 'to the rank of the supreme political passion' and 'the highest political virtue'[34] without however being embedded in a universalistic framework. Compassion is no longer tied to universalistic ethics and moral claims (*pietà, misericordia*) or the promise of liberation and salvation. Solidarity is no longer connected to critical analysis and its *grand récit* of revolution but to individual feeling and the displayed, mediatized authenticity of the other's suffering, the 'ironic spectator'. Thus, the call for solidarity in the 'era of post-humanism'[35] is to be kindled by dramatic, 'tragic' scenarios such as shipwreck, disaster and death and not by the discreet and 'invisible' day-to-day life of *sans-papiers* in search of a normal and ordinary life.

Next to the topic of emotion and the topic of aesthetic, the social imagination of the refugee as hero reworks the topic of denunciation and indignation.[36] The symbolic transformation elevates those who are excluded from 'legal' mobility and who seize the right to do so into modern heroes of an autonomous fight for opportunities and the realization of autonomous will—in short, the excluded become heroes of modern subjectivity.

Such representations do not refer to the humanitarian discourse and its—alleged—neutrality. However, and paradoxically, this discourse is a-political even if it seeks an antagonistic position. It is a-political because the figure of the hero is situated between the innocent victim of capitalism and neoliberal governance on one hand and the figure of threat, an enemy who menaces the existing order, on the other. Whereas some time ago the attention of activists has been directed to the movements of liberation in the 'Third World' and the hope that revolutionary élan of the periphery is to pressure the capitalist centre, the hero of liberation has been replaced by the fighting refugee. He is to take up the fight against power and capitalism and yet is being assigned to an asymmetric position which allows the activist to celebrate the (missed) triumph of the revolution and to assure himself the position of a protector, a guardian angel of a just and humanitarian cause.

The 'Declaration of Solidarity' of the committee 'Lampedusa is everywhere' runs as follows:[37]

> The inhumane events of Lampedusa during October of 2013 are only one example of how the 'fortress Europe' claims countless human lives every day. We are *shocked, angry and mournful* that the defence of western wealth is indiscriminately violating human rights.

Even if 'antagonistic' discourse establishes analytical connections to European policies and the border regime, it falls in with the pathos of humanitarian discourses of catastrophe and victimhood: it displays the authenticity of suffering in one's own shock, anger and mourning. By depicting victims whose autonomous actions end up in tragic fatality—even have to end up in tragic fatality if its legitimizing power is to be established—the tensions of the tragic humanitarian discourse are repeated. Taking up the topic of denunciation, it laments the defence of affluence, even if the co-suffering activists do participate in prosperity while they seek to exorcize such participation through the displayed authenticity of emotion.

Additionally, if power works through 'dispersed, heteromorphic and local procedures' which are 'adopted, enforced and transformed by strategies, resistance, inertia' and therefore do not lead to 'massive domination' or a binary structure of domination and subordination, as Foucault remarks,[38] the fighting hero is positioned within a binary structure. For some strands of activism, the fighting hero/non-citizen is to act on the behalf of those whose revolutionary practices and aspirations did not succeed. Therefore, such representations have to equip mobile people with revolutionary courage. In such a vein, Antonello Mangano describes the revolt of illegalized day labourers in the Calabrian town of Rosarno in 2010 in the following way: 'part of the Senegalese community cordoned off the villa of a capomafia ... no one ever dared to do such a thing. This is why *Africans will save us*'.[39] Against the superior might of circumstances, the foreigner, the victim, the sacrificed is transformed into a redeemer, a Salvatore of the enslaved and oppressed, he is the one who acts for others and speaks on behalf of those without a voice. The hero redeems from voicelessness, acquits from responsibility and the image of the hero who ceaselessly fights injustice, power and the state allows the spectator to celebrate victory, is even allowed to celebrate himself as a constant and victorious fighter for the just cause.

As Bonnie Honig demonstrates, the figure of the stranger as hero and/or liberator reflects that of the 'foreign founder' who inaugurates a political community, a figure therefore which is well-known in political thought. Rousseau's contract theory, for example, assures 'a foreign founder's foreignness ... the distance and impartiality needed to animate and guarantee a general Will that can neither animate nor guarantee itself'.[40] Following Honig, the figure of the stranger, the foreigner as founder and lawmaker, as immigrant reveals the problematic nature of democracy and the already mentioned paradox of democracy.[41]

The social imaginary depicts mobility either as aggression and invasion or draws on the figure of the hero of liberation. Between these gendered poles of significations, the figure of the victim and caring mother is inscribed into the social imagination.

3. Victim and Caring Mother

'The victim is ... the hero of our times', as Daniele Giglioli states.[42] The refugee as victim is depicted as the innocent object of appalling circumstances, victim of warfare and violence seeking to save his/her life and who is ready to take risks—who has to take deadly risks— in order to do so. In this way, the terrifying, threatening stranger is transformed into a ward and a supplicant, a passive, needy object of temporary care who in turn has to be grateful for the offering of shelter and asylum. Using the 'topic of emotion, sentiment and aesthetic',[43] the social imagination recognizes the victim in the figure of the miserable and turns the vulnerable and needy into an icon.[44] Victimhood: a generalized victim is not gendered. In the context of mobility however, '[w]hile the status of the female 'requires' shame and suffering, the contrary can be said of male victims. Stereotypes regarding men's demeanour as 'macho' often undermine their ability to self-identify as victims, thereby reaffirming the stereotype that it is predominantly women who are victims of trafficking.'[45]

Whereas 'public framing of human trafficking has changed over time from a human rights issue to a criminalization issue and now a national security issue,'[46] the figure of the victim as hero is applicable for mobile women. Invisible mobility of women is rendered visible only as victims. The dominant media gaze 'has inaccurately portrayed trafficked victims and focused exclusively on one issue (i.e., sex trafficking) while misrepresenting other types of labor exploitation.'[47] Mobile women are either portrayed as victims of trafficking and thus have to be rescued, or as the 'archetype' of the caring mother.[48] Whereas the first position also allows for the rescue of female purity, the second position transforms the (prospective) sex-worker, the prostitute into a caring mother.[49]

The figure of the mother, female sacrifice (Auf*opferung*) and the applied trauma tag, allow for humanitarian moral claims and refers to the rich Christian iconography of the holy and nurturing mother, *pietà* and *misericordia*.[50] In this context, the image of the caring volunteer also has an exculpating purpose. The brutal violence of the historical border regime is being taken by almost 'natural' female gestures of rescue and care and inscribed into Christian values and prescriptions.

The dominant image of suffering and the wide-open eyes of victims capturing the post-humanitarian spectator confirms Susan Sontag's remarks in *Regarding the Pain of Others* about the dominant 'shots' of suffering people in distant countries and the 'full frontal views'.[51] The spectator can hardly evade the direct gaze of suffering that calls for pity, and donations. In fact, Médecins sans Frontières, Save the Children and Terre des Hommes use these images. These organizations are active in taking care of vulnerable people on Lampedusa. Terre des Hommes also engages in commercial partnership for fundraising.[52] During the 'state of emergency regarding North Africa' in 2011, the organization started the project Faro (I-III) which took care of unaccompanied minors arriving on the island.[53] The organization cooperated with the company C&A, and for a short period the label offered 1% of its takings to Faro in order to 'sustain the psychological and psychosocial support of families and all children that flee from war, poverty and violence'—in buying new clothes, the consumer could contribute to the noble and humanitarian cause.[54] The 'emergency Lampedusa' moved to the checkout, connected the multinational enterprise and the corporate image. Consuming becomes the consumption of victims and a vendible moral.

The post-humanitarian discourse and its 'visual humanism' is a-political and a-historical.[55] Replacing one image of atrocious disaster with another, images are distributed around the globe with unprecedented speed and suggest authenticity and a fictitious co-presence. As it needs to attract attention and funding, emotion and authenticity, post-humanitarian discourse does not name responsibilities, does not ask for causes or consequences, it does not have a referent other than the conveying of authenticity; in short, it is auto-referential. Violence, ferocity, war, destruction, mobility, blind and merciless nature, pitiless fatality, catastrophe are not discriminated between and thus are mingled together without critical judgement in order to attract attention and subjective responsiveness.

> Another salient attraction of images of victims is that their closeness to physical pain creates a semblance of authenticity resulting from the unreflecting crudeness of the representation. …
> The representation of pain in images of victims does not tell a personal story, it rather generates

attention by means of its event character. It suggests evidences that are not meant to inform, but to create the impression that similar events have taken place since times immemorial. By means of their irrational perspective and the persistent repetition of their motifs, they achieve a narcotic effect. From this perspective, they could be compared to spiritual imagery and its language of ritual. Mostly, representations of suffering—as a kind of *visual humanism*—are deployed as a means to propagate proper ethical values. In scenarios generated by PR agencies, they become mere clichés of an aesthetics of pity geared to sell *issues*. The overstimulation of this emotional approach to ethics numbs the viewer until he becomes used to shocks.[56]

By exposing human plight, exposure and the bare life, such a discourse resembles mythical-religious narratives; it erases and overwrites time, history and post-colonial entanglements.

Within the accelerated economy of attention, the commodification of *pietà*, *misericordia* and solidarity, the selling of humanitarian issues via personal story-telling that is to render deplorable fate catchier for the consumer's subjectivity, (images) of humanitarian rescue and protection against blind fate and sudden catastrophe are the only possible offer. The identification with the (female) victim, its visibility, allow for subjectivity and, as Renata Salecl states, ultimately for the deviation of anxiety:

> There seems to be an attempt in today's society to find a cure for anxiety by constantly exposing the disturbing objects that might incite it (even in contemporary arts, for example, we try to figure out what is anxiety-provoking in death by exposing cadavers).[57]

The post-humanitarian discourse can be labelled as tragic because the actor has to bear responsibility for his acts and yet is entangled in fatal circumstances. From the comfortable and secure shores the spectator bears witness to shipwreck, death and destruction, is part of the commenting media chorus and the tragic border regime that assembles threats, heroes or victims.

The social imagination sets female vulnerability against male aggression and the threat of 'invasion', the transgression, the violation of borders and national sovereignty, an assault against the body of the nation.[58] Within the reiterated gender binarism and its symbolic order, the mother as well as vulnerable children are deprived of threatening agency, of autonomy. They do not menace the political order of the nation and its sovereignty. In other words, the female victim and her suffering do not belong either to historical time or to the political order.

The gendered non-actor, the ontologized female victim is an object of care and certainly not a political subject. With regard to the constitution of the 'political, the community, the subject' as a 'fully moral agent',

> reason is the truth of the subject and politics is the exercise of reason in the public sphere. The exercise of reason is tantamount to the exercise of freedom, a key element for individual autonomy. The romance of sovereignty, in this case, rests on the belief that the subject is the master and the controlling author of his or her own meaning. Sovereignty is therefore defined as a twofold process of *self-institution* and *self-limitation* (fixing one's own limits for oneself). The exercise of sovereignty, in turn, consists in society's capacity for self-creation through recourse to institutions inspired by specific social and imaginary significations.[59]

However, the foreigner as imagined hero, as figure of salvation, as icon of struggle is advised to arrange that which political circumstances deny. The cult of the hero blocks claims to a normalized life according to wishes and dreams.

Mobility challenges democracy; it constantly points towards the paradox of democracy and its inclusive-exclusive structure. In fact, current national-populist 'excitable speech'[60] and its emphasis on borders and national sovereignty, the sovereignty of an imagined homogeneous, identitarian demos to decide who belongs and who is excluded from the community, exhibits the paradox as well as the call for open borders or humanitarian impetus cannot escape this tension. Mobility challenges efforts to contain the excluded. The signifying processes of the social imagination that produce the racialized and gendered figures of mobile people as threats, heroes or victims reiterate and elaborate these tensions as well.

Disclosure statement

No potential conflict of interest was reported by the author.

Notes

1. *La Repubblica*, 15 April 2015, foto Igor Petyx), <http://palermo.repubblica.it/cronaca/2015/04/15/foto/emergenza_sbarchi_due_navi_cariche_di_migranti_al_porto_di_palermo-111998895/1/?ref=HREC1-11#1> (accessed 2 April 2016).
2. I prefer the term mobility to migration. Migration has largely been seen as a unilinear movement from a sending to a host country and has been framed by rather mechanical concepts such as push-and-pull factors that are to confirm the theoretical model of the *homo oeconomicus*. Today's transnational mobilities question such concepts. I hardly follow the juridical distinction between migrants and refugees/asylum seekers as well as they establish a hierarchy of mobilities and ultimately produce 'illegality'—the term 'economic migrant' is even used in a denigrating way by populist discourse.
3. L. Wolfe, 'The missing women of the Mediterranean refugee crisis', WMC's Women Under Siege, 2015 <http://www.womenundersiegeproject.org/blog/entry/missing-women-of-the-mediterranean-refugee-crisis> (accessed 2 May 2016).
4. Such a view corresponds to the separation of the private and the public sphere in political thought. Political thought is based on that division and the invisibility of care. For a brilliant and concise overview, see A. Loretoni , *Amplificare lo sguardo. Genere e teoria politica* [Amplifying Views: Gender and Political Theory], Donzelli editore, Roma, 2014, pp. 54–58.
5. Gian Carlo Blangiardo, *Gender and Migration in Southern and Eastern Mediterranean and Sub-Saharan African Countries*, Research Reports—Gender and Migration Series Demographic and Economic Module, 2012, CARIM-RR 2012/01, p. 5 <http://cadmus.eui.eu/bitstream/handle/1814/20834/CARIM_RR_2012_01.pdf?sequence=1&isAllowed=y> (accessed 2 February 2016, emphasis mine).
6. See F. Bettio, A. Simonazzi and P. Villa, 'Change in care regimes and female migration: the "care drain" in the Mediterranean', *Journal of European Social Policy*, 16(3), 2006, pp. 271–285, doi: 10.1177/0958928706065598; M. Ambrosini, 'Irregular but tolerated: unauthorized immigration, elderly care recipients, and invisible welfare', *Migration Studies*, 3(2), 2014, pp. 199–216, doi: 10.1093/migration/mnu042.
7. C. Gilligan and C. Marley, 'Migration and divisions: thoughts on (anti-)narrativity in visual representation of mobile people', *Forum Qualitative Social Research*, 11(2), 2010 (art. 32), p. 2.
8. M. Foucault, *Sicherheit, Territorium, Bevölkerung, Geschichte der Gouvernementalität I. Vorlesungen am Collège de France 1977–1978*, Suhrkamp, Frankfurt am Main, 2006 (published

in English as *Security, Territory, Population. Lectures at the Collège de France 1977–1978*, Palgrave Macmillan, Basingstoke, 2007).
9. C. Castoriadis, 'The Greek *Polis* and the creation of democracy', in *The Castoriadis Reader*, Blackwell Publishers, Oxford, 1997, p. 284.
10. Between 2000 and 2014 more than 30,000 people have been left to die at European borders: The Migrants Files <http://www.themigrantsfiles.com> (accessed 20 January 2016). Between 1 January and 29 October 2015 at least 3,329 died in the Mediterranean: IOM <https://www.iom.int/news/mediterranean-update-migrant-deaths-rise-3329-2015> (accessed 20 January 2016). We should not forget that freedom of movement within the space of Schengen goes hand in hand with the increasing surveillance of European external borders and a restrictive visa system for non-European citizens. The Schengen system is however increasingly challenged not least after Germany's decision to allow the entry of asylum-seekers and Syrian refugees in 2015.
11. C. Castoriadis, *The Imaginary Institution of Society*, Polity, Cambridge, MA, 1987.
12. See H. Friese, 'Spaces of hospitality', in A. Benjamin and D. Vardoulakis (eds), *Politics of Place*, special issue of *Angelaki. Journal of the Theoretical Humanities*, 9(2), 2004, pp. 67–79; H. Friese, 'The limits of hospitality. Political philosophy, undocumented migration and the local arena', in H. Friese and S. Mezzadra (eds), special issue of *European Journal for Social Theory*, 13(3), 2010, pp. 323–341; H. Friese, *Grenzen der Gastfreundschaft. Die Bootsflüchtlinge von Lampedusa und die europäische Frage* [The Limits of Hospitality. Lampedusa, Refugees and Europe], transcript, Bielefeld, 2014.
13. Y. Citton (ed.), *L'économie de l'attention. Nouvel horizon du capitalisme?*, La Découverte, Paris, 2014. (published in English as The Ecology of Attention, polity, Cambridge, 2016).
14. 'Refugee crisis: following the tragic journey of Aylan Kurdi's family from Syria to Kos. The death of Aylan al-Kurdi en route to the holiday island has made it a symbol of refugee misery', *The Independent*, Saturday 5 September 2015 23:13 BST <http://www.independent.co.uk/news/world/europe/refugee-crisis-following-the-tragic-journey-of-aylan-kurdis-family-from-syria-to-kos-10488358.html> (accessed 10 November 2015). Contemporary art—I'm referring to the rather disgusting fake of Ai Weiwei on the shores of Lesbos—is in line with this, it displays tragic misery, it seeks to transmit authenticity while it rests within the simulacrum of repetition.
15. For an elaboration of this relation, see J. Schaffer, *Ambivalenzen der Sichtbarkeit. Über die visuellen Strukturen der Anerkennung* [Ambivalences of Visibility. On the Visual Structures of Recognition], transcript, Bielefeld, 2008. See of course the seminal work of A. Honneth, *Kampf um Anerkennung. Zur moralischen Grammatik sozialer Konflikte* [The Struggle for Recognition. The Moral Grammar of Social Conflicts], Suhrkamp, Frankfurt am Main, 1994; and J. Butler, *Excitable Speech. A Politics of the Performative*, Routledge, New York, 1997.
16. L. Boltanski, *Distant Suffering. Morality, Media and Politics*, Cambridge University Press, Cambridge, 1999.
17. Ibid., p. 33.
18. For a historical account of the development from humanitarian rights to human rights, see B. Cabanes, *The Great War and the Origins of Humanitarianism, 1918–1924*, Cambridge University Press, Cambridge, 2014, pp. 300–313.
19. Chouliaraki looks at the 'institutional, political and technological' changes of communication and the modes by which humanitarian organizations represent distant suffering. Whereas once the appeal was to *pietà* and altruism, the 'ethics of pietà' has been substituted by an 'ethics of irony', 'individualistic moral' and 'often narcissistic' subjectivity and emotion. At the same time, 'the encounter with vulnerability' is part of its branding and the logic of the market. L. Chouliaraki, *Lo spettatore ironico. La solidarietà nell'epoca del post-umanitarismo* [The Ironic Spectator. Solidarity in the Era of Post-Humanitarism] (a cura di Pierluigi Musarò), Mimesis, Udine, 2014, pp. 24, 26.
20. Ibid., pp. 82–83.
21. It is not intended to engage the '"anti-trafficking" or "anti-anti-trafficking" position that at present limits most feminist debates on sex trafficking'. F. Laviosa (ed.), *Visions of Struggle in*

Women's Filmmaking in the Mediterranean, Palgrave, New York, 2010, p. xxx. For a global and policy-oriented overview, see L. Shelley, *Human Trafficking: A Global Perspective*, Cambridge University Press, Cambridge, 2010; L. Shelley, *Human Smuggling and Trafficking into Europe. A Comparative Perspective*, Migration Policy Institute, 2014 <http://www.migrationpolicy.org/research/human-smuggling-and-trafficking-europe-comparative-perspective> (accessed 2 April 2016); see A. Gallagher, 'Human rights and the new UN protocols on trafficking and migrant smuggling: a preliminary analysis', *Human Rights Quarterly*, 23, 2001, pp. 975-1004.

22. Presidenza del Consiglio dei Ministri, 'Dichiarazione dello stato di emergenza umanitaria nel territorio del Nord Africa per consentire un efficace contrasto all'eccezionale afflusso di cittadini extracomunitari nel territorio nazionale', *Gazzetta Ufficiale*, 83, 11 April 2011 <http://www.protezionecivile.gov.it/jcms/it/view_prov.wp?toptab=2&contentId=LEG24032#top-content>̲ (accessed 17 April 2016). Following suggestions of the Head of the Civil Protection and the Commissioner for the 'emergency of immigration', in January 2012, €300 million has been allocated to cope with the 'humanitarian emergency due to the exceptional influx of Northern Africans to Italy'. '€101 m. are designated to fulfil the accords with Tunisia which have been stipulated in April 2011, €197,4 m. for necessary measures to cope with the emergency and finally €8 m. for allowance of police forces and the fire department which assure the public order.' Lettera43, 'Immigrazione, il governo ha stanziato 300 milioni. Fondi per l'emergenza umanitaria legata ai flussi dal Nord Africa', *Martedì*, 10 January 2012 <http://www.lettera43.it/attualita/35997/immigrazione-il-governo-ha-stanziato-300-milioni.htm>̲ (accessed 17 April 2016).

23. As the Italian Revenue Agency started to recover taxes for locals, in 2015 the major opted for yet another extension of the moratorium to, 'help, sustain and compensate the economic damage incurred in 2011' <https://www.facebook.com/GiusiNicoliniSindacoDiLampedusaELinosa/posts/710054335774656> (accessed 9 January 2015).

24. For an account of the (local) migration industry and clientelistic networks, see H. Friese, 'Border economies. Lampedusa and the nascent migration industry', in A. Mountz and L. Briskman (eds), *Shima: The International Journal of Research Into Island Cultures*, special issue on 'Detention Islands', 6(2), 2012, pp. 66-84. In late 2014, Italy was shaken by the scandal *Mafia Capitale*. A network of politicians and businessmen influenced public tenders covering services for migrants and Roma. The web of corrupt city hall officials, neo-fascist militants and mobsters included Salvatore Buzzi, who was jailed for murder in 1984. He was alleged to have been the 'entrepreneurial right hand' of Massimo Carminati, the top mobster and a former member of the NAR neo-fascist terrorist group. 'His organisation is claimed to have bribed officials to win contracts, including for the management of migrant holding facilities and Roma camps. Evidence submitted by police in support of their application for warrants includes a wiretapped phone conversation in which one speaker is claimed to be 59-year-old Buzzi. "*Do you know how much you earn from immigrants?*" the speaker asks. "*Drug trafficking earns less.*" More than 100 other people have been formally placed under investigation, including Gianni Alemanno, the mayor of Rome from 2008 to 2013 and a former member of the neo-fascist Italian Social Movement (MSI)'. J. Hooper, and R. Scammell, 'Rome's 29 June co-operative alleged to be base of mafia- style gang', *The Guardian*, 7 December 2014 <http://www.theguardian.com/world/2014/dec/07/june-29-co-operative-italy-rome> (accessed 15 May 2015, emphasis mine). Connected to investigations regarding *Mafia Capitale*, relations between politicians and migration entrepreneurs in Sicily came under critical scrutiny. The largest camp in Europe for asylum seekers is the CARA in Mineo/Sicily. The mayor of Mineo, Anna Aloisio, member of the *Ncd* (Nuovo Centro Destra/New Centre-Right), the party of the minister of the interior Angelino Alfano, is head of the *Consorzio calatino terra di accoglienza* which runs the centre. A member of the consortium, the cooperative *La Cascina* which won a public tender worth €100 million, has been accused of corruption by investigators of *Mafia Capitale* because he had bribed the member of the commission with €10,000/month. Additionally, the undersecretary Giuseppe Castiglione (*Ncd*), Angelino Alfano's right-hand man, had nominated Luca Odevaine, an associate of the abovementioned Salvatore Buzzi as consultant to the centre and as a member of the National Roundtable on Immigration.

Odevaine confessed that he was 'compensated' by *La Cascina*: 'They gave me €10,000/month as… let's call it this way, "contribution".' *La Repubblica*, 3 December 2014 <http://palermo.repubblica.it/cronaca/2015/03/12/news/cara_di_min..._illegittima_otto_indagati_tra_cui_un_sottosegretario-109315938/> (accessed 15 March 2015).
25. See <http://www.etymonline.com/index.php?term=catastrophe> (accessed 18 October 2015).
26. A. Mountz, *Seeking Asylum: Human Smuggling and Bureaucracy at the Border*, University of Minnesota Press, Minneapolis, 2010, p. xv.
27. Border management and technologies of *gouvernementalité* are to detect and contrast strategies of border-crossings before they even occur and to fix mobile people. The production of knowledge thus becomes a remunerative resource and a product to place on the highly competitive market. Statistics, screening, mapping and visualization have a long tradition in techniques of surveillance and policing. It is not by chance that the ICMPD hosts an interactive map—its fancy name is *i-map*—entailing visualizations of movement, routes, 'hubs' and 'flows'. 'Implementing partners' on irregular and mixed migration are 'Europol, Frontex, Interpol, UNHCR and UNODC, Migration and Development: IFAD, IOM'. Main donors are the European Commission and co-funding states <https://www.imap-migration.org/> (accessed 10 March 2017) (emphasis mine).
28. Save the Children <http://images.savethechildren.it/f/download/bilancio/20/2011_bilancio.pdf> (accessed 10 March 2017). p. 25. In 2005, the first project *Praesiduum I* (Potenziamento dell'accoglienza rispetto ai flussi migratori) was financed by the EU ARGO programme and has been constantly renewed since then. The project is a joint collaboration between the International Organization for Migration, the Italian Red Cross and United Nations High Commissioner for Refugees (UNHCR) on Lampedusa (since April 2008 it has also involved Save the Children, which is in charge of taking care of unaccompanied minors). The aim of the projects is to 'improve reception' and services for unaccompanied minors. In 2008, the Ministry of the Interior requested €395,935 from the European Commission (ARGO). In order to promote 'an increase in communication between immigrants and the Ministry of Interior', to streamline procedures for the identification of migrants, and to reduce 'clashes between different ethnic groups and between immigrants', the Ministry requested another €371,827 (ARGO). In 2011 the annual budget of *Save the Children* included €52,348 for the 'emergency Lampedusa' (Save the Children <http://images.savethechildren.it/f/download/bilancio/20/2011_bilancio.pdf> (accessed 10 March 2017) p. 38).
29. For an account of the 'humanitarian industry', see Mesnard, who delineates a 'doubled typology: the first one corresponds to the specific visibility of victims and the second regards both the visibility of the NGO and their *own victims* and the relations to rival organisations'. P. Mesnard, *Attualità della vittima. La reppresentazione umanitaria della sofferenza* [Actuality of the Victim. The Humanitarian Representation of Suffering], ombre corte, Verona, 2004, p. 17.
30. For an account of international cooperation in the EuroMed region, see the contributions in F. Ippolito and S. Trevisanut, *Migration in the Mediterranean: Mechanisms of International Cooperation*, Cambridge University Press, Cambridge, 2015.
31. G. Simmel, 'Exkurs über den Fremden', [Excursus on the Stranger] in O. Rammstedt (ed.), *Soziologie. Untersuchung über die Formen der Vergesellschaftung*, Suhrkamp, Frankfurt am Main [1908] 1992, p. 760; published in English in K. Wolff (ed. and trans.), *The Sociology of Georg Simmel*, Free Press, New York, 1950, pp. 402–408.
32. Foucault, *Sicherheit, Territorium, Bevölkerung*, op. cit., p. 291.
33. F. Falk, 'Invasion, infection, invisibility: an iconology of illegalized immigration', in C. Bischoff, F. Falk and S. Kafehsy (eds), *Images of Illegalized Immigration. Towards a Critical Iconology of Politics*, transcript, Bielefeld, 2010, pp. 89, 90.
34. H. Arendt, *On Revolution*, Penguin, London, 1963, p. 75.
35. L. Chouliaraki, *Lo spettatore ironico. La solidarietà nell'epoca del post-umanitarismo* [The Ironic Spectator. Solidarity in the Age of Post-Humanitarism] (a cura di P. Musarò), Mimesis, Udine, 2014.

36. L. Boltanski, *La souffrance à distance. Morale humanitaire, médias et politique*, Métailié, Paris, 1993, p. 10 (published in English as *Distant Suffering*, op. cit.).
37. 'Refugee struggle for freedom' <http://refugeestruggle.org/en/solidarity/lampedusa-everywhere> (accessed 24 October 2015, emphasis mine).
38. M. Foucault, 'Pouvoirs et stratégies', [Powers and Strategies] in *Dits et écrits, 1970–1975*, Vol. II, D. Defert and F. Ewald (eds), Gallimard, Paris, 1994, p. 425.
39. A. Mangano, *Gli africani salveranno l'Italia* [The Africans Will Save Italy], BUR, Milano, 2010, p. 135 (emphasis mine).
40. B. Honig, *Democracy and the Foreigner*, Princeton University Press, Princeton, NJ, 2001, p. 21.
41. Ibid., pp. 15–41.
42. D. Giglioli, *Critica della vittima* [Critique of the Victim], nottetempo, Roma, 2014, p. 9.
43. Boltanski, *La souffrance à distance*, op. cit., p. 10.
44. Falk, op. cit., p. 86.
45. R. Vijeyarasa, *Sex, Slavery and the Trafficked Woman: Myths and Misconceptions about Trafficking and Its Victims*, Ashgate, Farnham, 2015, p. 38.
46. R. Bishop, C. V. Morgan and L. Erickson, 'Public awareness of human trafficking in Europe: how concerned are European citizens?', *Journal of Immigrant & Refugee Studies*, 11 (2), 2013, p. 115, doi: 10.1080/15562948.2013.759047.
47. Ibid.
48. For a discussion of the sometimes rather moralistic 'rescue industry', the role of media and NGOs, see Vijeyarasa, op. cit., pp. 31–39. The 'various categories analyzed ... (feminist academics, governments NGOs and related groups involved in raids and rescue, the UN, inter-governmental organization, donors and the media) identify, promote and amplify the attention given to various "causes" assumed to link with human trafficking, the moral panic of governments towards sex work and the demands from abolitionists for the criminalization of prostitution endorse the idea that prostitution and the underlying problem of gender equality are to blame for trafficking' (ibid., 39).
49. Images of the stranger as victim recall an inheritance situating the guest between friend and foe (*hostis/hospes*), on one hand. On the other hand, they recall the closeness of the stranger to the divine and sacrifice. In this context, yet another field of signification is opened, as the relationship between sacrifice and the scapegoat points towards the relations between the community, the divine gods, the stranger and the victim: *hostia* (sacrifice, sacrificial offering) signifies, 'in contrast to *victima*', a sacrifice that had to 'calm the anger of the gods', as Bahr notes, '*hostia*' is an atonement and offering for their non-aggression. H.-D. Bahr, *Die Sprache des Gastes: Eine Metaethik* [The Language of the Guest. A Meta-Ethic], Reclam, Leipzig, 1994, pp. 27–28. Christian iconography takes up the relations between the stranger and the holy.
50. Focusing on Giovanni Bellini's *pietà* and the photo of a Somali refugee arriving on Lampedusa, Fancesca Falk elaborates on the centrality of Christian iconography for the representation of migrants. Falk, op. cit., pp. 89–90.
51. S. Sontag, *Regarding the Pain of Others*, Picador, New York, 2003, p. 56 <http://monoskop.org/images/a/a6/Sontag_Susan_2003_Regarding_the_Pain_of_Others.pdf> (accessed 30 December 2014).
52. Save the Children, Bilancio al 31 Dicembre 2011, p. 38 <http://images.savethechildren.it/f/download/bilancio/20/2011_bilancio.pdf> (accessed 4 October 2012).
53. 'Terre des Hommes torna a Lampedusa per offrire un supporto psicologico e psicosociale ai minori migranti e alle famiglie con bambini', 2013 <http://terredeshommes.it/comunicati/terre-des-hommes-torna-a-lampe...co-e-psicosociale-ai-minori-migranti-e-alle-famiglie-con-bambini/> (accessed 1 March 2014).
54. 'C&A per i diritti die bambini migranti con Terre des Hommes', 2013 <http://terredeshommes.it/aziende-case-history/ca-per-i-diritti-dei-bambini-migranti-con-terre-des-hommes/> (accessed 27 February 2014).

55. S. Kafehsy, 'Images of victims in trafficking in women. The Euro 08 campaign against trafficking in women in Switzerland', in Bischoff, Falk and Kafehsy (eds), *Images of Illegalized Immigration*, op. cit., p. 76.
56. Ibid.
57. R. Salecl, *On Anxiety. Thinking in Action*, Routledge, London, 2004, p. 15.
58. In this sense, public outcry after the events in Cologne on New Year's Eve 2016 can be read as a reaction against the assault on the body of the nation, symbolized by the female body.
59. C. Castoriadis, quoted in J.-A. Mbembé, 'Necropolitics', *Public Culture*, 15(1), 2003, p. 13.
60. Butler, op. cit.

Back to Basics: Stateless Women and Children in Greece

Mariangela Veikou

ABSTRACT
European societies are effectively witnessing a growing refugee crisis in tandem with the ongoing economic crisis in recent years. Within this climate, migration is at risk of being seen more than ever before as an additional 'burden' that societies have to 'carry' and it is sometimes even questioned why it should be accommodated or respected at all. This paper draws on empirical research from Greece to examine changing European societies, with a particular focus on how the crisis is affecting the most vulnerable members of society, the stateless children and women migrants and refugees.

Introduction

The photos (above) are by the photographer Greg Constantine, at his exhibition 'Nowhere People: The World's Stateless' (2012).[1] The photographs document the impact that statelessness has on people and on entire communities around the world. This is an issue of many technical and legal aspects. The one thing that perhaps gets lost about statelessness worldwide is the impact that it has on people's daily lives. This is where this paper comes in, trying to provide evidence on how these people feel and the impact of statelessness on their lives. There are obstacles and boundaries that people find overwhelming, making it very difficult to navigate through their lives as they are frequently subjected to forms of civil and social discrimination. For example, they are often denied vital documents, such as birth certificates and passports, and this would not allow them to go to school, find legal employment or get a driver's licence, to secure housing or to travel freely from one place to another, etc. They are thus unable to return to their countries after having left them and often they might be subjected to detention since the state cannot resolve the question of their identity or nationality.[2] Tragically, many issues have a root cause in statelessness, such as child labour, forced migration and/or human trafficking; stateless people are vulnerable to any of these high-profile abuses. This paper tries to show some of the by-products of statelessness and lack of belonging, focusing on stateless women and children in Greece.

Currently, in Greece there are some 1000 stateless women and children, who have either migrated to the country without documents or overstayed their visa. Sometimes, they were born in Greece to parents without legal status. The denial of an identity is probably the most tragic element of statelessness.[3] Many stateless people are stateless in their country of birth. They never left the place where they were born, yet they are denied the right to belong to that place and of course this may end up having a big effect on people's psyches and motivation.[4]

People often take for granted the empowerment deriving from being the citizen of a state and the rights that go along with this. Not to have this connection to the place they call home marginalizes people to such an extent that they have no voice.[5] Citizenship is a fundamental condition that legally connects individuals to a number of rights, to the state and in essence to the rest of the world.[6] Hannah Arendt, the leading political theorist of the twentieth century, who has been stateless herself, when she was stripped of her German nationality, famously said that to be stripped of citizenship is to be stripped of worldliness.[7] In the modern political scene, citizenship is how one becomes a member of the state (and thus of the world) and this is how one is protected by the state.

The paper is structured as follows: the first section describes the political setting in Greece and the restrictive immigration/nationalization laws and policies, de-legitimizing the position of immigrants in society on the basis of ethnic and cultural arguments. The second section examines the background and the legal and social position of stateless women and children in Greece in the midst of the economic and refugee crisis. It enquires into the rights that children and women are entitled to as a matter of human rights law and contrasts this with the enforcement capabilities of the Greek state in practice. The discussion then turns to the consequences of rights denial, including non-access to economic and social rights. This is followed by a section on statelessness where the aim is to pick out some aspects of the work of different social theorists which may help in understanding and exemplifying the situation in Greece. This section includes stories by stateless women and children situated in the particular contemporary Greek social and political context, which provides the empirical evidence for this paper. These are all stories of invisibility and marginalization which exemplify life as experienced by stateless people.[8] As phrased by Arendt in *The Origins of Totalitarianism*: 'It seems that a man who is nothing but a man has lost the very qualities which make it possible for other people to treat him as a fellow-man'.[9] The concluding section pulls all the threads together and suggests ways to amend discriminatory laws to feed into analytical and relevant advocacy work.

The political and social setting

Immigration to Greece since 1990 has led to radical social transformations, as a previously homogenous society developed significant ethnic and religious diversity. Immigration is a polarizing issue in Greek politics. Centrist and leftist parties have adopted broadly pro-immigration policies, whereas right-wing parties have cultivated uniformly negative views of immigrants. Since 2009, the on-going debt crisis has exacerbated social problems (e.g. crime and unemployment), raising hostility toward immigrants to new levels, as populist right-wing political parties have successfully linked these two trends in public discourse.[10] As a result, weak state institutions cannot develop strategies to manage the social consequences and public perceptions surrounding immigration, which is an issue that is getting more pressing due to the growing refugee crisis.

In addition to the nine years of acute economic and social crisis, since 2014 Greece has been facing a rapid increase of refugee flows, is still in full swing in 2017. The country is witnessing a refugee emergency as people from the Middle East, Asia and Africa escape war and crisis by coming to Europe.[11] In earlier years refugees did not make it to Europe and hence Europe generally took a stance that could be summarized aptly as 'out of sight, out of mind'. Now that the crisis is finally here, European states do not seem able to react appropriately. Europe could have built an architecture that could have worked adequately, but instead the policy chosen was to fortify the Union's borders. Greece is profoundly affected. More than 800,000 people were estimated to have entered the country in 2015, via Turkey, to the Aegean islands.[12] The Greek islands predominantly bear the burden of providing the main host structures for these arrivals.[13] Additionally, in Athens there are three refugee centres with a total reception capacity of 2,300 persons. They operate under the responsibility of the Ministry of Migration Policy, the Greek police and the United Nations High Commissioner for Refugees (UNHCR) acting as a co-moderator. Alongside the official Greek authorities, many NGOs provide rescue services, reception, health care and solidarity, while local volunteers and international organizations have equally mobilized. Yet the situation remains critical.[14]

During the first three months of 2016, the challenge became even more critical, as the borders to northern countries closed in accordance to European management of transit flows. This meant, in practice, that Greece had to accommodate thousands of refugees by operating registration centres (hot spots), reception infrastructure and developing hospitality and integration infrastructure. This is in contrast to the previous position of the Greek government, which considered the fact that asylum seekers are not interested in remaining in the country as a positive development and attempted to facilitate their relocation to northern European countries through the Balkan route.[15]

One cannot but wonder whether we are experiencing a collapse of the humanitarian architecture. Intolerable images of children boarding fragile vessels and drowning in the Mediterranean[16] may tragically continue because there are no other exit options for refugees and migrants. Europeans are deliberating the alarming prospect of fences being erected between member states. Europe, an area of free movement, is becoming an area fortified by barbed wire.

EU governments have shown few integrated and systemic approaches to dealing with the situation. This crisis represents an enormous humanitarian and political challenge. There are such diametrically opposed views and political drivers within EU states about how to cope with refugees that it is a real challenge to find a unified response and approach.

Yet one has to note that making use of a crisis as a decisive factor for the development of immigration policies disguises social injustices with a serious impact on the most vulnerable. For example, the Greek state's prevalent approach on immigration policy over the years has been to de-legitimize the position of the migrants in the host society on the basis of ethnic and cultural arguments.[17] Greek ideological support for restrictive immigration/nationalization law and policies remains a significant issue, acutely apparent in the status of the stateless people, which focuses on the intersection between human rights and migration. The following section looks more closely at this theme.

Women and children in limbo

This paper distinguishes two contemporary manifestations of statelessness: *de jure* (legal) statelessness, when individuals lack any nationality because of the circumstances of their birth or political and legal obstacles; and de facto statelessness, when nationals of one country live irregularly in another and they lack or are denied the documentation to prove their right to state services where they are legal residents and/or citizens, and they cannot turn to the state in which they live for protection.[18] Put another way, there are those who are not considered as a national by any state under the operation of its law (i.e. those described as *de jure* stateless), and there are also those de facto stateless people who might have legal claim to the benefits of nationality but they cannot prove or verify it.[19] The term de facto stateless is, more often than not, applied to those persons who do not enjoy the rights of citizenship enjoyed by other citizens of the same state. Consequently, while *de jure* statelessness can result from the oversight of lawmakers who leave gaps in the law through which persons can fall, de facto statelessness typically results from state discrimination and most persons considered de facto stateless are victims of state repression.[20] They are, effectively, without a nationality and cannot rely on the state of which they are citizens for protection. Many of them suffer (in)formal discrimination of some kind regarding their claim for citizenship and they are not, for a variety of reasons, able to enjoy the benefits of nationality.[21] These reasons might be laws related to administrative practices (insuperable obstacles to documenting birth, marriage, parentage or residence), discrimination, restrictive naturalization laws and policies (*jus sanguinis*),[22] denationalization (automatic loss of citizenship by operation of law), etc.[23]

This section looks, in particular, at how statelessness intersects with migration and human rights protections. By focusing on stateless women and children in Greece, it tries to understand (a) what are the specificities that affect women (women as stateless migrant workers, family members, subjects encountering discrimination, what is distinctive about being a female as opposed to a male migrant/refugee, when most of the norms and the assumptions are that the man is the primary actor of migration) and (b) what are the challenges and lacunas in protection when children are involved.

Gender discriminatory laws in some countries, combined with ineffective legal safeguards in the EU states, can render a woman stateless by divorce or the death of the husband.[24] Women's inability to transmit nationality to their children on an equal footing to men can lead to statelessness which, in turn, results in severe consequences for individuals and their families.[25] For example, Syrian women refugees resettling in Greece, give birth to their children in Greece and they are *de jure* and de facto stateless (under Syrian law, only men can pass citizenship on to their children). Ameera, for instance, explains that she had to leave Syria without her husband. Her twin sons are stateless in Greece. They were not recognized as citizens of Syria and this makes a big difference in their everyday life in Greece. They are stateless and had they been able to prove their Syrian nationality they would have been entitled to register as Syrian asylum seekers, increasing their chances of legalizing their status in Greece.

Problems of de facto statelessness are especially highlighted among trafficked women in Greece. For many, nationality is not a means to assistance because often their passports are taken away and even if these women were to gain their freedom, they are faced with the difficulties associated with being unable to prove their nationality. Being without identity documents also makes it difficult for them to obtain basic social services. Moreover, without identity documents many of these women also find it difficult to claim or obtain political asylum. Nona, for example, was born in a small town in Georgia, and her mother left her in an orphanage. As a teenager she became—evidently—a victim of sex trafficking. Too afraid to admit it openly, she said that 'something happened in Georgia, making it dangerous for me to go back home'. She found herself in Greece and it was then that Nona fell into a strange crack in the law. She was hesitant to declare herself a victim of human trafficking in the country as she would possibly put her life at further risk due to the fact that her official recognition as a sex trafficking victim would endanger her life once the procurer found out. She only has a birth certificate with her. According to her, a birth record is not sufficient proof of citizenship and this makes it very difficult to claim a legal status in Greece.

The focus of the paper is also on children, adolescents and teenagers, of migrants/refugees (second-generation migrants).[26] These children are born in Greece or arrived in the country at a very young age, received all their education and socialization in Greece, and know no other place as their home, yet they are overlooked by the official government records.[27] These children often have the status of a non-citizen in Greece due to their parents' irregular status (as a result of undocumented migration, expiration of permits, transit migrations, unresolved asylum procedures, pending deportation status and so on) or due to their own status being contested (i.e. children with no nationality). These children are special in many respects, especially since they are missing the crucial evidence of their relationship with the Greek state. Without proof of these ties with the state they remain obscure in policies, which seriously impacts on their development and the problems they will face in the future.

These women and children are in practice (de facto) stateless. They 'lack their own government' in Arendt's sense and have to fall back upon their minimum rights, unable to enforce rights that are supposedly indisputable. For instance, the fundamental rights to protection, family life, education and health care that they have in theory (under international law) are unenforceable in practice.[28] As a consequence, they often live in a precarious situation on the margins of society, lacking identity documentation and frequently subjected to discrimination since their access to a state able to protect them is tenuous at best. Given their disenfranchised and precarious situation, these women and children have a strong claim to enforcement of their human rights within the Greek context where they live.[29] Faridah, a 29-year-old with a Syrian identity document, explains:

> My situation is weird. I do not know why they are treating me this way. They put me on hold. But… this is the law. I always have to wait; I cannot organize my life because when I try something, nothing seems to work. It makes me feel that I need some faith in my life—some religion. I need to find some proper job that I can provide for myself and for my family. I pray that I can always have all my family around me.

The UNHCR has warned about the dire consequences that these children and female migrants, who lack protection, face in Greece. They are at serious risk of being deprived of access to medical care, education and jobs while they are sentenced to a life of discrimination, frustration and despair.[30] They face physical, social and cultural barriers which permeate every area of life since there is a need either to conceal their legal status or to try to 'pass' as a citizen in daily interactions (with employers, with healthcare providers, etc.) in order to access rights that would otherwise be denied.[31] They often struggle to earn a living, commonly facing restrictions in accessing the labour market. Stripped of their rights, they are forced into menial jobs far beneath their qualifications, while also not qualifying for social security benefits, which are not designed to take into account their particular circumstances and vulnerability. Their statelessness also forms an obstacle to accessing financial services (bank accounts, loans, etc.), which can make it all the more difficult to break out of poverty.[32] Here people are completely stuck, unable to travel, unable to live their life to the full. Jamila is an example of a person who, as she describes, feels stuck in place: 'I also do not have travel documents. There is no hope that I will see my son and that we will meet again in this life'. On another occasion, a mother described how her husband is abroad and she cannot be properly reunited with him, nor can he see his child. These are inhuman situations that breach many legal international articles on the right to family life and reunification.

Thus, one major challenge these people face relates to the stress resulting from the fact that they are, in essence, invisible. Moreover, in addition to being invisible, they are also subjected to a condition of ambivalence. For example, the ambivalence in Greek policy exemplifies a society torn when dealing with these 'others': On the one hand, there are assumptions in policies that expect women and children outside of families to need special protection and to deserve the same rights to health care, education and shelter as any person. On the other hand, there are other assumptions reflected in governmental policies which consider undocumented women and/or unaccompanied/undocumented children of a different background as causing a sense of precaution, suspicion and, in turn, hostility on the part of the host society. This conceals the idea that these women and children might be deviant, juvenile delinquents, or, at any rate, not innocent people.

The invisibility and ambivalence regarding their status is a substantial issue and the Greek authorities have failed to systematically address it. For instance, until now, while unaccompanied child refugees in Greece have the right to legal counselling and a guardian *in loco parentis* through proceedings, in effect the authorities are unable to provide them with such a service, creating a huge vacuum of protection. Since April 2016, under the new immigration and asylum law, authorities became more proactive in increasing access to forms of counselling and representation (still within the limits of what is convenient or expedient for the system). This is of course a drop in the ocean, but at least it is an indication that the authorities are aware that there is need for some more concerted intervention.

Successive Greek governments over recent years have been enforcing restrictive immigration legislation. Currently, the government is enforcing the regularization of second-generation children and stateless people who want to live in Greece legally. According to statistics by the Generation 2.0 for Rights Equality & Diversity, there are about 200,000 children and young adults born to immigrant parents presently in Greece, that have been previously denied access to citizenship, with a precarious legal status. Before July 2015, citizenship acquisition for people of migrant origin in Greece was possible only by naturalization (*jus sanguinis*). In 2010, Act 3838/2010 was adopted by the Greek parliament which made the acquisition of citizenship on the principle of *jus soli* possible, allowing those who had been born to immigrant parents, legally living in Greece for at least five years, to be granted Greek citizenship, providing they had studied at a Greek school for a minimum of six years.[33] Following Greece's conservative-led government, this law was considered anti-constitutional by the State Council's ruling and, in 2013, the State Council overturned the articles that provided a path to citizenship acquisition (this meant that some who were granted Greek citizenship in accordance to the 2010 law provisions lost their respective rights). During that time, children born in Greece to immigrant parents received a so-called 'maternity clinic certificate' rather than a proper birth certificate, which awarded them no legal status other than basic rights. In 2015 the parliament approved a bill drafted by the Ministry of Interior granting Greek citizenship to migrant children of foreign nationals who were stateless, not covered by any legal framework, as long as they were born and/or raised in the country. The bill also included provisions and changes in the requirements for the acquisition of Greek citizenship by other stateless migrant groups. The legislation passed with 172 votes in the 300-seat parliament.[34] The bill introduced three main conditions for the acquisition of citizenship: (a) five-year legal stay in Greece; (b) children born within a five-year period, during which at least one parent lived legally in the country; (c) children enrolled in first grade and still attending school when they submit an application for the acquisition of nationality.[35]

Against this general background, the next section discusses from an analytical and empirical point of view how legal and de facto statelessness impinge on people's lives in Greece today.

On being stateless

The approach here concentrates on subjects of a polity who wish to have the same rights as citizens but, excluded from civil society, are instead managed by the state negotiating their relationships with it.

In the section above we looked at the boundaries of the Greek political community, the principles for political membership and the limits of incorporating others, such as stateless women and children, into the existing polity. We have also seen that the limits of political community and definitions of political membership may shift according to historical and political contingencies shaping accordingly the social arrangement of society, informing the identities and political subjectivities available to people.

The right to be a member of an organized political community, as Arendt reminded us, is a human right.[36] In terms of statelessness, this can get complicated because being an immigrant entering a state territory is a human claim, but not everybody who enters a state should automatically become a citizen. 'Statelessness' is constructed as an unstable social condition of social and political marginality, fixed in a binary opposition between the rights of citizenship rooted in a national territory and a 'stateless' condition outside the nation-state, which has, at its core, not only subordination and control, but also ambivalence and resistance.[37]

The stateless are a category of people created in and by a (international) state system (in crisis) and subjected to a precarious existence. The stateless persons and the displaced have become symptoms of the politics of late modernity which do not resolve but only exacerbate the conflict between the territorially demarcated system of state sovereignty and the universality of human rights claims. The distinguished political theorist Seyla Benhabib makes a plea for moral universalism and cosmopolitanism, advocating porous boundaries and the recognition of admittance rights of the displaced[38] by emphasizing that the predicament of the stateless, those who seem to possess only their human rights, stands at the very core of the distinction between human rights and the rights of the citizen.

From Arendt's famous discussion of the 'right to have rights' in *The Origins of Totalitarianism*, to Foucault's 'biopolitics',[39] to Agamben's *Homo Sacer*[40] to Benhabib's *Rights of Others*, to Butler's *Precarious Life*,[41] one may trace back a theoretical discussion on statelessness. In a much discussed passage in the *Origins of Totalitarianism*, Arendt wrote

> we become aware of the existence of the right to have rights and a right to belong to some kind of organized community … people emerge who had lost and could not regain these rights because of the new global political situation … these rights spring immediately from the 'nature' of man … and the right to have rights or the right of every individual to belong to humanity, should be guaranteed by humanity itself.[42]

The 'right to have rights', therefore, has become the well-known phrase through which to capture the condition of the stateless and the displaced persons—that is, those who have been cast out. According to Arendt, conceptions of human nature should not treat humans as if they were just things in nature. For her, it is with reference to the 'human condition' alone that we must try to justify the 'right to have rights'. Arendt writes that

> our political life rests on the assumption that we can produce equality through organization, because man can act, and change, and build a common world together with his equals, and only his equals. We are not born equal, we become equal as members of a group on the strength of our decision to guarantee ourselves mutually equal rights.[43]

Arendt and Agamben[44] identify statelessness as emerging under the sweeping logic of sovereignty. In Arendt's reflections on the modern state of sovereignty and Agamben's reflections on the state of exception, it is the state that creates the stateless. There is an intense contemporary debate among social scientists and political philosophers about how to characterize the apparent conflict between human rights and the rights of a citizen. Should we characterize it as a transformation in the regime of state sovereignty leading to a regime of 'legal cosmopolitanism', which, in turn, may give rise to a certain dualistic international order of global governance and the continuing state system?[45] Benhabib has defended such a position of moral and legal cosmopolitanism in her work *The Rights of Others*, and in an exclusive 2010 interview she argued that

> when you come to the land of 'another' and your intentions are peaceful, you have a moral and legal claim to be able to stay there. But whether you are permitted to stay when the danger is past, whether you can actually be a member of that society, is a sovereign claim. There must be an open, transparent, consistent way for the stranger to become a member of a state. We ought to consider each human being as a person entitled to basic human rights whether they are a national or a citizen of a state.[46]

She considers this claim a regulative ideal about the way the international state system should function. According to her, the issue is whether this ideal, which she describes as legal cosmopolitanism, can become not just a regulative ideal but also a constitutive ideal of the international community. Benhabib[47] points to the fact that the state is not the only domain of the political and public sphere of our times.[48] She is interested in the international and transnational politics of human rights that have emerged (different from humanitarianism, in her view) often impacting on human rights struggles within the states themselves. Sometimes, she argues, international politics oblige states to grant the stateless the right to stay, if they would most likely be in danger if sent back to their countries of origin. Individuals nowadays are (should be) recognized as holding human rights directly under international/transnational politics and international law.[49]

According to Agamben, states remain the principal actors to guarantee and respect human rights, as well as being the political domain within which human rights are enacted and interpreted.[50] States also impose reservations which allow them to avoid compliance with certain human rights clauses.[51] This becomes a very interesting area of analysis because on occasion states may put reservations on a legal or policy aspect and they may return and modify it years later.[52] Take the example of the changes in the naturalization policies of Greek state in recent years, as described above. Eventually, Agamben developed this thought into a more dynamic understanding with his notion of 'state of exception' in which he proposes that statelessness appears to be a status that is marked in a decisive way by the political system of the state.[53] The state of exception suspends the legal order and it is from this angle that it increasingly presents itself 'as the dominant paradigm of governing' by arguing that today's political conditions necessitate it. For example, the Greek state's legitimation for the State Council decision to annul the 2010 citizenship reforms was that naturalization according to the Greek state is recognized only when there is a 'real bond' between the foreigner and the Greek nation. Other ideological positions put forward by the right-wing government to legitimize such a decision at the time were that the state was gravely affected by what appeared to be a permanent financial crisis[54] and a mounting refugee crisis. The state of exception, Agamben argues, is what the sovereign each and every time decides, and takes place as the ultimate foundation of political power, capitalizing on the only form of legitimacy that seems to be accepted by it and that is usually the emergence of a crisis.[55] This increasingly widening gap between order and state (a state of exception during which the law may be suspended) becomes the new fact of politics. The state brings a crisis in as the reason for remaining outside of the normal order. As the crisis makes the state of exception the rule, rather than the exception, it brings about a new legal–political paradigm in which the norm becomes indistinguishable from the exception.[56] The state of exception, according to Agamben, is the legal form of that which cannot take on legal form: a legal category describing the absence of law.[57] In that way, the state of exception, which had initially been thought of as a temporary displacement of law, gradually becomes the normal practice of governance. The contribution of Foucault is relevant here in understanding the term 'crisis'. His concept of 'biopolitics' shows an understanding of modern politics as administrating, regulating, calculating and managing the life of the population.[58] Suspending people's human rights reduces certain groups of people to the status of being 'mere life', stripping these people of their rights, social positions and civil status, in the name of the 'life' of society. In this sense, life of society has become the highest good; it is not the life of the individuals but rather the life of society itself, which ranks as the supreme good.[59] Foucault thus diagnosed a specifically technocratic understanding of politics, linked to the 'governmentalization of the state'.[60] In this perspective, the crisis creates a condition of emergency also with regard to the rights of people. Agamben's 'state of exception' critically enquires into the sovereign's declarations and enactments of 'exceptions' to legal, political and social norms and by consequence individual rights, typically in the name of security imperatives or a 'state of emergency'. He borrows Foucault's concept of biopolitics to claim that in modern biopolitics it is the sovereign that decides on the value or the non-value of people's rights on its soil. The sovereign affirms its power over the people by withdrawing its protection, abandoning their lives to a realm of lawlessness.[61] Agamben largely succeeds in drawing attention to the stakes involved in contemporary deployments of exceptional sovereign lawlessness: The state of exception starts with a (security) threat and ends with an executive able to act against the people without the constraints of legislative checks or judicial review. The state of exception explains how this legitimation takes place and a modern society rapidly transforms from one where government owes protection and rights, to one where people are left unprotected, abused or detained at a whim.[62]

The human impact of such suspension of rights is proven to be more difficult for the segment of population under question, the stateless, who are those mostly affected. They often find themselves facing serious obstacles, they lack the required identification and they are typically required to go through lengthy security checks.[63] Fear and distress related to economic insecurity, and scarce resources, contribute to a life where basic rights are reduced to a minimum in the name of a state of exception. Hence, following Agamben's work, the stateless people in Greece resemble his *homo sacer*, reduced to 'bare life', and thus deprived of their basic rights.[64] Hala explains:

> we are like dust; wherever the wind blows I am going to go. I cannot settle properly to a home, because I have to constantly move around. They make you feel you are not human and you develop more animal instincts, that's it.

It is the sovereign privilege, which is still at work, governing, in Butler's sense, the 'precarious life' of the stateless.[65] A process of rough tolerance has been exercised for years (under the pretence of humanitarian reasoning) to enable stateless people to disappear into the folds of civil society and live there below the radar of legality. Raja shockingly describes her life in Greece:

> It is a struggle; like being a ghost forced to live in the shadows. You do not become stateless purposely, you feel you have freedom but you don't. My mother went to work and they got her. At the police station she cried. She faced threats of detention or deportation and separation from her children. The police officer told her to change residence. He said: it is very difficult to trace you if you change your address. This is what we did.

Yet one has to stress that human basic rights are not an abstract, discretionary concept. It is a claim of right by the people on the state. These individuals have been demanding their rights from the Greek state, where they have been residing for long. Consider the story of Sanaa, who has spent her whole life so far without citizenship in Greece, which highlights the fate awaiting her children if their nationality is not resolved:

> I don't know how me and my family became stateless. I never knew a different life. For more than 20 years, I lived without a resident permit in Greece, constantly afraid of being found out. Only recently I realized that another life is possible.

There is a need for the Greek state to respond to the social and emotional needs of this part of its population, the stateless women and children, which may lead to further immigration policy reforms and a redefinition of Greek citizenship to include both ethnic and civic features. Kicking it off, the recent restoration of the *jus soli* principle for some in the new immigration law which passed on April 2016 reflects the capacity of state to engage with the concerns of people in need of protection and safety residing in Greek soil, or at least to engage with substantive political issues and human rights lacunas with regards the stateless women and children in Greece.

Conclusion

The paper engages in understanding statelessness especially of women and children in Greece, its challenge and impacts, as a mutual accommodation and adjustment between concepts such as Agamben's 'state of exception' and '*homo sacer*', Foucault's 'biopolitics', Butler's 'precarious life', Arendt's 'the right to have rights' and Benhabib's 'rights of others'.

The machinery for protection for the displaced has been broken in Greece in recent years. Getting the government to agree to accept in the polity a substantial number of others/immigrants/refugees has proven hard because politicians are looking to their electorates and the groundswell for humanitarian support is matched by the groundswell for xenophobia. The failure to protect the stateless by obscuring the political and moral recognition necessary for their basic rights to be exercised, abandoning them in an in-between reality, is understood as a betrayal of the most basic duty of a liberal democratic society, which is a tacit understanding that the state should hold together as a political community and uphold to basic rights and conditions of safety for all. By dismantling this basic duty, the Greek state was able to push through, and further consolidate, its ideological conservatism with regard to who belongs and who does not belong to the political community.

A democratic polity within an international global community has an obligation to think about vulnerable populations dependent on protection. It cannot just think of citizens as being the target of its attention. It has also to think about populations that move across borders. Democratic polities have an obligation to think outside the box and to be more broad-based and syncretic, inventing different tools and avenues to use regarding the stateless.

Finally, we need a robust normative framework, and to generate strategies for preventing traumatic situations and work upstream with a reactive focus to make society more sensitive. It is impossible to turn the clock back once children have been separated from their parents or women have been victims of abuse. When these problems occur, then it is often too late and people have suffered irreparable trauma and it is very hard to get back on track. It is up to liberal democratic states to create the social and economic rights to protect stateless people from these situations.

Disclosure statement

No potential conflict of interest was reported by the author.

Notes

1. The exhibition was hosted by UNHCR Ireland as part of the Photo Ireland Festival 2012, at the Department of Justice and Equality, Dublin, Ireland.
2. David Weissbrodt and Clay Collins, 'The human rights of stateless persons', *Human Rights Quarterly*, 28, 2006, p. 245 <http://scholarship.law.umn.edu/faculty_articles/412>.

3. 'The world's stateless', Report, Institute on Statelessness and Inclusion, December 2014 <http://www.institutesi.org>.
4. Ibid.
5. Most countries in EU do not have a procedure put in place to determine who are the stateless persons. It is very difficult to estimate with any precision the numbers of de facto stateless people, even in countries where data on statelessness is collected on immigration systems. There are complexities of categorization and often there are overlaps between refugees, displaced persons, asylum seekers and stateless people when some people fall under more than one category at a time. For example, while clearly not all stateless people are refugees and not all refugees are stateless, the overlap has meant that some stateless people fall through the cracks (UNHCR, 'Special Report: The strange hidden world of the stateless', *Refugees*, 147(3), 2007.). Statelessness might also be a taboo subject for states because it often refers to discriminatory policies.
6. Seyla Benhabib, 'Borders, boundaries, and citizenship work(s)', *Political Science and Politics*, 38(4), 2005, pp. 673–677.
7. Hannah Arendt, *The Origins of Totalitarianism*, Harcourt, Brace and Jovanovich, New York, 1968.
8. UNHCR, Special Report, op. cit.
9. Arendt, op. cit., p. 300.
10. High unemployment and problems of social order in urban areas with high concentrations of immigrants have been manipulated by conservative politicians and extreme right-wing groups to gain electoral support among voters while deflecting attention from more pressing problems.
11. Mark Tran, 'Dozens drown off Greek islands in deadliest January for refugees', *The Guardian-Migration*, Friday 22 January 2016 <http://www.theguardian.com/world/2016/jan/22/dozens-dead-as-two-boats-sink-off-greece>.
12. The main countries of origin of migrants seeking international protection in Greece are Syria (about 50% of the total number of arrivals), Afghanistan (30%) and Iraq (10%), IOM, Missing Migrants Project, 2015 <http://missingmigrants.iom.int/>.
13. On the island of Lesvos, for example, there are two reception centres with a total capacity of 2,800 people. The reception infrastructure on other islands—Chios and Samos—is even smaller (about 300 people in each) (UNHCR, News and Stories, Migrants facing shameful conditions in Greece, 7 August 2015).
14. UNHCR, 'News and Stories', UNHCR - Press Conference (Geneva, 7 August 2015) Subject: Europe's refugee crisis: Greece and Calais. Speaker: Vincent Cochetel, UNHCR Director for Europe, <http://www.unhcr.org/ibelong/news-and-stories/> (accessed June 2015); UNHCR, 'The sea route to Europe. The Mediterranean passage in the age of refugees', 2015 < http://www.unhcr.org/5592bd059.pdf>; UNHCR, 'Number of refugees and migrants arriving in Greece soars 750 per cent over 2014', News and Stories, 2015 <http://www.unhcr.org/55c4d1fc2.html> (accessed August 2015).
15. Migrants and asylum seekers arriving in Greece continue their journey via South-East European countries (Macedonia, Serbia, Croatia, Slovenia) on to Central Europe (Hungary, Austria, Germany and Sweden). There seems to be a trail to seek refugee status in countries where the state structures and overall support for refugees and migrants is attainable, contrary to the conditions in Greece, which is a region affected by the economic crisis. As a consequence, despite the high number of arrivals, asylum requests remain low in Greece. People entering Greece, in a few days or weeks (depending on resources and their networks) go through the Balkan route to other European countries, especially Germany (UNHCR News and stories, press conference, op. cit.).
16. <http://www.theguardian.com/world/2016/jan/22/dozens-dead-as-two-boats-sink-off-greece> (accessed January 2016).
17. Anna Triandafyllidou and Mariangela Veikou, 'The hierarchy of Greekness: ethnic and national identity considerations in Greek immigration policy', *Ethnicities*, 2(2), 2002, pp. 189–208.

18. Jacqueline Bhabha, 'Arendt's children: do today's migrant children have a right to have rights?', *Human Rights Quarterly*, 31(2), 2009, pp. 410–451; Jacqueline Bhabha, *Children Without a State: A Global Human Rights Challenge*, Massachusetts Institute of Technology, Cambridge, MA, 2011; Weissbrodt and Collins, op. cit.
19. Bhabha, 'Arendt's children', op. cit.; Hugh Massey, 'UNHCR and de facto statelessness', *Legal and Protection Policy Research Series*, Division of International Protection, April 2010.
20. Bhabha, *Children Without a State*, op. cit.
21. Massey, op. cit.; Bhabha, 'Arendt's children', op. cit.
22. *Jus soli* and *jus sanguinis* are principles that dictate the criteria used to grant or deny citizenship. *Jus soli* literally means law of the land and, according to this principle, citizenship is based on place of birth; *jus sanguinis* dictates that citizenship is based on family heritage or descent.
23. Weissbrodt and Collins, op. cit.
24. Alice Edwards and Laura Van Waas (eds), *Nationality and Statelessness Under International Law*, Cambridge University Press, Cambridge, 2014.
25. UNHCR, 'Nationality and statelessness. Handbook for parliamentarians N° 22', UNHCR –Inter-Parliamentary Union, 2014; UNHCR, 'Global action plan to end statelessness: 2014–2024', 2014.
26. Most studies do not address children as discrete agents in the migration or asylum-seeking process, see a useful overview in *Forced Migration Review* special issue on statelessness, issue 32, April 2009.
27. 'Migrant groups slam government over Greek citizenship law', e-kathimerini.com, 27 February 2013.
28. Ilias Trispiotis, 'Socio-economic rights: legally enforceable or just aspirational?', *Opticon1826*, 8, 2010.
29. 'Immigrants press children's Greek citizenship', *Greek Reporter*, 27 February 2013 <http://greece.greekreporter.com/2013/02/27/immigrants-press-childrens-greek-citizenship/#sthash.F94nq597.dpuf> (accessed February 2015).
30. UNHCR, 2015 News and Stories, 2015 <http://www.unhcr.org/55c4d1fc2.html>.
31. <http://www.unhcr.org/ibelong/news-and-stories/> (accessed June 2015).
32. Ibid.
33. 'Equal citizens: campaign for the right to citizenship', 2010, <http://www.ithageneia.org/en>.
34. 'Greek government divided over migrant law but measure passes', Reuters, US, Thursday 25 June 2015 <http://www.reuters.com/article/us-greece-migrants-idUSKBN0P52CV20150625>. Reporting by Karolina Tagaris; editing by Andrew Roche (accessed 27 June 2014).
35. <http://greece.greekreporter.com/2013/02/27/immigrants-press-childrens-greek-citizenship/#sthash.F94nq597.dpuf> (accessed 27 February 2014).
36. Arendt, op. cit.
37. Victoria Redclift, *Statelessness and Citizenship: Camps and the Creation of Political Space*, Vol. 5, Routledge, Florence, KY 2013.
38. Seyla Benhabib, *The Rights of Others: Aliens, Residents, and Citizens*, Vol. 5, Cambridge University Press, Cambridge, 2004.
39. Michel Foucault et al., *The Birth of Biopolitics: Lectures at the Collège de France, 1978–1979* (ed. M. Senellart), Palgrave Macmillan, Basingstoke, 2010.
40. Giorgio Agamben, *Homo Sacer: Sovereign Power and Bare Life*, Stanford University Press, Stanford, CA, 1998.
41. Judith Butler, *Precarious Life: The Powers of Mourning and Violence*, Verso, New York, NY. 2006.
42. Arendt, op. cit., pp. 177–178.
43. Ibid., p. 181.
44. Giorgio Agamben, *State of Exception*, University of Chicago Press, Chicago, 2005.
45. Benhabib, *The Rights of Others*, op. cit.
46. Seyla Benhabib, 'Dialogues on civilizations: migrations and human rights', March 2010 <http://www.resetdoc.org/story/00000021116> (accessed 5 June 2015).

47. Seyla Benhabib et al., *Another Cosmopolitanism*, Vol. 3, (ed. R. Post), Oxford University Press, Oxford, 2006; S. Benhabib, 'From the right to have rights to the critique of humanitarian reason. Against the cynical turn in human rights discourse', lecture Seyla Benhabib delivered upon receiving the Meister Eckhart prize on 19 May 2014 in Köln, Germany.
48. Seyla Benhabib, 'Dialogues on civilizations: migrations and human rights', March 2010 <http://www.resetdoc.org/story/00000021116> (accessed 5 June 2015).
49. Benhabib, lecture, op. cit.
50. Agamben, *Homo sacer*, op. cit.
51. Giorgio Agamben, 'Means without end. Notes on politics', in *Theory Out of Bounds*, Vol. 20, University of Minnesota Press, Minneapolis, 2000.
52. In 2016 the Greek economy entered an eighth year of recession, relying on international rescue loans. The crisis is not merely some acute moment in the history of Greece but is most likely to be a deep and prolonged period of recession <http://www.vox.com/2015/6/29/8862583/greek-financial-crisis-explained> (accessed 29 June 2015).
53. Agamben, *State of Exception*, op. cit.
54. Foucault et al., op. cit.
55. Agamben, *State of Exception*, op. cit.
56. Here I paraphrase Agamben's thought to examine the state of exception with regard to the stateless and its effect on granting them (basic) rights.
57. Agamben, *State of Exception*, op. cit.
58. Ibid.
59. Michel Foucault, *Society Must Be Defended: Lectures at the Collège de France 1975–1976*, Picador, New York, 2003.
60. Michel Foucault, 'Governmentality', in J. D. Faubion (ed.), *Power: Essential Works of Michel Foucault, 1954–1984*, Vol. 3, pp. 201–22, The New Press, New York, 2000.
61. Agamben, *State of Exception*, op. cit.
62. Ibid.
63. Weissbrodt and Collins, op. cit.
64. Agamben, *Homo sacer*, op. cit.
65. Butler, op. cit.

The Conflict between Education and Female Labour in Turkey: Understanding Turkey's Non-compliance with the U-shape Hypothesis

Miray Erinc

ABSTRACT
Female labour force participation rates (FLFPRs) are known to be exceptionally low in Turkey by international standards. The general consensus is that the catalyst behind FLFPRs is the level of educational attainment. In the academic literature, the relationship between the two factors—education and female labour force participation—is explained under what is known as the U-shape hypothesis. Although female education has increased over the past years, the U-shape is not observable in Turkey. This research scrutinizes the economic and social characteristics of the labour markets in Turkey and finally seeks to demonstrate how women in Turkey are trapped in a vicious cycle. The U-shape theory is insufficient to explain FLFPRs in Turkey. Turkish women, although well educated, face cultural barriers in entering the labour markets. They present a form of passive human capital, whose skills are underutilized. Thus, the curve remains an L-shape rather than a U.

1. Introduction

With the beginning of the industrialization era in 1955, Turkey began to experience a drastic decline in the female labour force participation rate (FLFPR). Female labour force participation constitutes an important determinant of economic development. Greater economic equality between women and men is linked to poverty reduction, higher gross domestic product (GDP) and better governance. The latest World Bank analysis (2001) on Turkey and female labour force employment reveals that by increasing the rate significantly, poverty could be reduced by 15 per cent. Whereas the average FLFPR in developed economies and the European Union (EU) was 52.7 per cent, Turkey had a rate of 24.4 per cent in 2007[1] making up only a third of what it was more than half a century ago in 1955, and thus falling far behind many of today's developing country rates. The strikingly low participation rate plays an essential role in strengthening the overall economy, and thus requires an analysis with special regard to country-specific attributes unique to Turkey's social and economic factors.

Developing countries undergoing industrialization experience a steep decline in terms of labour force, followed by a sudden hold and then an extremely fast recovery. This particular observation is commonly observed in economics and is better known as the U-shaped female participation curve or the U-shape hypothesis. The simple reasoning behind this phenomenon is that FLFPRs first decline with industrialization, which is mostly accompanied by a demographic shift from rural to urban areas, and then rise again as the country develops by expanding its industry and improving female education. However, in Turkey's case, even though female education has almost converged with male education, the female participation rate still has not recovered from its steep fall in the 1980s. The non-recovery of the female labour participation rate may be justified by arguing that Turkey is still categorized as a developing country and is not yet fully industrialized. However, in Turkey's case, the long unchanged low rate, enduring from 1980 to today, is disproportionate to the steep decline, which lasted 25 years. According to the U-shape hypothesis, recovery must take place within a relatively short span of time once industrialization has begun. The implications are that entry into the labour market is interrupted by external variables. The rich literature about the female labour force in Turkey agrees that education is the main determinant of the curve, fuelling FLFPRs. This paper will scrutinize the impact of education on the FLFPR in Turkey. Although Turkish women are better educated than ever, education levels still have not translated into a higher FLFPR.

This study opens with a brief theoretical overview of the U-shape hypothesis. After this brief introduction, the function of the general U-shape hypothesis is presented. A brief literature review follows, examining previous studies about female labour force participation and fitting them into this paper's context. Next, the current FLFPR in Turkey and Turkey's education levels are discussed. The failure of the U-shape hypothesis is portrayed, and the most obvious barriers to re-joining the labour force exposed in the literature are discussed. The following section illustrates the aforementioned vicious cycle. The inconsistencies with Turkey are further revealed, and a new type of theory, an L-shape (instead of a U-shape), is discussed. The research concludes by criticizing the insufficiency of the U-curve hypothesis, namely, that education does not necessarily lead to a higher FLFPR. The paper finally points out factors that need to be considered if the current government wants to achieve a higher FLFPR.

2. The U-shape hypothesis

The U-shape hypothesis was proposed for the first time in 1967 by Sinha[2] and explains the following phenomenon: in a country prior to industrialization, the FLFPR is high. The rate starts to fall with the industrialization process, but then it increases again with the education of the female population. Henceforth, the U-shape hypothesis contends that there is a U-shaped relationship between the level of education (as a consequence of economic development) and women's participation in the labour force. This relationship between the FLFPR and economic development has been well researched, for example, by Goldin (1994), Durand (1975), Pampel and Tanaka (1986) and Schultz (1990)[3].

Figure 1 showsgraphs a typical U-shaped female labour force participation curve. The FLFPR is governed by the national income and the female labour force participation force. The vertical axis provides the FLFPRs, whereas the log of GDP per capita lies on the

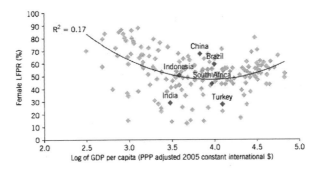

Figure 1. Data for 169 countries showing a U-shaped relationship, that is, a decline and then a rise in female labour force participation as economies develop (2010). Source: International Labour Office, *World of Work Report*, Geneva, 2010.

horizontal axis. By the nature of the curve, developing countries usually lie on the falling slope, whereas developed countries lie on the rising arm.

The following correlations of incidents are responsible for the shape of the U-curve: in regions where agriculture dominates as an economic activity and incomes are low, women account for a very large share of the total labour force, thus presenting high labour force participation rates. This condition represents the starting point of the U-shape on the left-hand side. Women are working mostly in family businesses as unpaid family workers, but still contributing actively to economic activities. With economic development, that is, industrialization, economic activity shifts from home-based production to market-oriented activities.[4] Hence, mass factory production substitutes for family production. The population moves in massive numbers to urban areas, where rising wages seem highly attractive. New technologies are introduced, substituting for manual work, which was previously done mostly by women. In addition, women lack most of the skills which are now required in the new industry, thus hindering them from entering the labour market in urban areas. Consequently, the participation rate of women falls as indicated by the downward slope of the curve.

The rise of the slope results from changes in education levels and their effect on the female population: at times of relatively low income and low male schooling levels, the ratio of male to female education is strikingly high.[5] Increased incomes through economic development reduce the constraints on both male and female education, but female education, especially, rises unusually fast. After this point, Goldin (1994) argues that increased education automatically expands the worker supply for the white-collar sector, and demand and supply continue working in tandem. At higher income levels, the demand for educated workers is greater, and with increased incomes, the supply of female-educated workers expands. Thus, both effects—increased education as well as increased white-collar employment—have a positive impact on the labour force participation rates of women. With economic development, labour reserves are called into use by higher wages, benefitting the unused female labour force.[6] From Goldin's (1994) point of view, there is no social stigma attached to the clerical sector. This means that occupations in offices or sales sectors are generally acceptable forms of employment for women. Accordingly, increased education of women, particularly at the secondary school level, will raise the female share of office and sales employment. The increase will be almost immediate, since these women often take such positions directly after their school years.[7] The U is thereby traced out.

Figure 1 presents a large data-set of countries for 2010 with evidence for a (somewhat weak) U-shape relationship between the log of GDP per capita (in purchasing power parity-adjusted 2005 constant international dollars, a proxy for economic development) and the FLFPR. A few outliers, such as India, China, Brazil and Turkey, can be observed. The outliers India and Turkey have far lower participation rates than most countries at the same income level.

One of the strongest determinants of labour market outcomes in both developed and developing countries is educational attainment. The general consensus is that education is a key factor behind the U-shaped hypothesis: women's education lags behind improvement in educational attainment among men, but once women's education levels catch up with men's and job opportunities emerge, women start to participate in greater numbers. Related to this, Hill found that a significant share of GDP is generated in the agricultural sector in the countries around the falling portion of the slope while in the rising arm agriculture constitutes a low share of the GDP and industrial activities dominate.[8] Another interpretation of the U-shape is that high-income and low-income countries have high FLFPRs, whereas middle-income countries experience low FLFPRs. The FLFPR in the United States provides a very good exemplification of the U-shape theory.[9] With the industrialization era, the FLFPR in the United States experienced a deep fall, but soon recovered in a very steep fashion. Goldin (1994) accounts for the rise of the slope, the incline of which is visually almost congruent to the fall, by citing the major factors of female education overtaking male education and female white-collar employment rising. Secondary school levels will provide women easy access to the white-collar sector. The general argument that social stigma may exist for women and inhibit their entry into the labour market is eliminated in Goldin's research study, thanks to increased education. The validity of this argument as a universal hypothesis in regard to Turkey is challenged in the later parts of this study. Kottis interprets the curve from a supply and demand side of labour.[10] He postulates that the demand for female labour in the market will increase with more dynamic economic development. This will enhance the FLFPR. Boserup works out the downbeat of industrialization, arguing that it marginalizes women in the sense of hindering their participation in work for wages.[11] This interpretation fits into Turkey's framework on female labour force participation. More evidence on education and a positive impact were brought forward by Psacharopoulos and Tzannatos (1989). Using income, age, fertility, religion and education as explanatory variables, they found ambiguous effects, except for the education variable. They came to the conclusion that since controlling the education variable is more efficient than controlling other variables, educational policy should be the first applied in order to increase FLFPRs.

Regarding studies analysing the U-shape in Turkey, Tansel (2002) used time-series evidence and cross-province estimates to outline the relationship between economic development and female labour force participation. Her technique was to estimate four different models by pooling the data of six provinces in Turkey for the years 1980, 1985 and 1990. The regional dummies revealed regional differences, demonstrating significant regional disparities. Tansel's studies revealed that unemployment rate, education, urbanization rate and industrial share make up the main determinants of female labour force participation in Turkey. Unlike Kottis' findings, Tansel's calculations showed that the female illiteracy rate hinders labour force participation.[12] The variable 'education' delivers a different outcome between the two case study countries, despite agriculture being for both of the countries the major employment sector for women. Ince and Demir (2006) provide further evidence for higher female labour force participation given higher education levels.[13] Using time-series regressions with eight indicators, their results lead to the finding that graduates from higher education institutions, particularly, are associated with higher FLFPRs. One year of additional female schooling has a positive impact on the FLFPR. Cultural factors, which play a significant role in society, are ignored in their study. Goksel (2010) investigated the main determinants causing mothers to decide to participate in the labour force in Turkey.[14] She added a new variable, namely, conservatism, and the role of traditional and social norms. Her results led to the conclusion that childcare institutions and education play important roles in the participation of women. Her paper presented new aspects like social norms, religion and men's higher bargaining power. According to her study, all these variables have negative effects on the probability of women working in urban areas. Interestingly, they have opposite effects in rural areas.

In sum, the literature agrees that female labour force participation is fuelled by higher levels of education. Why does the U-shape theory not apply to Turkey? The non-correlation of the factors education–FLFPRs in Turkey asks for a deeper analysis, including other possible external factors specific to the socio-economic structures in Turkey.

3. Labour markets and women in Turkey

Female labour supply is both a driver and an outcome of development. As more women enter the labour force, economies grow faster in response to higher labour inputs. For this reason, policymakers need to understand the nature of women's labour supply and to monitor women's labour force participation. This section of the paper looks at the development and current status of the FLFPR in Turkey. The following section outlines the most specific characteristics of the labour markets in Turkey in relation to the female population.

In Turkey, labour markets are dominated by the services sector. Although male workers continue to dominate the services sector (making up 73 per cent of the sector in 2012), the number of women employed in the services sector doubled between 2004 and 2012, and increased 21 per cent more than the number of men increased.[15]

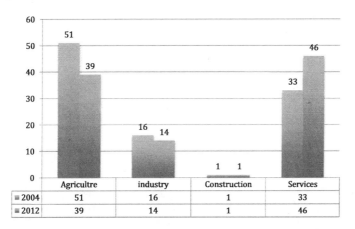

Figure 2. Female employment by sector (per cent): 2004 vs. 2012. Source: TurkStat Labour Force Statistics and TEPAV calculations.

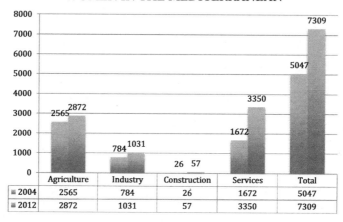

Figure 3. Female economic activity by sector and by selected years (thousands of people, 15+ age). Source: TurkStat Labour Force Statistics.

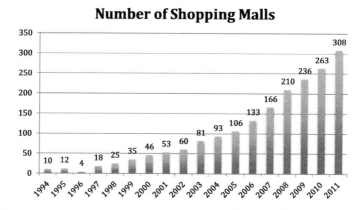

Figure 4. Number of shopping malls in Turkey. Source: Jones Lang LaSalle.

On the basis of aggregate data from 2004 and 2012, Figure 2 provides the percentage share of various sectors in the female labour market. As shown in the figure, in 2012, the female labour market was dominated by the services sector.

Comparing the female economic activity in the four sectors—agriculture, industry, construction and services—these sectors experienced increases of 307,000, 247,000, 31,000 and 1.68 million jobs, respectively, in absolute terms (see Figure 3).

Noteworthy is the fact that Turkey recently experienced a highly significant growth in the number of shopping malls. As shown in Figure 4, whereas the number of shopping malls in Turkey was 53 in 2001, exactly 10 years later, in 2011, the number had reached 308 (of which 144 were located in Anatolia and 258 in Istanbul). The creation of shopping malls establishes an excellent environment in which women can work: most clients in the malls tend to be women, and the positions in malls present a formidable way for these women to socialize. Moreover, shopping malls can be very appealing to women as places in which to work, as they present a relatively secure and safe environment. In addition, working in a shopping mall may be regarded by society as more prestigious compared to other low-paid jobs, for example, cleaning. Ultimately, the exponential increases in the number of shopping malls may in theory add up to the FLFPR in Turkey. In order to support this assumption, it would be interesting to conduct further research on the distribution of male and female workers in shopping malls.

The growing trend concerning shopping malls coincides with the growing number of women working in occupations such as wholesale and food services. Looking at service sector jobs more closely, women have outpaced men in growth rates in all of the categories. The most dramatic growth in terms of number of jobs has been in wholesale & retail trade and in accommodation & food service activities. The highest growth rate in female employment, however, has been in administrative & support service activities. The number of positions held by women in public administration (generally deemed safe) grew by 71 per cent compared to 18 per cent for men.[16]

A major issue in the labour market is the underrepresentation of females in the skilled sector. Males continue to be disproportionately represented in higher-end positions (i.e. as legislators, senior officials and managers, professionals, etc.). A study done by the non-governmental organization (NGO) KAGIDER (2012) points to the underrepresentation of women in decision-making positions. For instance, only 23 per cent of women make up boards of the largest listed companies, and the proportion of women presidents of the largest publicly quoted companies is only 12 per cent.[17]

Moreover, another issue in the Turkish labour market is the large size of informal work. In their study, Uraz et al. (2010) emphasized how informal work remains high, particularly among women in Turkey, with 66 per cent of female employment being unregistered employment (compared to 34 per cent for men). The proportion of women employed informally decreased from 71 per cent in 2003 to 66 per cent in 2006. At the same time, as of 2003, 48.3 per cent of women employed in Turkey worked as unpaid family workers. In 2006, this level had gone down by 10 percentage points to 38.3 per cent. In the same time period, this trend was accompanied by an increase in the percentage of employment—discouraged female workers in the population from 0.6 to 4.6 per cent.[18]

The fact that most of the women in Turkey are largely employed in the services sector[19] may in fact be further discouraging women from working. However, this argument is still not sufficient to explain the lack of impact of the 'improved' education levels on the FLFPR. The FLFPR for female university graduates has indeed increased, but how is it that this has no effect at all on the aggregate level of the FLFPR?

3.1. The development of the FLFPR curve in Turkey until 2000

Figure 5 shows the FLFPR in the period 2000–2012. During a time span of over 12 years, the FLFPR in Turkey, overall, had increased by only 4.6 per cent, with a very minor, though noticeable, change after 2009–2010. Inan and Asık (2015) agreed in their study that 'the U-shaped pattern generally relates to the relationship of female labour force participation rates to the process of economic development', and they further stated in that study that 'economic growth and development dynamics in the Turkish context are too complex and insufficient to explain the changing patterns of FLFP'.

It was only shortly after 2008 that a slight increase was noticeable, with a peak of 29.5 per cent for the first time in post-industrialization history. Obviously, these numbers are still far below average, and remain incompatible with the proportionately high rises in educational levels. It can be said that it is still too early for this minor change to project an optimistic forecast. Thus, if further increases in the FLFPR are desired, scholars need to determine why the rates are still at only 29 per cent as of 2014.

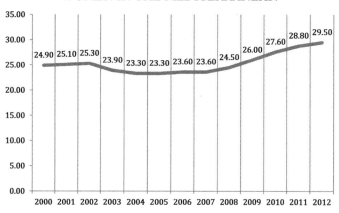

Figure 5. Female labour force participation rate, 2000–2012 (Turkey, urban, rural). Source: TurkStat Labour Force Statistics.

According to the U-shape hypothesis, the curve must have been declining since the beginning of the industrialization era in the 1960s. The explanation for the fall, the downward slope, is in accordance with the U-shape hypothesis. Women, who made up the main workforce in agriculture before 1960, experienced a fall in their labour force participation due to the shift of labour composition in the cities. A major reason was that jobs in the cities could not accommodate the almost 100 per cent workforce from agriculture. Secondly, as the following part of this paper will show, women in the 1960s fell far behind their male counterparts regarding educational attainment. The often-suggested argument that Turkey might still be on the downward-sloping part of the curve[20] is invalid for several reasons. Firstly, according to the U-shape hypothesis, the falling arm of the slope has the following characteristics: it lies in the initial stages of economic development, and more importantly, female education at that time lagged significantly behind male education. Neither of these two conditions is entirely true regarding the present situation in Turkey (Turkey is not a newly industrialized country, and female educational levels have not increased, as will be shown). Secondly, according to the theory, the climax of the fall lasts for a relatively short period. In Turkey, however, it has lasted now for over 40 years; although a continuing but minimal increase can be observed after 2008, it may be still too early to speak of ground-breaking changes regarding female employment in Turkey.

In regard to the coming decades, how realistic is it to expect a steeper decrease? As Turkey represents an outlier, what kind of conditions must be met in order to meet the demands of the U-curve hypothesis—the correlation of education and FLFPRs? According to the current status, the upward slope is still lacking. Does this mean that the education levels of women in Turkey have not improved at all? The next section scrutinizes the educational attainments of Turkish women in recent decades in order to answer that question.

4. Educational attainment of women in Turkey since 1960

Education as an economic good was discussed for the first time in the theory of human capital.[21] A greater level of education—which is in practical terms the development of skills—is a leading factor in contributing to high labour productivity and aggregate growth

Table 1. Number and ratio of secondary and tertiary level graduates in Turkey: 1960–2000.

Year	Education Gender	High school Male	High school Female	Ratio (M/F)	Vocational school Male	Vocational school Female	Ratio (M/F)	University Male	University Female	Ratio (M/F)
1960/61		8649	3328	2.6	17,974	5533	3.3	4864	1161	4.2
1965/66		18,257	6611	2.7	24,247	9361	2.6	8127	2484	3.3
1970/71		31,860	13,818	2.3	34,292	18,860	1.8	18,440	4416	4.2
1975/76		57,911	30,738	1.9	53,949	34,465	1.6	23,069	7789	3
1980/81		64,335	44,795	1.4	69,027	32,213	2.1	23,319	8522	2.7
1985/86		71,942	60,068	1.2	90,845	37,848	2.4	37,700	20,148	1.9
1990/91		161,283	128,246	1.3	135,250	73,442	1.8	54,461	29,394	1.9
1995/96		159,113	137,717	1.3	149,060	86,354	1.7	84,702	64,428	1.3
2000/01		155,696	133,604	1.2	146,384	96,818	1.5	133,781	100,400	1.3

Source: Own calculations/processed from 'Turkish Statistical Institute: Statistical Indicators 1923–2008'.

in the entire nation.[22] Education is thus an input in skill and leads directly to an increase in the labour force, see Talani, this issue. Henceforth, it can be said that the greater the amount of educational attainment, the more skilled, knowledgeable and productive people in society there will be.[23]

In order to answer the question of whether women in Turkey possess the necessary skills to enter the (skilled) labour market, an assessment of their educational background will be appropriate. In the following section, women's educational advancement will be portrayed and compared to that of their male counterparts. The general assumption is that the higher the supply of educated people, the higher the labour force participation rates.

As a prominent characteristic of most developing countries, access to education was not equal for both genders before industrialization.[24] Table 1 gives the change in the male–female ratios[25] in both secondary and tertiary levels of education. The ratio in 1960 reveals that men in Turkey graduated from high school at almost three times the rate as women. It was after the 1970s that the difference between male and female high school graduates started to gradually narrow. Girls' education continued to increase faster than boys'. The ratio reached 1.2 by 2000. In other words, males graduated from high school only 1.2 times more in 2000 in contrast to 2.6 in 1960.

As for vocational and technical schools, in 2000 women were still a third behind male graduates. However, the gap has narrowed significantly over the years.

Tertiary education delivers the most skilled labour. On a comparative basis, university levels increased the most for girls. Whereas the male–female ratio was 4.2 in 1960, it shrunk significantly and constantly to 1.3 in 2000. From 1960 to 2000, the supply of female skilled labour increased exponentially, as can be seen from the table. In their studies, Dayıoglu and Kırdar (2009) provide similar findings, namely, that the share of women with a university education increased from 1.8 per cent in 1988 to 4.3 per cent in 2000, and to 5.8 per cent in 2006. Whereas the proportion of female university graduates almost tripled between 1988 and 2006, the proportion for men only doubled.[26] Based on these results, a report by the State Planning Organization (SPO) from 2009 agreed that 'educational attainment has been improving in Turkey, especially for women'.[27]

Figure 6 illustrates the drop in the male–female ratios for the three school types. In 1960, the average ratio for the three school types on the vertical axis was 3.3 but decreased gradually to slightly above 1 in 2000, almost converging with the educational attainment of the male population.

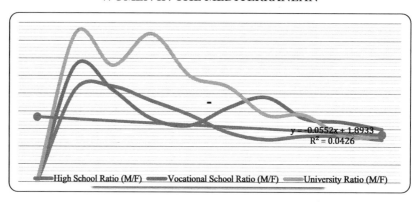

Figure 6. Male–female ratio of secondary and tertiary graduates, Turkey: 1960–2000. Source: Own calculations.

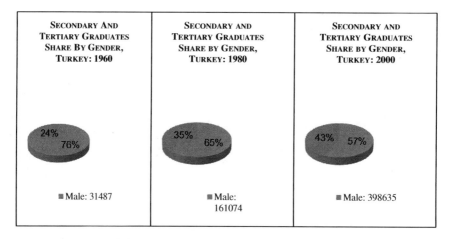

Figure 7. Secondary and tertiary school graduates over time divided by gender, Turkey: 1960–2000 (secondary level includes high school and vocational school education levels). Source: Own calculations.

The total share of secondary and tertiary female graduates has converged significantly with the male's share compared to the 1960s and 1980s data (high school and vocational school). Female students shared in all three educational attainments and improved significantly from 24 to 43 per cent, which is almost evenly balanced to half and half. This numerical increase complies with the theoretical literature, namely, female education increases much faster than male education with economic development (Figure 7).[28]

Recent literature commonly argues that attainment in higher education levels for 'urban' women is still very low[29] and this is the cause behind the low FLFPR. Although this may be true, still, it is not sufficient to explain the conundrum of why improved education levels in Turkey on an aggregate level have not had any positive impact at all on the FLFPR.

The most important conclusion to be drawn from this analysis is that female education has increased rapidly over the last decades. It increased at a much faster rate than did male education, which leads to the conclusion that the gap between the genders has narrowed significantly. Although it may still not have reached optimum enrolment rates, Inan and Asık (2015) claim that only small portions of the female population reach higher education

Table 2. Distribution of labour force by education, urban areas, Turkey.

Educational attainment	Labour force in 1988 (%)	Labour force in 2000 (%)	Labour force in 2006 (%)
High school	19.3	21.1	15.8
Vocational school	7.7	10.3	12
University	12.9	26.5	28.5

Source: Processed from Dayioglu and Kirdar (2009).

Table 3. Female labour force participation by educational profile, 2012.

	Inactive (%)	In labour force (%)	Total (%)	In labour force/total (%)
Illiterate	9.2	1.7	10.9	16
No diploma	14.2	3.1	17.4	18
Primary (5 years)	29.8	9.2	39.1	24
Secondary and vocational secondary (8 years)	9.6	2.5	12.1	21
Regular high school	5.8	2.5	8.3	30
Vocational or technical school	3.1	1.9	5	28
Tertiary, higher education or above	2.2	5.1	7.3	69

Source: TurkStat Labour Force Statistics and TEPAV calculations.

levels, especially in urban areas. Based on the results above, Turkish women are significantly better educated today than they were in 1960. By 2000, their education level had almost converged with the male education level. The implications of this advancement for the labour market are a substantial increase in the relative supply of skilled female workers. Next, it is interesting to scrutinize the impact of these educational attainments on the FLFPR in Turkey. Ttable 2 provides an interesting insight.

Whereas the female labour force participation of university graduates was relatively low in 1988, compared to that of high school graduates, by the year 2000, the participation of university graduates was the only category in which female labour force participation increased significantly, namely, from 12.9 to 26.5 per cent. By 2006, almost 20 years since 1988, university leavers almost doubled their rate of female labour force participation, reaching 28.5 per cent. High school leavers dropped to 15.8 per cent for urban areas.

One possible explanation behind this non-linear change may be that the higher the education of the female, the lesser the presence of social stigma in urban areas for women working outside the informal sectors. Bulutay confirmed that female university graduates were more open minded and less affected by constraints arising from social norms.[30] Thus, negative impacts of perceptions and conservatism in society decreased with education.[31] The figures shown in Table 3 lead to a similar interpretation.

At first glance, one may agree, as is commonly argued, that those with higher educational levels have a higher FLFPR. As is evident from the figures in Table 3, the better-educated portion of the total sample exhibits a higher participation rate. Particularly, higher levels of education matter more for women than for men; 22 per cent of women with a college education are employed compared to 16.5 per cent of men. A larger share of women with a tertiary education has a paid job (20.7 per cent) compared to men (14.1 per cent). On an aggregate level, however, this has no effect on the total sum of the FLFPRs. The U-curve is still not traced out, and the FLFPRs in Turkey are still far below the global average. In addition, it is interesting to ask why those portions with non-university backgrounds are more resistant in joining the labour market compared to their male counterparts, and also especially if the service sector constitutes the greater share of the labour market.

The following conclusions can be drawn: the education levels for girls have improved in Turkey significantly, almost converging with those of men by 2000. Although some sources still claim that in terms of university degrees, women remain far behind men, particularly in urban areas, other sources show how women are almost equal to men on an aggregate level, and education in Turkey has improved immensely. In any case, the supply of skilled female labour has increased along with the education levels. Moreover, female education improved much faster, relatively, than men's education. The main point of concern is why the increase has no positive effect on the FLFPRs. Why are women in Turkey still not well represented in the labour market? The causality that education alone leads to higher female labour force participation seems less valid for Turkey. Additionally, the claim that education fuels FLFPRs does not seem fully justified. Evidently, some inhibitors exist that cause the flat right-wing slope (rather than upward) in the U-curve. The next section discusses the possible constraints.

5. Constraints on Turkish women entering the labour market

5.1. Gender differences in earnings

The neoclassical theory of allocation of time proposes an explanation for the labour supply decision of individuals along the following lines: time is valued according to preferences that maximize the utility of the individual. Comparing the values of time spent in the labour market with the values of time spent on non-market activities, individuals decide to participate or not. Participation depends on the higher value of the activities. The value of market activities depends on the prevailing wage rate while the value of non-market activities is determined by the tastes and preferences of the individual as well as by the demands placed on an individual's non-market time, such as number of children and dependants in the family, and non-market income of women. Since women are primarily expected to be homemakers and caretakers, the reservation wage for the value at home has been high for women, restricting the participation of women in the labour market.[32]

Consequently, one of the most important results of gender discrimination in the Turkish labour market is the wage differential between men and women. Even within major occupational groups significant pay gaps exist (hierarchical segregation). The largest wage gaps are observed for 'plant and machine operators, assemblers' and for 'professionals'. The only occupational group where women were at an advantage regarding wage levels compared to men was at managerial positions, but very few women reach managerial positions. Furthermore, the gender pay gap takes education into account. Wages rise with the level of education for both men and women. However, the return to education is higher for men than for women. Hisarcıklılar and Ercan's research implies that the wage gap between men and women is not due to women's respective human capital levels but to their differential treatment.[33] Uraz et al. (2010) point out that there is a large gap in hourly earnings between low-skilled men and women in Turkey, underlining that this gap is not observable for highly skilled workers. The hourly earnings for low-skilled men in urban areas is 1.4–1.5 times that of hourly mean earnings for women, while for high-skilled men and women in urban areas the difference in hourly wages remains insignificant. The earning potential from available jobs for women with low skills is particularly low.[34] Uraz et al. underline that another aspect that needs to be considered is the opportunity cost of working in urban and rural areas. If in urban areas, the opportunity cost of working for women is high (with low availability of day-care options for children and the inability to share responsibilities with extended family members on household chores), the probability rises that women with lower earnings will choose to stay home rather than take low-paid jobs. In other words, the earning potentials for low-skilled women in urban areas may not be 'high enough' in Turkey to justify them leaving home for work.[35] This observation may explain the lower participation rates in the services sector of women compared to men. It would be interesting to analyse this hypothesis further with qualitative data.

5.2. Marriages and their negative consequence on FLFPRs

A further condition, which may hold back women from entering the job market, is related to a 'life event'—getting married. A recent report prepared by the SPO in Turkey, in collaboration with the World Bank, states that 'marriage seems to be a strong determinant for FLFP'.[36] The SPO found that in urban areas, married women are less likely to participate in the labour market than are single women for the corresponding age groups. According to the study, married women aged 25–29 display very low participation rates. Single women in the same age bracket have much higher participation rates, at 60 per cent. The participation gap diminishes at later ages as women with a high propensity to work get married. In another report conducted by the SPO in Turkey, Uraz *et al.* (2010) found that women who are currently not working (and who are between the ages of 20 and 65 years old) overwhelmingly stated 'being a housewife' or taking care of children as the main reason for not working. Of the women in the working age group who have ever been married, 58 per cent stated 'being a housewife' as a reason for not working, while 9 per cent stated 'taking care of children' as the reason for not working. Only 6 per cent of those who are currently not working are looking for jobs, hence indicating the low rate of 'undesired' unemployment among women.[37] For men in the same age group, the story is quite different: of the men in the same age group who are currently not working, 32 per cent 'do not have a job and are looking for a job'; 28 per cent are 'retired'; and 12 per cent are 'handicapped/sick or too old to work'.[38]

So why do Turkish women not re-enter the labour market once they get married? The observation of strikingly low numbers of kindergartens and lack of other childcare facilities may provide a plausible answer. Marriage, most often, entails childbirth. Regarding childcare facilities, public provision of daily childcare in Turkey is very low[39] with only a very small percentage of children aged 0–3 in formal day-care or crèche facilities and only half of all children aged 4–5 taking part in preschool education (about 90 per cent of these are receiving education in state schools, and four out of five of them are in nursery classes attached to primary schools).[40] This may indeed present a serious barrier to the re-entry of married women (with children) into the labour market. Uraz *et al.* (2010) drew the following conclusion from their study, namely, that pregnancy and childbirth were associated with lower probabilities of women working in Turkey.[41] Their studies also tested the correlation between having an additional woman in the household (above the age of 20 and who could act as a carer for children) and labour force participation and found that having such a person in the household is associated with a 4 per cent increase in the probability of women working in the overall sample.

5.3. Social norms

Walby pointed out that factors such as patriarchy or culture are determinants for the women's labour supply, affecting it negatively.[42] Hence, whether women will work or not is not their own decision. Rather, it is influenced by external factors within a society. This is also mostly true for Turkey. In Turkey, the social norm in society is such that people believe that women should stay at home and take care of the house, as confirmed by various studies.[43] Thus, women are less likely to find access to jobs. In addition, the nature of industry or factories is a strong determinant.[44] Much of the manual work was considered at that time as typically 'male work'. Other sectors such as the textile sector were almost exclusively occupied by female workers, due to a sense of safer work atmosphere. However, sectors that were acceptable for women were very limited. A plethora of studies have explored the reasons Turkish women do not participate in the labour force. The women's role as wives and mothers is the most important factor influencing the woman's labour supply decision in urban areas.[45] This is an indicator of the high value of non-market activities for women in Turkey.

6. Educated but trapped: the underutilization of human capital

Irrefutably, the course of economic development can be affected by social norms. Evidently, despite the increase of educational levels, the FLFPRs in Turkey have remained unchanged for the last 40 years. The large differences in wages, the strong existence of the informal sector, which provides a pull factor for Turkish women, as well as the substantial lack of childcare facilities may all present barriers for Turkish women, even educated women, to take up employment. These external factors may well explain the unchanged FLFPR in Turkey. Figure 8 shows the conditions and givens in the socio-economic sphere as outlined above and illustrates their interrelation. A vicious cycle emerges, explained as follows: Turkish women seek education, with the hope or intention of finding employment opportunities, however, they are inhibited from entering the labour market through external barriers. Hence, they remain an untapped potential. The curve is an L-shape, instead of a U-shape.

Figure 8 shows the cycles and interrelation of the factors in a progress chain. The flow of the cycle can be explained as follows: educational attainment for women improves as a result of economic development. Economic progress enables women to attend school and university. Upon graduation, instead of following the norm and joining the employment sector, Turkish women face constraints due to the given norms in their culture as well as to other external factors. Therefore, they are not free now to make their decision, but are limited by unattractive wages in the services sector or even by a lack of childcare facilities. Turkish women face substantial differences in wage gaps, as compared to men, and this can greatly discourage them from entering the job market. Secondly, society's traditions or cultural values predetermine a woman's work environment, which is mostly pre-set in the informal (or low-skilled sector), regardless of her educational background. The low-skilled sector is often restricted to jobs in services or retail. The (urban) informal sector as a primary source of employment for women rather than for men is valid for many developing countries.[46] The downside is that these jobs are mostly low paid and frequently have no health insurance or skill requirements.[47] The higher the wage rate, the more attractive work becomes.[48] Informal employment includes all remuneration work, both self-employment and wage employment, that is not recognized, regulated or protected by the existing legal or regulatory framework, and non-remunerative work undertaken in an income-producing

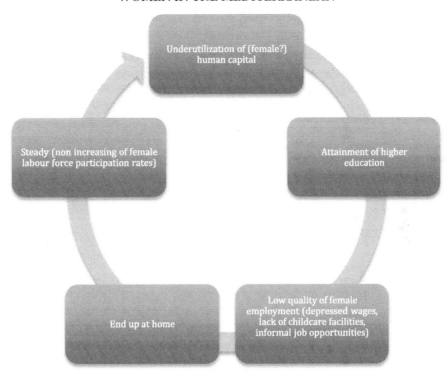

Figure 8. The underutilization cycle. Source: Own derivation.

enterprise. Most informal workers, including both self-employed and wage-workers, are deprived of secure work, workers' benefits, social protection and representation or voice. They are still accepted because they contribute to growth. Even though the average earnings of women in the informal sector are low, the female informal workforce contributes significantly to the GDP,[49] which might be also regarded as explanatory for the strong existence of this sector. Goksel (2010) notes that social norms against women working means employers set lower wages for females and female returns to education are therefore lower.[50] Educated women, that is, especially women with secondary education backgrounds, very often find themselves in the predetermined sectors. Basically, they are not employed by education, but by social norms. Henceforth, their 'skills' are underutilized. The few women who obtain managerial positions or similar white-collar jobs are generally less affected or not affected at all by the social stigma. This may also explain the relatively higher FLFPR for women from the tertiary education levels (with university degrees). Men, for instance, do take skilled jobs after secondary education since they do not experience the same constraints as women do and find it easier to move around within the labour market. Their employment field has no restrictions, which in turn may indeed have a highly positive impact on the male labour force participation rates. Thirdly, the latest studies on the FLFPR in Turkey reveal the extremely limited number of childcare facilities in Turkey. In linkage to this limited access to childcare, the FLFPR decreases once Turkish women get married. All these factors added together present barriers to women entering the labour market.

Education is universally associated with better life quality and prospects for more freedom in better work. Thus, better education opportunities will always be passed down to

WOMEN IN THE MEDITERRANEAN

children. If the aforementioned characteristics, which may be considered as hindrances to opportunities, continue to exist, then a vicious cycle evolves, and although women get educated, they are unable to translate their skills into economic activities. They remain caught in the cycle. Rather than a U-curve, the shape remains an L, as explained in the following section.

7. The L-shape hypothesis

Turkey, as stated in the beginning of this paper, is an outlier when it comes to the U-shape hypothesis. The previous section described how Turkish women are trapped in a vicious cycle, despite being relatively well educated.

From a purely economic perspective, according to the U-shape theory, in an optimal condition, the slope is supposed to increase with the provision of more skilled labour (through more education). In suboptimal levels, such as in Turkey, the rise of the slope is not causally related to economic development/increase in the GDP. Hence, the line will remain an L-shape, as is the case in Turkey. Figure 9 illustrates the curve according to the level of skill on the vertical axis and advancement in education on the horizontal axis.

The figure can be divided into two periods, namely, before and after economic development. The fact that the FLFPR was high before the industrialization era does not mean that women then were more educated and thus possessed the right skills. Rather, with economic progress together with industrialization, the nature of 'skill' changed. What it means to be 'skilled' is entirely different today; the ability to do farm work, for example, no longer qualifies an individual as competitive in the job market. Industrialization, the introduction of machinery and new technology, required new types of skills. Education is henceforth essential as it can be seen as a 'tool' that translates agricultural workers into urban workers.

The L-shaped line can be interpreted as follows: before industrialization, female labour force participation was high because women were fully employed in the agricultural sector. Over time, the country underwent economic development and in the later stages, education for the female population began to catch up with the male population.[51] According to the U-shape hypothesis, as soon as female education started to improve, the slope of the curve was supposed to rise, since more skilled female workers were available to fill the demand of the newly emerged, more technology-based labour market. Both of these conditions are met in Turkey's case: Turkey underwent an industrialization period; new labour markets emerged in the urban areas and education improved at the same time. All these factors are applicable for Turkey. However, what results is that education does not translate into a higher FLFPR in Turkey, and the FLFPR is disrupted by other external factors. The shift from the

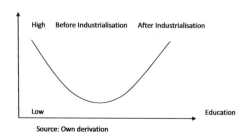

Figure 9. Female labour force participation curve according to skills and education. Source: Own derivation.

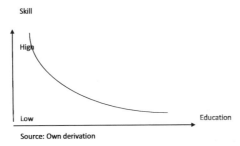

Figure 10. The L-shape curve. Source: Own derivation.

high levels of agricultural work to high levels of employment in urban areas is lacking and does not take place. Conclusively, the slope does not rise, but remains an L-shape (Figure 10).

8. Concluding remarks: untapped potential

This study has examined the U-shape hypothesis and then analysed its position in the framework of the Turkish labour market. The following conclusions can be drawn: in terms of the theoretical framework, the U-shape hypothesis is highly questionable. Although it may provide some (weak) evidence for some countries in the world, it is not sufficient to explain the FLFPR across all economies. Hence, the generalization of the U-shape theory is highly questionable. Regarding its applicability to Turkey, the first part of the curve in Turkey complies with the U-shape theory. The second part, however, is not compatible and is out of harmony with the U-shape hypothesis.

Education does not, necessarily, translate into a higher FLFPR among women in Turkey. Factors such as wage gap, attractiveness of the working sectors for women, social stigma and even childcare facilities play an immense role when women want to enter the job market. Once these restrictive factors in entering the labour market exist, no correlation can be traced between increased education levels and labour force participation. Also noteworthy is the finding that higher educational attainment leads to higher FLFPRs, as some of the hindrances are eliminated (such as social stigma), however, not all barriers are fully eliminated, such as the lack of childcare facilities, which seems to make a significant difference. One argument that may speak in favour of the U-shape hypothesis is that Turkey is not a fully developed economy yet, and so the fruits of the rise in education levels are still to be earned. This is a highly optimistic forecast. Although it may come to be true, the probability is still low as long as the so-called 'barriers' are not addressed. In addition, a counter-argument that follows is that the low periods of the FLFPR have lasted for too long already. The bottom line is that, no matter what, the labour force levels of women significantly influence the level of economic development. Given that skilled labour is a global scarcity, Turkey, as well as other countries with low FLFPRs, suffers from a double loss, as its human capital remains untapped 'gold'. It is thus highly recommended that one understand that education alone does not lead to a higher FLFPR, as suggested by the U-shape hypothesis, but other criteria must also be fulfilled if there is to be a positive impact on education. As long as the factors hindering the socio-economic structure in Turkey are not addressed, the FLFPR will continue to remain an L-shape instead of turning into a U-shape, leading to a loss of highly valuable human capital in Turkey.

Disclosure statement

No potential conflict of interest was reported by the author.

Notes

1. M. Dayioglu and M. G. Kirdar, *Determinants of and Trends in Labour Force Participation of Women in Turkey*, Middle Eastern Technical University, Ankara, 2009.
2. Sinha noted such a U-shape pattern in the cross section of female standardized activity rates from censuses taken around 1950, compiled by the United Nations.
3. C. Goldin, 'The U-shaped female labor force function in economic development and economic history', NBER Working Paper Series, No. 4707, 1994, p. 7; J. D. Durand, *The Labor Force in Economic Development*, Princeton University Press, 1975; F. C. Pampel and K. Tanaka, 'Economic Development and Female Labor Force Participation: A Reconsideration', *Social Forces*, 64(3): 599–619, 1986; T. P. Schultz, 'Women's Changing Participation in the Labor Force: A World Perspective', *Economic Development and Cultural Change*, 38: 457–488, 1990.
4. A. Tansel, 'Economic development and female labor force participation in Turkey: time series evidence and cross-province estimates', ERC Working Papers in Economics, 2002.
5. Goldin, op. cit., p. 7.
6. G. Psacharopoulos and Z. Tzannatos, 'Female labor force participation: an international perspective', *The World Bank Research Observer*, 4(2), July 1989, pp. 187–201, p. 192.
7. Goldin, op. cit., p. 13.
8. M. A. Hill, 'Female Labor Force Participation in Developing and Developed Countries', *Review of Economics and Statistics*, 65: 459–467, 1983.
9. Ibid.
10. A.P. Kottis, 'Shifts Over Time and Regional Variation in Women's Labor Force Participation Rates in a Developing Economy', *Journal of Development Economics*, 33: 117–132, 1990.
11. E. Boserup, *Women's Role in Economic Development*, New York: St. Martin's Press, 1970.
12. Kottis, op.cit., pp. 117–132.
13. M. Ince and H. D. Demir, 'The Determinants of Labor Force: Empirical Evidence from Turkey', *Eskisehir Osmangazi Universitesi IIBF Journal*, April 2006, Vol. 1 (1), pp. 71–90. 2006.
14. I. Goksel, Conservatism and Female Labor Force Participation in Turkey, *IUE Department of Economics Working Paper Series*, 2010.
15. F. Inan and G. Asık, *Making Economies Work for Women: Female Labour Force Participation in Turkey*, Tepav, Ankara, 2015.
16. See ibid. for a more detailed analysis.
17. KAGIDER (Women Entrepreneurs Association of Turkey), *Status of Women in Turkey: Existing Situation and Policy Proposals*, Ankara, 20–21 December 2012.
18. A. Uraz, M. Aran, M. Hüsamoğlu, D. O. Şanalmış, S. Çapar, *Recent Trends in Female Labor Force Participation in Turkey*, State Planning Organization of the Republic of Turkey and World Bank, Ankara, 2010.
19. E.g. Inan and Asık, op. cit.
20. E.g. Tansel, op. cit.
21. G. Becker, 'A theory of allocation of time', *Economic Journal*, 75, 1965, pp. 493–517.
22. Ibid.
23. Ibid.
24. Goldin, op. cit.
25. The number who were male times 100, divided by the number who were female.

26. Dayıoglu and Kırdar, op. cit.
27. State Planning Organization (SPO), *Female Labor Force Participation in Turkey: Trends, Determinants, and Policy Framework*, T. R. Prime Minister, SPO and World Bank, 23 November 2009, p. 7.
28. E.g. Goldin, op. cit.; Ince and Demir, op. cit.
29. SPO, op. cit.
30. T. Bulutay, *Kadın Istihdamı*, DIE, Ankara, September, 2002
31. Goksel op. cit., 2000, p. 15.
32. For more information on the theory, see F. D. Blau, M. A. Ferber and A. E. Winkler, *The Economics of Women, Men, and Work*, 3rd edn, Prentice Hall, London, 1998, pp. 86–111.
33. M. Hısarcıklılar and H. Ercan, 'Gender Based Wage Differentials in Turkey', *Bilgi Sosyal Bilimler Dergisi*, 10, 45–62, 2005.
34. Uraz *et al.*, op. cit.
35. Ibid.
36. SPO, op. cit.
37. Ibid.
38. Ibid.
39. Uraz *et al.*, op. cit.
40. UNICEF, Annual report for Turkey, CEE/CIS, 2012.
41. 'A woman who is currently pregnant is 8% less likely to be working, controlling for all else, and a woman with one child below the age of 5 is 6% less likely to be working compared to a married woman with no children' (Uraz *et al.*, op. cit., p. 10).
42. S. Walby, 'Methodological and Theoretical Issues in the Comparative Analysis of gender Relations in Western Europe'. *Environment and Planning*, 26, 1339–1354. 1/05, 1994.
43. Such as I. Goksel, Determinants of Demand for Education In Turkey, Working Paper, 2009; Tansel, op. cit. or Goksel 2010, op. cit.
44. Women are known for being well represented in the textile sector, but less so in male-intensive industries like mining, iron and steel.
45. Ş. Özar and G. Günlük-Senesen, 'Determinants of female (non-)participation in the urban labour force in Turkey', *METU Studies in Development*, 25(2), 1998, pp. 311–328.
46. E.g. M. A. Chen, 'A global picture, the global movement', *SAIS Review*, 1(1), 2001, pp. 71–82 and International Labour Office (ILO), *Decent work and the Informal Economy*, Geneva, 2002.
47. A. Bugra, 'The Turkish welfare regime in transformation', *Journal of European Social Policy*, 16, 2006, pp. 211–228, p. 207.
48. Psacharopoulos and Tzannatos, op. cit., p. 190.
49. Chen, op. cit.
50. Tansel, op. cit., states that this is indeed the case in the private sector in Turkey.
51. The trend in the previous section proved the significant and positive change of female education.

Index

Note: **Boldface** page numbers refer to tables and italic page numbers refer to figures. Page numbers followed by "n" denote endnotes.

Abduh, Muhammad 10
adult literacy *47*
Afshar, Haleh 34, 38n32
Agamben, Giorgio 104–6
Agenda for Sustainable Development 74
Age of Rights, The (Bobbio) 8
AHDR *see* Arab Human Development Report
alam 9
al-Banna, Hassan 52, 54, 55
al Haddad, Tahir 10
almaniyya 9
al-Nahda movement 9, 17, 18
Amin, Qasim 10
Amor, Abdelfattah 4
An-Na'im, Abdullahi 13, 17
Anwar, Zainah 5
Anwendung 35
Arab Human Development Report (AHDR) 41, 47, 53
'Arab Spring' countries 72
Arab world 41, 44; knowledge dissemination processes 47; literacy rates *48*; lower literacy levels 47
Arendt, Hannah 87, 98, 101, 103, 104
Asık, G. 120–1
Ausübung 35
autochthonous feminist 9, 24
Ayubi's conceptualization 51

Badran, Margot 5, 8, 11, 14, 15, 17, 20n12
Balchin, Cassandra 29, 31, 37n22
Belli, Alessia 2
Benhabib, Seyla 26, 103, 104
'biopolitics' 105
Blangiardo, Gian Carlo 83, 91n5
Boltanski, Luc 84
Boserup, E. 114, 128n11
Bourdieu, P 49
Bulutay, T. 121, 129n30
Butler, Judith 33, 104

Castoriadis, Cornelius 83, 84
catastrophe: contamination and 86; notion of 85–6; victimhood and 88
Chouliaraki, Lilie 84, 92n19
citizenship, Greek policies 98, 102–3
civil society: in faith-based organizations active 50; Gramsci conceptualized 49; idea of 49; internal value of 50; Islam and 51–8; re-Islamization of 51; role of 61n80; social cohesion of 50
Civil Society Facility (CSF) 72
Clark, J. 54
Clash of Civilizations (Huntington) 25
Coleman, J. 49
colonialism 5–7, 26
Constantine, Greg 97
CSF *see* Civil Society Facility
cultural diversity, feminist approach to 2, 35

Dayioglu, M. 119
'Declaration of Solidarity' 87
Declaration of the Rights of Man and of the Citizen (1789) 16
'deconstructive strategy' 23–4
de facto statelessness 100–1
de jure stateless 100
Demir, H. D. 115, 128n13
democracy 25, 83; mobility challenges 90–1
demos, constitution of 83
Deveaux, M. 34
Dicken, P. 41

Ebadi, Shirin 18
economic migrant 86–7
educational attainment, of women 118, 122; distribution of labour force **121**; female university graduates 121; male-female ratios 119, **119**, *120*; secondary and tertiary female graduates 120; State Planning Organization report 119; tertiary education 119; U-shaped female participation curve 114
EED *see* European Endowment for Democracy

INDEX

Egypt 44, 45, 48, 52; case of 54–5; Islamic medical clinics in 54; Jamma Islamiyya 56; Muslim Brotherhood 55, 56; re-Islamization of 53
Egyptian Feminist Union (UFE) 11, 29n21
Elimination of All Forms of Discrimination against Women 71
'emergency Lampedusa' 89
'emergency' of immigration 81, 85
ENP *see* European Neighbourhood Policy
Enric, Miray 3
Ercan, H. 122
EU *see* European Union
Euro-Mediterranean Partnership 79n34
European Commission 74
European Council 79n38
European Endowment for Democracy (EED) 72–3
European External Action Service 74
European Institute for Gender Equality 67
Europeanization, concept of 67, 78n1
European Neighbourhood Policy (ENP) 2, 65; actor-centred approach 73; analysis of 74; Barcelona Process 71; elite-driven process 76; financial crisis 72; flexibility of 65; and gender mainstreaming 69–74; give-and-take bargaining process 70; implementation of 71; international human rights 71; 'joint ownership' 70; Optional Protocol 71; revisions 72; tailor-made policy 65; terrorism 74
European Union (EU) 68, 111; absorption of 69; finance gender policies 74; Gender Action Plan 73; gender equality law 64, 78n5; gender mainstreaming 65; gender strategy 2; law, fundamental principles of 66; Lisbon Treaty 66; Ministers of Foreign Affairs 71; narrow perspectives 64; neighbourhood policies 73; new framework 75; policy strategy for 66; political-legal constitution 64, 67–8; relationship 70; securitization, concept of 80n42; structural foreign policy 68; Treaty of Amsterdam, Article 141 66; Treaty of Rome, Article 119 66; women's empowerment 65–6; women's rights 71
European West, cultural heritage of 6

female education 3, 112, 113, 118, 120, 122
female labour force participation rate (FLFPR) 3, 111, 112, 120, 124, 125, 127; by educational profile **121**; evidence for 115; marriages and negative consequence on 123; in Turkey 115; in 2000–2012 *117,* 117–18; in United States 114
female mobility 82–3
feminine conscience 10, 11, 14
fluid identity, concept of 2, 32–3
Foucault, Michel 83; 'biopolitics' concept 105
Friese, Heidrun 3
Frontex (European border agency) 86

Gaddafi, Muammar Mohammed Abu Minyar 56, 62n122
Gender Action Plan 73, 74
gender differences, in earnings 122–3
gender discrimination 19, 100
gender equality 14, 15, 33, 35, 66, 67; Article 49 of 69; bottom-up changes in 72; development of 66; economic and political life 71; employment and social policy 69; financial crisis 72; important advancement in 66; new framework 75; political game of 72; structural foreign policy 69; and women's empowerment 74–6; women's rights 71
Gender Equality Index 67, 78n6
gender gap 43, 66, 67
Generation 2.0 for Rights Equality & Diversity 102
Ghanoushi, Rachid 56
Giglioli, Daniele 88
Giusti, Serena 2
glocalization 20n1
GNI *see* Gross National Income
Goksel, I. 115, 125
Goldin, C. 113, 114
gouvernementalité of mobility 83, 94n27
Gramsci, A. 49, 50, 57
Greece, stateless in *see* stateless women and children, in Greece
Gross National Income (GNI) 42

harragas 85
Harvey, D. 51, 60n48
Henry, Barbara 2
hermeneutics 15, 17
heroes-liberators, mobile people as 85–8
Hill, M. A. 114, 128n8
Hizb' Al Nahda 55, 56
Honig, Bonnie 88
human capital, underutilization of 124–9, *125*
'humanitarian crisis' 85
Hisarcıklılar, M. 122

identity 23–4
IGOs *see* intergovernmental organizations
ijtihad 6, 17–19, 20n14
immigration policies, Greece 98, 99
Inan, F. 120–1
Ince, M. 115, 128n13
inequality, in Mediterranean countries 1 *see also* gender discrimination
information and communication technology (ICT) indicators **40**, 41, 43; access and use of 44; adult literacy *47*; by businesses 45; category of 44; in education 48; internet 43, *43, 44,* 44, *45*
intergovernmental organizations (IGOs) 86
International Telecommunication Union (ITU) 41, 42
intersectionalism 27, 28

INDEX

ISI *see* Islamic social institutions
Islam 18, 25; business sector 55; civil society and 51–8; law 17; modernism 16; political ideology 52; political Islam, programme of 53; radicalization of 56; waqf system 53
Islamic Center Charity Society 54
"Islamic Civilisation" 52
Islamic feminism 2, 18, 25; autochthonous tradition of 8, 9; auto-ethnography 6–8; century of nationalism 11; colonialism 5–7; criticism of 18–19; cultural heritage of European West 6; definition of 8, 15; democratization 12; discourse of religious reform 11; discrimination 7; dual citizenship 12–14; Egyptian women 11; epistemic revolution 6; equality for women 17; gender equality 14, 15; human rights 12; internal criticism of 18–19; in Iran 18; in MENA region 8–12; *Mu'tazilites* period 8, 9; patriarchalism 14, 16; polygamous marriage 10; religious beliefs 12, 13, 19; resistance 7; secularism 9, 11–14, 17; state feminism 10; syntagma 5; women's rights 7, 10, 12, 14, 15, 17
Islamic headscarf 30, 34
Islamic rebirth (*al-Nahda*) 9
Islamic social institutions (ISI) 52, 54, 55, 57
Islamic Tendency Movement (MTI) 56
Islamism 52, 53, 57
Islamist movements 5, 52, 56
Islam Women's Charitable Society 54
Istanbul 71
Italian Civil Defence Department 85
Italy: Catholic Church 30; feminism 30; language of Islam 33; Muslim women 30, 31, 36n15
ITU *see* International Telecommunication Union

Jamma Islamiyya 56
Joint Staff Working Document 75
jus soli principle 101, 106

KAGIDER 117
Kirdar, M. G. 119
Kondratiev wave (K-wave) 41, *42*
Kottis, A. P. 114, 128n10
K-wave *see* Kondratiev wave

labour markets and women 115; female economic activity by sector *116*; female employment by sector 115; gender differences in earnings 122–3; 'marriages' and negative consequences 123; shopping malls *116*, 116–17; social norms, in Turkey 124
lesbian, gay, bisexual, transgender and intersex (LGBTI) 71
LGBTI *see* lesbian, gay, bisexual, transgender and intersex
Libyan civil society 56

Libyan Islamic Fighting Group (LIFG) 62n122
Libyan Islamic Group 62n122
LIFG *see* Libyan Islamic Fighting Group
Lisbon Treaty 66, 68
Loretoni, Anna 2
L-shape hypothesis *126*, 126–7, *127 see also* U-shaped female participation curve

male superiority 15, 16
Mangano, Antonello 88
Marrakesh Conference 71, 72
marriages, negative consequence on FLFPRs 123
maternity clinic certificate 103
Médecins sans Frontières 86, 89
MENA area *see* Middle East and Northern Africa area
Mernissi, Amina 15
Mernissi, Fatima 5, 25
Middle East and Northern Africa (MENA) area 1, 2, 4; Arab education 48; businesses 45; civil society 48, 50; gender divide 43; global political economy 40, 41; Islam and civil society 51–8; knowledge-based society 47; manufacturing exports 45, *46*; non-religious civil society organizations 53; patents, number of *46*; in regional integration project 51; social and geographical wealth gap 40; socio-economic group 49; techno-economic structure of 40; technological marginalization 40–8, 51; technological starvation of *46*
Middle East Islamist groups 53
migration 91n2
Mittleman, J. H. 40, 58n1
modernity 24–6
Moghadam, Valentine 12, 18
Morocco 71
Mountz, Alison 85
MTI *see* Islamic Tendency Movement
Muslim Brotherhood: Islamic state 54; leaders of 55; objectives of 54; social and economic reform 54; social solidarity system 55; violent sections of 52
Muslim-majority societies 52, 54
Muslim women 2, 25, 28, 30–3

nafsin 16
Nahda 8, 9, 12
Nasser, Gamal Abdel 55
nationalism 11
Nationality Code 71
Neighbourhood Civil Society Facility 79n37
'new barbarism' 25
NGO *see* non-governmental organization
non-governmental organization (NGO) 86, 117
non-Western feminism 24, 26
'Nowhere People: The World's Stateless' 97

133

INDEX

Occidentalism 6
Organisation for Economic Co-operation and Development (OECD) 45
Orientalism 23; bargaining with Muslim communities 31–2; concept of 24; 'deconstructive strategy' 23–4; dualistic thinking 25; feminist research 27–8; fluid identity 32–3; gendering 24–6; identity 23–4; limits of Western feminist 26–7; modernity 24–6; 'new barbarism' 25; positionality and power 28–9; secular feminists relationship 29–30; unveiling Muslim women 30–1
Origins of Totalitarianism, The (Arendt) 104

patriarchalism of Islam 14, 16
Pepicelli, Renata 8
political Islam 51, 52, 55, 57
polygamous marriage 10
post-Gaddafi Libyan political 57
post-humanitarian discourse 3, 89, 90
Psacharopoulos, G. 114
Putnam, Robert 49

Qur'an 2, 9, 10; gender equality for women 8, 15; genuine faith 14; *ijtihad* 6; languages translation 9; *min nafsin wāḥidatin* 16; *Mu'tazilites* 9; religious faith 18

radicalism 12
Regarding the Pain of Others (Sontag) 89
religious identity 12, 29, 30, 32
religious social capital (RSC) 50
Rights of Others, The (Benhabib) 104
'right to have rights', Arendt's discussion of 104
Rorty, Richard 84
Rousseau's contract theory 88
RSC *see* religious social capital

saeculum 9
Said, Edward 24, 33
Salecl, Renata 90
Salih, Ruba 25
Save the Children 86, 89, 94n28
secularism 9, 11–14, 17, 25, 29–30
Sherkat, Shala 5
shopping malls, in Turkey *116*, 116–17
Simmel, Georg 86
'sisterhood' 27
social capital: cumulative dimensions of 49; definition of 49; external value of 50; internal value of 50
social imagination, representations of gendered mobility 3; Castoriadis' work on 83; catastrophe, notion of 85–6, 88; democracy 83, 90–1; female mobility pattern 82–3; *gouvernementalité* of mobility 83, 94n27; mobility challenges 90–1; post-humanitarian imagination 84; solidarity 87; *Souffrance à distance*, Boltanski's notion of 84; threat and hero-liberator 85–8; and tragic border regime 81–5; victim and caring mother 88–91, 95n49; (in)visibility and recognition 84, 89; visual representation of mobility 81–2, *82*
social norms, in Turkey 124
Sontag, Susan 89
Souffrance à distance, Boltanski's notion of 84
state feminism 10
stateless women and children, in Greece 3, 97–8, 108n5; acquisition of citizenship, conditions for 103; Act 3838/2010 102; Agamben's 'state of exception' 104–6; ambivalence 102; asylum seekers 99, 108n15; being 'statelessness' 103; 'biopolitics' concept 105; citizenship policies 98, 102–3; de facto statelessness 100–1; *de jure* stateless 100; denial of identity 98; '*homo sacer*' 106; immigration and asylum law (2016) 102; immigration policies 98, 99; *jus soli* principle 101, 106; maternity clinic certificate 103; migrants 108n15; non-citizen status 101; *Origins of Totalitarianism* (Arendt) 104; overview of 98; political and social setting 98–100; political community 103; refugee centres 99; refugee crisis 99; 'right to have rights' 104; Syrian refugees 100–1; UNHCR's warning 101
State of Exception (Agamben) 104–6
State Planning Organization (SPO) report 119, 123
structural foreign policy 68–9
Sunni Islam 9
syntagma 5
Syrian refugees, in Greece 100–1

Talani, Leila Simona 2
Tansel, A. 114, 115
technological marginalization: capitalist development 41; fixed-broadband services 42, *45*; internet subscriptions *44*; internet usage *43*; technological anorexia 41; telecommunications revolution 41
Terre des Hommes 89
TEU *see* Treaty of the European Union
TIMSS *see* Trends in Mathematics and Science Study
Tohidi, Nayereh 19
tragic border regime, social imagination and 81–5
Treaty of Amsterdam, Article 141 66
Treaty of Rome, Article 119 66
Treaty of the European Union (TEU): Article 2 of 66; Article 3(3) of 66; Article 8 of 67
Treaty on the Functioning of the European Union (TFEU), Article 8 of 67
Trends in Mathematics and Science Study (TIMSS) 48
Tuksal, Hidayet 15
Tunisia: action plan 70; *al-Nahda* in 17, 18; Islamism 57

INDEX

Turkey, education and female labour in 111; educational attainment of women 118–22, **119**, *120*, **121**; L-shape hypothesis *126*, 126–7, *127*; underutilization of human capital 124–6, *125*; U-shape hypothesis 112–15, *113*; *see also* female labour force participation rate; labour markets and women

Tzannatos, Z. 114

UFE *see* Egyptian Feminist Union
UfM *see* Union for the Mediterranean
ummah 9, 14, 15
UN Beijing Platform for Action 74
UN Convention Elimination of All Forms of Discrimination against Women 71
underutilization of human capital 124–6, *125*
UNDP *see* United Nations Development Programme
UNHCR *see* United Nations High Commissioner for Refugees
Union for Foreign Affairs and Security Policy 72
Union for the Mediterranean (UfM) 71, 72
United Nations Development Programme (UNDP) 53
United Nations High Commissioner for Refugees (UNHCR) 99, 101
United Nations Security Council Resolution (UNSCR) 73
UNSCR *see* United Nations Security Council Resolution
Uraz, A. 117, 122, 123, 128n18
U-shaped female participation curve: correlations of incidents 113; educational attainment 114; education levels, female population 113–14; female labour force participation 114–15; log of GDP per capita *113*, 114; time-series regressions 115; *see also* L-shape hypothesis
U-shape hypothesis *see* U-shaped female participation curve
U-shape theory 3, 114, 115, 126, 127

Veikou, Mariangela 3
victim, mobile people as 88–91, 95n49
'visual humanism' 3, 89

Western constitutionalism 4
Western feminism 2, 14, 18, 24, 26, 27; third world woman 26, 27, 29
Wolfe, Lauren 82
women's empowerment 65–6, 74–6
women's rights 7, 8, 12, 14, 15, 17, 19, 25, 30
World Bank 45, 111

Zaid, Abū N. 15